The Ramessides, Medes and Persians

THE RAMESSIDES, MEDES AND PERSIANS

Vol. 4 in the series
Ages in Alignment

Emmet Sweeney

Algora Publishing
New York

No portion of this book (beyond what is permitted by
Sections 107 or 108 of the United States Copyright Act of 1976)
may be reproduced by any process, stored in a retrieval system,
or transmitted in any form, or by any means, without the
express written permission of the publisher.
ISBN-13: 978-0-87586-542-3 (trade paper)
ISBN-13: 978-0-87586-543-0 (hard cover)
ISBN-13: 978-0-87586-544-7 (ebook)

Library of Congress Cataloging-in-Publication Data —

Sweeney, Emmet John.
    The Ramessides, Medes, and Persians / Emmet Sweeney.
        p. cm.
    Includes bibliographical references and index.
    ISBN 978-0-87586-542-3 (trade paper: alk. paper) — ISBN 978-0-87586-543-0 (hard
cover: alk. paper) — ISBN 978-0-87586-544-7 (ebook) 1. Middle East—History—To 622.
2. Middle East—History—Errors, inventions, etc. I. Title.

    DS62.23.S94 2007
    939'.4—dc22
                        2007016277

Front Cover: Wall Relief Depicting A Mede Officer with Two Persian Guards Before
King Darius the Great, ca. 5th century B.C. Image: © Gianni Dagli Orti/CORBIS

Printed in the United States

TABLE OF CONTENTS

Introduction

In the course of the past few decades it has become increasingly obvious, to all but the most closed-minded, that there is something radically wrong with our chronology of the ancient (pre-Christian) world. The more demanding methods of 20th century scholarship have exposed embarrassing anomalies in the accepted scheme of things, and it is evident that the attempts of some academics to patch up the problems — usually by some *ad hoc* theory or other — have served only to increase the confusion. It is clear that we have reached the stage where, rather than trying to force-fit the pieces, we must dismantle the whole picture and begin the work of reassembling the historical jigsaw from the beginning.

The present work represents the fourth volume of a series of books ("Ages in Alignment") intended to do just that. The first of these, *The Genesis of Israel and Egypt*, examined the history of the origins of Egyptian civilization through to the end of the Third Dynasty, a point in time which, it was shown, corresponds to the Israelite Exodus. Volume 2 of the series, *The Pyramid Age*, looked at the epoch of the pyramid-builders, kings normally placed in the 3rd millennium BC, but here revealed to belong in the 9th and 8th centuries BC. Volume 3, *Empire of Thebes*, dealt with the rise of Imperial Egypt and the mighty Eighteenth Dynasty, which was revealed (as Immanuel Velikovsky argued) to be contemporary with the Early Kings period of Israel. Yet these rulers are rightly placed in the 7th century BC, not in the 10th and 9th, as Velikovsky believed.

Ramessides, Medes and Persians represents the final volume in the reconstruction of Near Eastern antiquity, bringing us from the start of the 6th century down to the end of the 4th.

The history presented here will appear at the same time both familiar and startlingly new. The reader will see how Ramses II, normally believed to have reigned during the 14th/13th century BC, was actually a contemporary of Cyrus the Great, founder of the mighty Persian Empire. He shall find how during the latter years of Ramses II, Cyrus usurped the Median throne and, under the Assyrian title of Tukulti-apil-esharra (Tiglath-Pileser), conquered Lydia, Babylon, and all of Palestine as far as the borders of Egypt.

All the Neo-Assyrian, as well as Neo-Babylonian kings who followed Tiglath-Pileser III, will be revealed as alter-egos of the Persian Great Kings. Names well-known from biblical history, such as Sargon, Sennacherib, Esarhaddon and Nebuchadrezzar, will be shown to be identical to characters equally well-known from classical history — Darius I, Xerxes, Artaxerxes I and Artaxerxes III. All these and other identifications are argued in some detail.

Evidence of many different types has been called upon in order to complete the picture here presented. The much-neglected ancient historians have been an invaluable source of evidence, and I have found myself quoting them alongside up-to-date modern scholars. Very frequently the cuneiform and hieroglyphic sources do not present enough information to properly reconstruct a history, and we are compelled to turn to the ancient authors to bring the whole thing to life. This is normal practice. We should know precious little (actually nothing at all) of the Persian War against Greece, or Alexander's conquest of Persia, had we to depend on the contemporary monuments of either land. In my reconstruction of a history hitherto unknown I have therefore found it necessary to turn to the ancient authors. The chapter on the fall of the Nineteeth Dynasty for example could not have been written without the combined insights provided by Manetho and Herodotus, as well as the hieroglyphic documents of Egypt.

Throughout the work I have made frequent use of the evidence presented in ancient art. The design of chariots, for example, went through a very definite evolution, an evolution accurately depicted by the artists of the time. Examination of this type of evidence may help us to date the reign of a king with a high degree of accuracy. Thus for example artistic and technological parallels prove beyond question that the so-called Neo-Assyrian Empire established by Ashurnasirpal II was contemporary with the Nineteenth Dynasty of Egypt.

It is evident that in a pioneering work such as this mistakes are inevitable. What is presented here is by no means an exhaustive or definitive history. Rather it is a broad outline, a blueprint along whose lines a new understanding of the ancient Near East's past can be built. There are those, particularly those with a little knowledge, who will object to much of what they will read. Many will perhaps reject the whole concept of royal alter-egos, a concept central to the reconstruction herein advanced. I have stated that the Mede kings used Assyrian names in their capacity as kings of Assyria. The Great Kings of Persia, I suggest, did exactly the same thing. To those who might instinctively be opposed to this concept, we must ask the following: Do they thereby suggest that ancient kings had but a single name (though we know that pharaohs regularly had several), or that they did not employ different names in the different regions and cultural areas over which they ruled (though Tiglath-Pileser III called himself Pul as king of Babylon and Ashurbanipal named himself Kandalanu as ruler of the same city)? Did the Semitic-speaking Assyrian subjects of Xerxes (Khshayarsha) really call him by this name — a name which was for them meaningless and probably unpronounceable? Is it so hard to believe that the Assyrian people would have had their own titles for Xerxes and the other Achaemenids, titles that meant something to them?

Perhaps an even more visceral opposition may be elicited by the suggestion that the Persians (under their "Assyrian" guise) were the real enslavers of the peoples of Israel and Judah. After all, in the reconstruction proposed here, it was Cyrus the Great, Cambyses and Darius I who destroyed the northern kingdom of Israel, and Artaxerxes III (Nebuchadrezzar) who enslaved and deported the inhabitants of Judah 150 years later.

Quite apart from throwing overboard Cyrus' and Darius' reputations for religious toleration, this proposal suggests that the Jews actually forgot who had enslaved them, as well as who had liberated them (i.e., Alexander of Macedon). Even worse, how could the writers of the Septuagint, just a few decades after the return from Babylon, have got the facts so hopelessly confused?

In reality, and contrary to popular belief, the original Septuagint authors did not translate to Greek the whole of what we call the Old Testament. Their remit, as the ancient sources make perfectly clear, was to translate the Books of the Law, the Torah, the first five books of the Bible. In later years, it is true, other books, including the Judges, Kings and Prophets, were added to the "Septuagint"; but the compilation we call the Jewish Bible did not take its final form before the first century BC, or perhaps even the first century AD — a full three centuries after the Babylonian Liberation. Since the people of Judah really were transported to the city of Babylon, and since the king responsible (Artaxerxes III) had one of his capitals (in fact, his chief seat of government) in that city, it would have been the easiest thing in the world for them to view him as a "Babylonian." This transformation would have been all the easier, had the king also possessed a Babylonian name — which in fact he did.

So the objections, I contend, which may initially seem to rest on powerful foundations, will be seen to be not nearly so solid as they appear. And this has been my own experience in writing and researching this work. Following the broader picture, which clearly demands a great reduction in antique chronology, the details have one by one, sometimes to my own astonishment, fallen into place. When we bring together all the evidence, from whatever source, the picture gradually becomes almost crystal clear. What I have been left with, basically, is a synthesis of the written history, as it appears in the classical and Hellenistic writers, with the archaeology. It is, I suggest, a reclaiming of ancient history along the lines understood by the ancients themselves.

The work that follows is divided into two parts, each performing a separate function. Part 1, consisting of Chapters 1 to 3, deals predominantly with a reconstruction of Egyptian history. Part 2, Chapters 4 to 7, deals on the whole with the reconstruction of Neo-Assyrian, or more properly, Persian history.

The reader will soon find why this division was necessary. As described in Part 1, both the histories of Egypt and Persia (Neo-Assyria) are distorted, but they are distorted by differing degrees. The kings and dynasties of the Egyptian New Kingdom are placed in the textbooks, as a general rule, about seven and a half to eight centuries too early. Thus the pharaohs of the Eighteenth, Nineteenth and Twentieth Dynasties, normally placed between the 15th and 12th centuries BC, actually belong in the 7th to 4th centuries. The great rulers of the Eighteenth and Nineteenth Dynasties were contemporaries of the "mighty Medes" of the 7th and 6th centuries, whilst the kings of the Twentieth Dynasty were contemporaries of the Persians (actually the latter Persians)

The empires and peoples of Asia however are dated quite differently to those of Egypt. Their kings and potentates, beginning with the Neo-Assyrians of the 9th and 8th centuries, are dated according to the chronology of the Bible. Yet the chronology of the Bible is also distorted, this time by just over two centuries. This in effect means that Neo-Assyrian kings who figure in the pages of the Bible, such as Tiglath-Pileser III and Sargon II, do not belong in the 8th century where they have been placed, but in the 6th. Thus Tiglath-Pileser III is revealed to be an alter-ego of the Persian Cyrus the Great, whilst Sargon II is an alter-ego of Darius I Hystaspes.

Here then there enters the potential for great confusion. Egyptian rulers such as Ramses II and Merneptah are brought down the timescale by seven and a half centuries into the 6th century to make them contemporaries of Cyrus the Great. Yet they *also* interact with "Neo-Assyrian" kings like Adad-Nirari III and

Tiglath-Pileser III, who are generally believed to have lived in the 8th century. Rather than throwing all of this together in one promiscuous mass, it is clearly preferable to try, somehow, to differentiate the two adjustments. Thus Part 1 of the book, generally speaking, deals with the Egyptian history and chronology, where we find the Nineteenth Dynasty terminated by the Persian Invasion of 525 BC and the Twentieth Dynasty in rebellion against the Persians from circa 400 BC onwards.

Part 2 deals mainly with the second adjustment, showing that the Neo-Assyrians and Neo-Babylonians of the 8th, 7th and 6th centuries, are alter-egos of the Persians of the 6th, 5th and 4th centuries respectively. Yet clearly it has not always been possible to thus neatly compartmentalize the two areas of the reconstruction. Of necessity, there has been a great deal of overlap; and we find in Part 1, for example, that we have much to say of the "Neo-Assyrian" kings who ruled Egypt immediately after the fall of the Nineteenth Dynasty and during the times of the Twenty-First to Thirtieth Dynasties.

I freely admit that all of this might appear impenetrably confusing to the general reader, especially if he has no prior knowledge of Egyptian or Near Eastern history. However, it was not I who wove this chaotic web. My task has been to untangle it; and if the reader will bear with me, he will find that the argument unfolds in a rational and logical manner, and is not nearly so difficult to understand as it may now appear.

Chapter 1. Egypt's New Kingdom in History

End of the Nineteenth Dynasty

The long and stable reign of Ramses II came to an end. Egypt's allies in Palestine must have wondered whether the new pharaoh Merneptah, already a mature man, would continue his father's successful policies, which had brought prolonged peace and prosperity to the region. Scarcely could they have foreseen the dramatic events that were about to unfold.

History says that near the end of Merneptah's reign, corresponding roughly to the end of the Nineteenth Dynasty, Egypt was engulfed in a veritable tide of violence and chaos. A mysterious group of peoples, known generally as the "Sea Peoples" or "Peoples of the Sea," descended on Egypt from the north. These invaders were eventually stopped and repulsed by pharaoh Ramses III of the Twentieth Dynasty, but only after they had brought the Hittite Empire and much of northern Mesopotamia to ruin.

The identity of these "Peoples of the Sea" is a question that has exercised the minds of scholars for over a century. The invaders are depicted in the dramatic bas-reliefs of Ramses III at Medinet-Habu, where they are shown in combat both against and (in some cases) on the side of the Egyptians. There the piratical marauders are named: there are the Pereset, the Tjeker, Shekelesh, Denyen, Sherden and Weshesh. Their appearance and equipment is observed and recorded in detail by the Egyptian artists. They wear a sophisticated type of segmented body armor, rather like the *lorica segmentata* of the later Roman legionaries, and they carry immensely long slashing swords. On their heads, as a rule, they wear a kind of horned helmet, reminiscent of those popularly (and wrongly) believed to have been worn by the Vikings. Other groups of the Sea Peoples, particularly the tribe known as Pereset, wear a crown-like helmet, often described as a "feathered crown," which is strangely reminiscent of the feathered crown worn by Persian gods and kings.

Where could such an unusual and exotic race or races of conquerors have come from? There is no doubt that some of the names provided by the scribes of Ramses III point to Greece and the Aegean, and indeed the Aegean peoples are often described in the writings of Near Eastern races (such as the Hebrews) as the "peoples of the islands" or "peoples of the sea." Furthermore, the Sea Peoples of Ramses III are also described as Haunebut, a term well attested from Ptolemaic times as referring to the Greeks.[1] Since these events are placed by historians in the 13th century BC, the Sea Peoples are generally believed to have been Mycenaean Greek marauders, who were perhaps uprooted from their homelands by famine or invasions from still further north. Thus it is assumed that the Tjeker might be Homeric Teucrians, the Shekelesh might be Sicilians, or perhaps from Sagalassos in Asia Minor, the Denyen Homeric Danaans, the Sherden from Sardinia or perhaps Sardis in Lydia, and the Weshesh a tribe from Assos or Iasos also in Asia Minor. It is often assumed that a great migratory horde of barbarians, similar to that which later brought the Roman Empire to an end, engulfed the whole of the Near East. Originating to the north of Greece, the barbarians are seen as making their way, both by land and sea, to the southern centers of civilization; namely the Hittite Land, Assyria and Egypt.

Amongst this group of peoples the Pereset, or Peleset, are popularly identified with the biblical Philistines, who are said in the Bible to have migrated sometime in the 15th century from the island of Caphtor (Crete or perhaps Cyprus).

But there appeared in 1977 another, radically different, interpretation of the Sea Peoples. In his *Peoples of the Sea*, Immanuel Velikovsky argued that the maritime invaders were indeed Greeks — but not of the Mycenaean Age. According to him, the "Sea Peoples" were mercenaries from Greece and Asia Minor of the 4th century BC, in the pay of the Persian Great Kings; and their Pereset allies, who

---

1 The Egyptian word now universally rendered as *Haunebut* was originally transcribed as *Helou-nebut*, and translated roughly as "Hellenic coast." This translation was perfacetly justified, for the term also appears in the Canopus Decree of Ptolemaic times, where a Greek version of the text accompanies the Egyptian. There, where the Egyptian has *Haunebut* or *Helou-nebut*, the Greek reads "Hellenic coast." At a later time, however, the same term was also appears in much older Egyptian documents, even on one of the early 18th Dynasty — believed to have flourished in the mid-second millennium BC. After this, Helou-nebut was dropped and Haunebut adopted. This was unjustified; and I have explained elsewhere how the 18th Dynasty rose to power around 720 BC, right in the period during which the Hellenes began their piratical raids on the Egyptian coastlands.

wore the strange "feathered crown," were none other than the Persians themselves, regular troops of the Great King.

In another volume, *Ramses II and his Time*, published in 1978, Velikovsky argued that the Nineteenth Dynasty came to an end not in the 13th century, and not at the hands of some barbarians from Greece, but in 525 BC, at the hands of the Persian King Cambyses.

In the work that follows, the present writer hopes to show that Velikovsky was right on both counts. Egypt's Imperial Age was indeed brought to a close by invaders from the north, but they were Persians, not Mycenaean Greeks.

Parallel Histories

Whilst the textbooks place the Eighteenth and Nineteenth Dynasties between the 16th and 14th centuries BC, there is in fact much that would suggest placing them in an age a great deal closer to our own — in the time of the Medes and Persians, as a matter of fact. So, for example, the greatest power in the Fertile Crescent during the time of the Eighteenth Dynasty was the so-called Mita or Mitanni. The Mita people, whose name is indistinguishable from that of the Medes, worshipped Indo-Iranian gods and were ruled by kings who bore Indo-Iranian names, names strangely reminiscent of those of the Great Kings of the Medes. And indeed the Mitanni emperors actually used the title "Great King" as part of their royal nomenclature. Similarly, just as the Medes of the 7th century had conquered the Assyrian Empire, so the Mitanni people had conquered the "Old Assyrian" Empire, whose kings bore names like Sargon and Naram-Sin.

During the time of the Eighteenth and Nineteenth Dynasties the greatest power in Anatolia was that of the Hittites, a people known to the Egyptians as Kheta or Khita. But the Hittites were in many respects reminiscent of the Lydians, the great power which, according to the classical authors, reigned over Anatolia between the 7th and 6th centuries BC. The "Hittite" language, known as Neshili, was in fact found to be virtually identical to that of the Lydians of the 6th century BC,[2] whilst their kings bore typically Lydian names such as Myrsilos (Mursilis)[3] and worshipped Lydian deities like Cybele (Kubaba).[4] In addition, the well-known enmity between the Hittites and Mitannians was strangely reminiscent of the Mede/Lydian rivalry referred to by classical authors like Herodotus.

---

2 See e.g., J. G. MacQueen, *The Hittites* (London, 1975), p. 59.
3 Herodotus (i. 7) names Myrsilos (Mursilos) as one of the most important of the early Lydian kings. Mursilis was the name borne by at least three of the greatest Hitttite monarchs.
4 "Originally a Phrygian goddess, Cybele ... is more widely considered of Luwian [Hittite] origin, from Kubaba." Wikipedia en. wikipedia. org/wiki/Cybele.

During the days of the Eighteenth and Nineteenth Dynasties the whole of the Fertile Crescent, as well as Anatolia, seemed to be beset by a group of barbarian tribes variously described as Sa.Gaz (in the Amarna Letters) or Gas-ga/Gasgas (in the Hittite Boghaz-koi documents). These nomads, who appear to be complete outsiders and much feared by all, sound very much like the barbarous Scythians (Persian Saka, Akkadian Ashguza), whom the classical writers tell us ravaged the whole of the Near East during the 7th and 6th centuries BC.

Now the parallels thus outlined between the histories of the 16th-14th centuries and those of the 7th-6th centuries could perhaps be dismissed as mere coincidence were it not for the fact that they are further confirmed by almost innumerable other kinds of evidence. Thus we may note that the artwork of the Late Bronze Age (16th-13th centuries) finds its closest parallels in that of the 7th-5th centuries.

It would be impossible to go into this question — essentially that of art styles as well as the technology of art — in detail without devoting many volumes to it. A reasonably thorough, though by no means exhaustive, overview of the evidence is presented in Chapter 4 of the present work. A few examples should here serve to illustrate the point.

During the days of the Eighteenth and Nineteenth Dynasties, Egypt and its civilization had a major impact on the peoples of Syria/Palestine. Great quantities of Egyptian artifacts of New Kingdom date are found in this region, and indeed the Egyptian material is routinely used to date the excavated sites. Yet in numerous cases the native Palestinian and Syrian work seems to be centuries younger than the Egyptian material with which it is associated.

A striking example of this phenomenon occurs in the case of Ugarit, an ancient northern Syrian port discovered near the village of Ras Shamra in 1929.

The most important and opulent level of the ancient city was found by its French excavator to date from the Late Bronze Age, contemporary with the Egyptian Eighteenth and Nineteenth Dynasties. One of the city's greatest kings, Nikmed (or Niqmaddu), was a contemporary of pharaoh Akhnaton, and a number of letters exchanged by the two kings have survived. In spite of suffering serious damage after an attack by the king of Hatti (Suppiluliumas I), Ugarit survived as an important and prosperous city right to the end of the Nineteenth Dynasty.

Yet it was from just this period that the archaeologists discovered various features which pointed to the 7th/6th century, rather than the 15th or 14th.

Most important in this regard were the sepulchral chambers. These, clearly of aristocratic provenance, were equipped with orifices which could be used to pour offerings to the dead. Astonishingly, these chambers find their closest parallels in tombs from Cyprus, which are there however dated to the 6th century.[5]

A great library, dating from the time of Nikmed, was found at Ugarit. The texts were written in cuneiform on tablets of clay. Some of the material was found to be in Sumerian, the ancient language of southern Mesopotamia, and some were found to be in Akkadian. Others, however, were written in Hebrew/Phoenician. These, even before they were translated, were known to have been composed in an alphabetic script, owing to the relatively small number of characters used. This was not expected in a library of the 14th century BC. Yet when scholars translated the texts, they were in for an even greater shock. It was discovered that the Phoenician/Hebrew of the documents bore striking similarities to the Hebrew of the Old Testament — even to parts of the Old Testament, which could not have been composed much before the 6th century BC. This at least had been the previous wisdom of biblical exegesis. Now, with the texts from Ugarit, and other parts of the Near East, experts were faced with an embarrassing dilemma. All of their knowledge and wisdom had compelled them to progressively lower the date of the Old Testament's composition. Yet these texts seemed to prove the precise opposite: that biblical Hebrew was much older than anyone had expected, older even than biblical fundamentalists had claimed.

The alphabetic texts from Ugarit provided another surprise. In order to facilitate reading, words were separated from each other by a characteristic stroke — a stroke identical to one used in the writings of the people of Cyprus, just a short distance across the sea from Ugarit. Yet the Cypriot strokes dated from as recent as the 4th or even 3rd century BC. How could it be that an epigraphic tool, abandoned eight or nine centuries earlier in Phoenicia, should survive unchanged for another millennium just across the sea in Cyprus?

But Ugarit had many more surprises in store for the archaeologists.

The king who founded the library, Nikmed, bore a name that sounded very similar to the Greek Nikomedes, and indeed in some texts he was actually called Nikmedes. Even worse, some of the texts referred to a group of people in the city named Jm'an, a word which could only be interpreted as "Ionian," identical in fact to the normal Akkadian rendering of this name. In biblical Hebrew the word is written as "Javan." And sure enough, the translators of the text rendered it as "Ionian."[6] Yet soon the question was asked: How could there be Ionians in a Phoenician city of the 14th century BC?

5 The question of these tombs is examined in detail in Chapter 4, 'Cypriot Tombs'.

6 See e.g., Hrozny, «Les Ioniens à Ras-Sharma,» *Archiv Orientální* Vol. IV (1932) also Dhorme, *Revue biblique* Vol. XL (1931) 37-39.

Along with a king with a Greek name and a Hellenic population, translators also found evidence of a Greek deity. One of the tablets speaks of a god
named Ddms. This was rendered quite simply as Apollo Didymeus by the scholars working on the text. Didyme was a city of Asia Minor/Ionia and a cult-center
of the god Apollo. Yet once again, this raised the vexed question of dates. No one
would place the establishment of the Greek colonies of Asia Minor (Ionia and
Aeolia) much before the 8th or 9th centuries BC.[7] How then could a god of one of
these cities be named on a text of the 14th century?[8] Worse still, how could Ionian Greeks have been present in force in Phoenicia in the 14th century BC, when
historians had reliably dated the Greek presence in that region to no earlier than
the 7th century?

And so the problems mounted. Each and every discovery at Ugarit presented
its own problems. Again and again archaeologists were confronted with material
which, according to its association with Egyptian remains, was dated to the 15th
and 14th centuries BC, but which, according to its association with Cypriot and
Greek-related remains, would have to be dated to the 7th and 6th centuries BC.
Unable to solve these conundrums, scholars eventually pretended they did not
exist; and one after another, the anomalies were relegated to footnotes, before
finally being effaced from the textbooks altogether.

Velikovsky's Chronology

As noted, the first writer to suggest that the accepted textbook chronology
of the ancient world might be wrong was Immanuel Velikovsky, a writer much-
maligned in his own lifetime and still regarded as *persona non grata* to the world of
academic respectability.

In his *Ages in Chaos* (1952) Velikovsky unveiled a radical reconstruction of
Egyptian and Hebrew history which involved subtracting over five centuries
from the length of New Kingdom Egyptian chronology. The histories of Egypt
and Israel did not "fit," according to Velikovsky, because they were out of sync
by half a millennium. Therefore it was not surprising, he said, that scholars could
find no mention in the hieroglyphic records of the great events (such as the Exodus) which the Bible claimed affected both Egyptians and Hebrews. In *Ages in
Chaos* Velikovsky showed how the Egyptians did indeed refer to catastrophic
events which concurred very well with those described in the Book of Exodus.

---

7 Actually, archaeological evidence suggests that the Ionic colonies could not have been established much before 700 BC.
8 According to Hrozny, «La colonié égéenne d'Ugarit semble donc avoir été composé spéciale-
ment par les Ioniens originaires de Didyme près de Milet... Nkmd ... pourrait être consideré
comme le roi des Ioniens qui s'emparèrent d'Ugarit au 13-ème siècle.» Hrozny, loc cit.

The problem of course was that these texts were dated centuries before the accepted date of the Exodus.

Bringing Egyptian chronology forward by five centuries in fact solved a whole host of problems, and in *Ages in Chaos* Velikovsky presented a detailed synchronization of Egyptian and Hebrew histories from the Exodus to the time of kings Ahab and Jehoshaphat, whom he believed to be contemporaries of the heretic pharaoh Akhnaton. He thus made the early Monarchy of Israel contemporary with Egypt's glorious Eighteenth Dynasty, and the wonderful picture he painted brought both the Egyptian and Hebrew histories to life in what can only be described as spectacular fashion. In this way the mysterious Queen of Sheba, who visited Solomon in Jerusalem, was identified with queen Hatshepsut, whose famous expedition to the Divine Land is depicted on the walls of her monument at Deir El Bahri. Thus too the pharaoh Shishak, who plundered the temple of Jerusalem after the death of Solomon, was shown to be Hatshepsut's successor Thutmose III, who records the vast quantities of treasure he looted from the great temple of the 'Holy City' of Palestine — Kadesh.

The reconstructed history presented by Velikovsky was hailed by many at the time as signaling the beginning of a radically new view of the ancient past. But the jubilation was short-lived, and major difficulties were soon to arise.

Because of his unquestioning support for traditional biblical chronology, Velikovsky left the early Hebrew monarchs in the 10th and 9th centuries, where he now also placed the Egyptian Eighteenth Dynasty. However, his researches soon made it equally clear that the Nineteenth Dynasty of Egypt belonged squarely in the 6th century BC, and that is precisely where he placed it in *Ramses II and His Time* (1978). This of course forced him to separate the end of the Eighteenth Dynasty from the beginning of the Nineteenth by two centuries — a separation which neither archaeology nor historiography could support — and which eventually led to the discarding of virtually every volume of *Ages in Chaos*, even amongst those who had been its staunchest supporters.

In the years since then researcher after researcher has grappled with the problem. Dynasties and king-lists have been shuffled backwards and forwards like historical playing-cards. Recognizing that the Nineteenth Dynasty must immediately follow the Eighteenth, the instinct of most scholars was to leave the Eighteenth Dynasty where Velikovsky had placed it and bring the Nineteenth Dynasty into the 8th century to join up with it. But such endeavors failed to result in a satisfactory picture, and one by one Velikovsky's supporters began to abandon even Volume 1 of his reconstruction.

A Double Adjustment

The problem, which for many years seemed insoluble, was that while both *Ages in Chaos* Vol. 1 and *Ramses II and His Time* were excellent pieces of scholarship with much to recommend them, one reduced Egyptian history by five centuries, the other by seven. What was the solution? Trying to reconcile the two seemed to be akin to squaring the proverbial circle.

Enter Gunnar Heinsohn. By the late 1980s, the work of the German Professor Gunnar Heinsohn began to cast an entirely new light on the problem. Heinsohn's Mesopotamian work made him realize that all literate civilizations belonged in the first millennium BC. This involved a contraction of history much more dramatic than anything even Velikovsky had envisaged. From there it was but a short step to recognizing that Velikovsky's date for the Eighteenth Dynasty, which involved taking five centuries off the length of history, was too high. By 1987 Heinsohn had equated the Mitanni people with the Medes, conquerors of the Assyrian Empire in the 7th century. Since the Mitanni were contemporaries of the Eighteenth Dynasty, it became imperative likewise to place that line of kings in the 7th century.

In effect then what Heinsohn had done was what the other researchers had failed even to consider: leave Ramses II and the Nineteenth Dynasty where Velikovsky had placed them in the 6th century, and bring the Eighteenth Dynasty downwards into the 7th century to link up with it. Following this conceptual leap it has become possible, I shall argue, to complete the reconstruction of ancient history which had commenced so promisingly in 1952.

As we proceed through the present study we shall discover why Velikovsky, with equal validity, was able to reduce New Kingdom dates by both five and seven centuries. In fact, he was working with two entirely different dating blueprints.

In *Ages in Chaos*, Velikovsky had labored to synchronize Egyptian history with biblical history, whilst in *Ramses II and his Time*, he had labored, in the main, to synchronize Egyptian history with classical history. It is indeed true that the synchronisms established in *Ages in Chaos* between Egypt and the Bible were correct. Bringing the great pharaohs of the Eighteenth Dynasty forward in the timescale by five centuries did make them contemporary with the early biblical kings. The problem was that the Bible itself was not synchronized with the classical world. It too, just like the Egyptian history, was unnaturally lengthened. Not indeed by the seven plus centuries of Egyptian chronology, but by just over two centuries. Thus the Israelite King Ahab and his Assyrian adversary Shalmaneser III, although normally dated to the second half of the 9th century BC, actually belong near the end of the 7th century. Thus too the Neo-Assyrian kings Adad-Nirari III and Tiglath-Pileser III, normally placed (by synchronization with biblical timescales) in the early to middle 8th century BC, actually belong in the early to middle 6th century.

As we shall see, the king known in the Bible as Tiglath-Pileser III is none other than the king known to the Greeks as Cyrus the Great of Persia.

The application of these two separate dating blueprints, the classical and the biblical, has had a devastating effect on the historiography, as well as the archaeology, of the Near East. Numerous cultural and artistic features of the (biblically and Assyriologically dated) 8th and 7th centuries are found to occur again in the (classically) dated 6th and 5th centuries. Even more to the point, cultural features from the Ramesside (Nineteenth Dynasty) period, supposedly of the 14th century, will be found to reoccur in the late 9th/8th century, after a gap of just over five centuries, and again in the late 7th/6th centuries, after a gap of a further two centuries. Again and again this strange five- and seven-century echo is heard.

In terms of absolute dates, then, it is true (as Velikovsky argued in *Ramses II and his Time*), that Ramses II reigned in the 6th century, just prior to the rise of the Persian Empire. In terms of biblical dates, however, the so-called Glasgow Chronologists, who wanted to make the Nineteenth Dynasty follow the Eighteenth in the latter 9th century, were right in making Seti I and Ramses II contemporaries of the Neo-Assyrian kings Shalmaneser III and Adad-Nirari III. All of these men were contemporaries; only they reigned in the 6th century, not in the 8th, as conventional history believes.

As a corollary to this, we shall find that the Neo-Assyrian kings from Tiglath-Pileser III onwards were identical to the Persian Great Kings, and that it was these men who brought the Nineteenth Dynasty to an end.

We shall find too that the so-called "Libyan" kings, of the Twenty-Second Dynasty, were actually Persian vassals, installed in the Nile Valley by Cambyses and his successors, and that these men, as well as the Nubian kings of the Twenty-Fifth Dynasty, were contemporaries of the last rulers of the Nineteenth Dynasty — Siptah, Tewosre and Seti II, all of whom, as descendants of Ramses II, struggled to reassert Egyptian independence in the early years of the 5th century.

Our proposed reconstruction may be formulated thus:

CONTEMPORARY EPOCHS AND HISTORICAL ALTER-EGOS

Dates BC (approx.)	Egypt	Contemporary with Mesopotamia/Persia
600	Seti I	ShalmaneserIII/Cyaxares (II)
	Ramses II	Shamshi-Adad IV/Arbaces
	Ramses II	Adad-Nirari III/Astyages
550	Merneptah	Tiglath-Pileser III/Cyrus
	Amenmesses/Amasis	Shalmaneser V/Cambyses
	Siptah and Shabaka	Sargon II/Darius I
	Seti II and Tirhaka	Sennacherib/Xerxes
450	Necho I	Esarhaddon/Artaxerxes I
	Psamtek and Ramses X	Ashurbanipal/Darius II
400	Setnakht/Nepherites	Nabopolasser/Artaxerxes II
	Ramses III/Nectanebo I	Nebuchadrezzar/Artaxerxes III
350	Nectanebo II/Ramses IV	Nebuchadrezzar/Artaxerxes III
		Nabonidus/Darius III

Chapter 2. The Fall of Imperial Egypt

The "Israel Stele" of Merneptah

Ramses II, we have seen, did not reign in the 13th century but in the 6th, and his lifetime, along with that of his son Merneptah, was contemporary with the end of Median power and the rise of Persia under Cyrus. In our reconstruction, therefore, Ramses II and Merneptah reigned at the same time as the so-called Neo-Assyrian rulers stretching from Shamshi-Adad IV through to Tiglath-Pileser III, whom we also recognize as alter-egos of Arbaces the Mede and Cyrus the Persian.

In *Ramses II and his Time* Velikovsky equated Ramses II's heir Merneptah with the king known to Herodotus as Apries, who reigned just before the Persian conquest. The present author concurs with this identification and we shall now see how Merneptah/Apries alludes in one of his most famous monuments to the despoliation of Syria/Palestine, as well as the kingdom of Lydia (Hatti), by the nascent power of Achaemenid Persia.

Pharaoh Merneptah is perhaps best known for the "Israel Stele," an inscription discovered by Flinders Petrie in 1896, whose main purpose was the glorification of the pharaoh's achievement in saving Egypt from Libyan invasion. By rights, the inscription should therefore really be called the "Libya Stele." In the text, Merneptah is called:

> the Sun, driving away the storm which was over Egypt, allowing Egypt to see the rays of the sun, removing the mountains of copper from the neck of the people ...

That Egypt had been directly threatened with conquest is obvious. The lines preceding the mention of Israel are:

> One comes and goes with singing, and there is no lamentation of mourning people. The towns are settled again anew; as for the one that ploweth his harvest, he shall eat it. Re has turned himself to Egypt; he was born, destined to be her protector, the King Merneptah.

The concluding lines of the inscription follow at this point:

> The kings are overthrown, saying: "Salam!" Not one holds up his head among the Nine Bows. Wasted is Tehenu, Kheta is pacified, plundered is Pekanan [i.e., "the Canaan"], with every evil, carried off is Askalon, seized upon is Gezer, Yenoam is made as a thing not existing. Israel ('-s-r-'-r) is desolated, his seed is not; Palestine (H'-rw) has become a widow for Egypt. All lands are united, they are pacified; everyone that is turbulent is bound by King Merneptah, given life like Re, every day.

The inscription is of course named the "Israel Stele" for these lines, which are widely believed to constitute the one and only mention of the Israelites in Egyptian hieroglyphic literature. In 1978 John Bimson made a detailed study of the stele and concluded that the despoliation and pacification of Syria and Palestine described on the monument was the work not of Merneptah himself, but of Tiglath-Pileser III. Bimson was able to show, in some detail, that both Assyrian and biblical sources could be made to concur with the stele in identifying Tiglath-Pileser as the author of Palestine's woes. According to Bimson, the "outcome of [Tiglath-Pileser's first] ... two incursions into the West corresponds exactly with the Asian events referred to on the 'Israel stele'."[9] As well as the claim that "Hatti is pacified" (which Tiglath-Pileser did indeed pacify), the stele tells us that "the Canaan is plundered with every evil." There follow a number of specific statements about that region. Two Philistine cities, Ashkelon and Gezer, are mentioned, and both these cities also occur in the annals of Tiglath-Pileser. Next we hear of Yenoam, which, Bimson notes, is a region of Israel. Both Tiglath-Pileser and the Book of Kings refer to Assyria's despoliation of this area and how the inhabitants were carried captive to Assyria. "There can be no doubt" says Bimson "that this devastation is the 'laying waste' of Israel to which the stele refers after the mention of Yenoam."[10]

Bimson of course does not actually prove that Merneptah and Tiglath-Pileser III were contemporary, but he certainly shows that they could well have been. The Egypt of Merneptah was a much diminished power, an empire that had already relinquished all pretence to influence in Syria/Palestine, areas long re-

9 John J. Bimson, "An Eighth-Century Date for Merneptah," *SIS Review* Vol. III No. 2 (1978) p. 58.

10 Ibid.

garded as her rightful sphere. The main purpose of the Israel Stele, we recall, is to record how Merneptah had saved Egypt in a *defensive* war against the Libyans. This alone should preclude the notion, commonly accepted in the scholarly community, that the despoliation of Palestine (as well as the pacification of Hatti) mentioned in the text was the work of Merneptah. Such a feat, worthy of a Thutmose III or a Ramses II, would have been immortalized in a grander way than upon a paltry stele.

We know in any case, from other sources, that the pacification of Hatti mentioned on the inscription was the work of an Assyrian king. Merneptah reigned during the destruction of the Hittite Empire whose last king, Tudkhaliash IV, we have already identified with Croesus. The end of Hittite power at this time can, we have seen, be linked to the activities of the Assyrian Tukulti-Ninurta, a man whom we shall also demonstrate used the appellation Tukulti-apil-esharra, Tiglath-Pileser.

An air of impending doom seems to pervade the "Israel Stele." The pharaoh records the destruction of Hatti and the nations of Syria and Palestine simply as a matter of fact, and the only sense of pride or self-glorification we detect is that Egypt, alone among the nations, still survives. That, however, was an achievement whose days were numbered.

Amenmeses the Usurper

According to Herodotus, Egypt survived against the growing might of Persia only a short time after the reign of Apries. The latter waged a disastrous war against the Greeks of Cyrene and was faced with a rebellion led by one of his generals, a commoner named Amasis. The story goes that the pharaoh sent Amasis (Ahmose) in the hope of winning back his rebellious troops. Instead, however, the rebels won over Amasis, whom they proclaimed king. Apries now sent his vizier to arrest Amasis, who returned him to the pharaoh with the message that when he did come it would be with his troops. Enraged at this reply, Apries had the vizier's nose and ears cut off, a move which made him deeply unpopular. A fierce battle was then fought between the rebels and the king's Greek and Carian bodyguard, from which the rebels emerged victorious. The pharaoh was soon a prisoner of the rebels, though for a while he remained nominal ruler of the country, under house arrest in his palace. In face of popular demand, however, Amasis eventually delivered him to the mob.[11] Shortly thereafter, Amasis himself was declared pharaoh. He was to be the last independent king of Egypt, if we discount the very brief reign (a few months) of his son Psammenitus.

---

11 Herodotus, ii, 63.

Having identified Merneptah with Herodotus' Apries, we must expect him, like Apries, to have been overthrown by a usurper, a usurper we must be able to equate with Amasis. What do the Egyptian sources tell us?

After Merneptah/Apries, the Egyptian monuments variously record a list of names whose importance and relationship with each other is by no means certain. The significance of Amenmeses, Seti II, Siptah, and Tewosret has been debated since the early years of Egyptology. Even the order of their succession is unclear.[12] Whilst Seti II and Siptah are unquestionably related to the royal line of Ramses II and Merneptah, the same cannot be said of Amenmeses. Indeed there is clear evidence to suggest that the latter was a usurper.[13] Even more intriguingly, this king, whose name we could reasonably imagine a Greek hearing as Amasis, actually appears to have used the latter part of his name — Mose — as a title. A document of the time, which mentions a ruler (not necessarily a king) named Mose, prompted discussion as to whether a king of that name could have reigned near the end of the Nineteenth Dynasty. In the words of R.O. Faulkner, "Mose was apparently a nickname of the king then ruling," and "It is assumed that Mose is an abbreviation of Amenmeses."[14] However, another document of the same period, which is almost certainly dated to the time of Merneptah, also mentions a ruler named Mose.[15] Scholars wondered how Mose, who clearly performed functions only a ruler could have, could nevertheless be placed at the same time as Merneptah. But the problem is resolved if Amenmeses, or Mose, is Amasis (Ahmose), the usurper who imprisoned his royal master Apries, according him, for a while, the honors to which he was entitled by birth, before eventually delivering him to the mob.

The evidently short reign of Amenmeses/Mose is reconciled to the 44 years that Herodotus accorded to Amasis by the simple proposition that *Herodotus got it wrong*, as he did with so much else of Egyptian history. The vast number of monuments said by Herodotus to have been erected by Amasis are nowhere to be found, for the simple reason that in all probability they never existed. It would seem that much of what was erected by Ramses II (Ra-moses) was attributed in the popular imagination to the much more colorful figure of Amasis, and that his supposed reign of forty-four years is likewise a reflection of the long reign of Ramses II. Four years (the span of Amenmeses' reign) is perhaps a better estimate.

---

12 R. O. Faulkner, "Egypt: From the Inception of the Nineteenth Dynasty to the Death of Ramesses III" in *CAH* Vol. 2, part 2 (3rd ed.) p. 236.

13 Ibid. p. 237.

14 Ibid. p. 236. The document concerns accusations against one Paneb by a vizier named Amenmose, and a ruler Mose, who dismissed the vizier.

15 Ibid. The papyrus is Papyrus Anastasi No. 1.

Amasis died only a matter of months before Egypt was overwhelmed by the victorious armies of Cambyses, whom we shall argue has an alter-ego in Shalmaneser V of Assyria. Seti II and Siptah, two other names linked to the Nineteenth Dynasty, were as we shall see, contemporaries of the Persian Great Kings. Cambyses styled himself an implacable foe of Amasis, and in such circumstances we might expect the Persians to promote any surviving scions of the old Tanite royal line as puppet monarchs. Sure enough, the monuments of Amenmeses, including his tomb, were wrecked on the orders of Siptah.[16] That Siptah and his mother Tewosret were of Tanite lineage is clearly demonstrated by their royal titles. Thus Siptah's full throne-name was Merneptah-Siptah, whilst the other king of the time, Seti II, called himself Seti-Merneptah. The adoption of Merneptah's name also illustrates the fact that they looked to him, not Amenmeses, as the last legitimate pharaoh.

Both Siptah and Tewosret, though not Seti II, were probably direct descendants of Merneptah. Queen Tewosret, we shall find, was almost certainly one of his grand-daughters.

Egypt Invaded by Asiatics

If Amenmeses/Mose is the same person as Amasis, the last king of an independent Egypt prior to its conquest by Persia, we must of course expect this to be reflected in the native source-material. The immediate aftermath of Amenmeses' reign, we should find, saw Egypt subdued by a great Asiatic power. Once again, our room for maneuver is rather limited. If we cannot find clear and unequivocal evidence of an Asiatic conquest coinciding with the end of the Nineteenth Dynasty and prior to the rise of the Twentieth, our reconstruction is in serious trouble. Such a major catastrophe could not have been ignored in the hieroglyphic records. What then do the records tell us?

The facts are clear. Very soon after the death of Amenmeses/Mose Egypt was invaded and conquered by an Asiatic power. Two quite distinct sources confirm this. On the one hand a great official with an apparently Asiatic name, Bey, now appears as the chief authority in the land. This man was a king-maker who placed his name beside that of the reigning monarchs and who erected a tomb for himself in the Valley of the Kings — the only non-royal personage in the history of Egypt to do so. Bey was called the "Great Chancellor of the entire land," and after the death of Amenmeses it was he, along with the queen (or princess) Tewosret, who set Siptah on the throne.[17] In the words of the inscription mark-

---

16 F. Petrie, *A History of Egypt* Vol. 3 (1905) pp. 129-131.
17 R. O. Faulkner, loc cit. p. 238.

ing the event, he "established the king on his father's throne."[18] According to R.O. Faulkner, "To have played the role of king-maker Bay must have been a man of immense influence."[19]

But what kind of man could perform the role of king-maker, and excavate for himself a tomb in the Valley of the Kings without actually being of Egyptian royal blood? Even worse, how could a man of apparently Asiatic origin, a foreigner in the kingdom of the Nile, assume such a position — if Egypt herself were not a conquered state?

Another source, entirely separate from the material relating to Bey, and of a later date, confirms that in the immediate aftermath of the collapse of the Nineteenth Dynasty Egypt became subordinate to a great Asiatic power. The Papyrus Harris, a massive document inscribed on a scroll some forty meters in length, written during the reign of Ramses III (whose last will and testament it appears to be), speaks very graphically of the horrors experienced by the people as a result of conquest by an Asiatic power. The papyrus begins, however, by praising the contributions Ramses III made to the temples of Amon-Ra, Mut, and Khons, the triad of Thebes, as well as to the temples of various other deities throughout the length and breadth of Egypt. The text was written by several hands, and concludes with a survey of past times, which from our point of view is the important section. Here the distress and humiliation of the country before the reigns of Ramses III and his predecessor Setnakht are described in vivid detail.

> The land of Egypt was overthrown from without and every man was thrown out of his right; they had no chief mouth for many years formerly until other times. The land of Egypt was in the hands of chiefs and rulers of towns, one slew his neighbor, great and small.

The country, it is evident, had been subdued by a foreign power ("overthrown from without"). The term "they had no chief mouth for many years" implies that there was no king and no central government. Lawlessness prevailed. The papyrus continues:

> Other times having come after it, with empty years, Arsa, a certain Syrian, was with them as chief. He set the whole land tributary before him together; he united his companions and plundered their possessions. They made the gods like men, and no offerings were presented in the temples.

It was some time after this distressing epoch that King Setnakht (Usikhaure-meramun-setpenre Setnakhte-merrere-meramun), first pharaoh of the Twentieth Dynasty, "set in order the entire land which had been rebellious; he slew the

---

18 Ibid.
19 Ibid.

rebels who were in the land of Egypt; he cleansed the great throne of Egypt." Royal authority was re-established and law and order was restored after the many years of chaos and exploitation. Setnakht's successor, Ramses III, we are told by the papyrus, was successful in further improving the order and defense of the country.

Scholars were surprised by the Harris Papyrus' reference to foreign invasion, the country being overthrown "from without." In the accepted scheme of things, the Nineteenth Dynasty progressed more or less peacefully, with perhaps one or two short interregnums, into the Twentieth Dynasty. Certainly no one had anticipated a foreign invasion at the time. It is held that there exists no other document, foreign or Egyptian, which would corroborate this statement of Ramses III. "Not the slightest hint is to be found" that would support Ramses' testimony of foreign domination under Arsa.[20] Even worse, the accepted version of history leaves only a few years between the end of the Nineteenth Dynasty and the beginning of the Twentieth; yet the papyrus speaks of a long period of anarchy, without any established authority, culminating in the domination of Arsa, the Asiatic potentate. The identity of Arsa is regarded as mystifying, though "the rule of an otherwise unknown" foreign usurper "is certain," because of the explicit statement of the papyrus.[21]

As early as 1977 Velikovsky presented fairly exhaustive evidence to show that Arsa of the Harris Papyrus, who plundered and oppressed Egypt in the years between the end of the Nineteenth Dynasty and the rise of the Twentieth, was none other than Arsames, the well-known satrap of Egypt appointed by Artaxerxes I after his reconquest of the country. The identification is well founded and fully supported by the present author.

Thus two entirely different sources confirm a lengthy and brutal Asiatic occupation of Egypt after the time of the Nineteenth Dynasty.

In the scheme of things proposed here, Bey, who assumes control of the kingdom sometime after the death of Amenmeses, would have come before Arsa/Arsames. Investigation will reveal him to be the Persian satrap appointed by Xerxes, whom we shall shortly see was one and the same person as the Neo-Assyrian King Sennacherib.

In the remainder of the present chapter we shall follow the fortunes of the various characters whose lives impacted on the Nile kingdom in the century which followed the reign of the usurper Amenmeses/Amasis. A rich variety of sources are available to aid in the task of untangling the web of events. Kings

20 H. Junker, "Die Aegypter," in Junker and Delaporte, *Die Völker des antiken Orients* (Freiburg, 1933) p. 153.
21 J. Wilson in J. B. Pritchard (ed.) *ANET* (Princeton, 1950) p. 260 n. 6.

placed centuries apart in the textbooks are shown to be contemporaries, whilst other rulers, believed to be Assyrians, are revealed as Achaemenid Persians.

Persians and "Libyans"

According to the scheme of things proposed here, the Nineteenth (Tanite) Dynasty was followed immediately by the Neo-Assyrian (i.e., Persian) epoch. During the Neo-Assyrian age, it is known, a dynasty of kings from Nubia ("Ethiopia") clashed repeatedly with the invaders for control of the Nile valley. This dynasty, known to historians as the Twenty-Fifth, is thus placed by us immediately after the Nineteenth Dynasty. Yet the Ethiopian pharaohs were also contemporary, in part, with a line of kings that has come to be known as "Libyan." It is not known how the Libyans of North Africa invaded Egypt, nor is any such conquest recorded in the classical authors. From the point of view of the reconstruction presented here, it will be obvious that the only conquest which could have brought foreign princes to power at this time was the Persian. We hold then that the "Libyan" dynasty (actually dynasties) was a line of Persian vassals awarded slices of Egyptian territory in the aftermath of Cambyses' conquest.

The names of the Libyans — Sosenk, Osorkon, Takelot and Nimrot — immediately mark them out as foreign. The supposed Libyan connection is fairly tenuous, to say the least, and is based on the fact that the term "chief of the Ma" — interpreted as chief of the Meshwesh, or Libyans, is a common title of the period. I would suggest however that the name "Ma" is a contraction of Mariyanna, the Iranian nobility. It should be remarked here that no less a person than Flinders Petrie argued at some length for an Asiatic origin, equating Osorkon with Akkadian *Sharrukin* ("Legitimate king"), Sosenk with Akkadian *Shushanku* ("Man of Susa"), Nimrot with the Akkadian *Nimr* ("Leopard"), and Takelot with Akkadian/Assyrian *Tukulti* ("Helper" or "Trusted One").[22] In the same place Petrie wondered about the origin of the line and stated his belief that "we must look to some Babylonian or Persian adventurer in the service of the Tanite kings for the source of the dynasty."

Having said all that, it must nevertheless be conceded that this family of princes may have had some Libyan connections, for Herodotus refers to the fact that Inaros, one of the most powerful Egyptian leaders in the Persian epoch — where we place the Libyan Dynasty — was himself of Libyan extraction.

---

22 Petrie, *A History of Egypt* Vol. 3 (London, 1905) p. 232. The supposed Libyan ancestry of Sosenk I (on the Pasenhor genealogy he is recorded as six generations removed from one Buyuwawa, who is described as *Thnw*, "the Libyan"), Petrie notes, is tenuous evidence for describing the dynasty as Libyan. Just as tenuous as the "Chief of the Ma" title. Sosenk I's grandfather was called Pallashnes, a name which, like the other royal titles of the dynasty, sounds very Assyrian, most probably being transliterated as Bel-nisheshu.

Nonetheless, the links between the "Libyans" and the Persian epoch are numerous. At an early stage, for example, certain correspondences were noted between the art and architecture of the Persian era and the Libyan.[23] Furthermore, there is clear proof that Libyan-style names were popular even during the Ptolemaic age, as at least one papyrus from the British Museum shows.[24]

Other evidence for placing these men in the age of the Persian Empire is not lacking. On the outside of the southern wall of the great temple of Amon at Karnak Sosenk I carved a much-debated list of Palestinian and Syrian cities subject to him. These cities are represented by human figures like those on the nearby bas-relief of Thutmose III, and it is obvious that Sosenk copied the earlier pharaoh's work. Because of this relief it has been assumed, since Champollion's day, that Sosenk was the Shishak of scriptural sources who plundered Solomon's temple in Jerusalem. Apart from the fact that Jerusalem is not even mentioned in Sosenk's list, one other factor should convince us of the impossibility of such an identification. Among the list of Palestinian towns (very few of which could be identified with known biblical settlements) there was a *p'-hw-k-rw'* — *'b'-r'-m*, or Hekel Abram, "the field of Abram." There are, in fact, quite a few *p'-hw-k-rw'*, and each of them is identified as *hekel*, or "field," in Aramaic. Yet Aramaic, the Semitic dialect of Syria, was not spoken in Palestine until after the Assyrian and Babylonian captivity, when the depopulated land of the Bible was settled by Syrian newcomers. In fact, Aramaic was to become the *lingua franca* of much of the Near East during the Persian epoch, and the discovery of Palestinian cities bearing Aramaic names on the list of Sosenk is virtually irrefutable evidence that the "Libyan" pharaohs could not possibly predate the Persian Empire.

Yet more evidence comes in the royal burials of the Twenty-First and Twenty-Second Dynasties at Tanis. The priest-kings of the Twenty-First Dynasty, which Velikovsky placed in the Persian and Ptolemaic ages, were buried in the same temple-precinct at Tanis as kings named Osorkon and Sosenk. Psusennes, who bore the Persian title *Shahedet*, or *Shahdidit* ("king's retainer"),[25] was interred next to a king named Sosenk-heka-kheper-re. This "otherwise unknown" monarch was buried (as was Psusennes) with artifacts inscribed in cuneiform.[26] The language used has not been disclosed, but we may guess, along with Velikovsky, that it was Persian. Further close links between the 21st Dynasty and the Libyans are not lacking. A statuette of the Nile god, a pilgrim's votive offering, was found to have been dedicated by the High Priest Meriamun Sosenk, who

23 See e.g., I. Woldering, *Egypt: The Art of the Pharaohs* (Baden-Baden, 1963) p. 196.

24 The papyrus, number 10508, is an instruction by one Onkh-sosenky for his son, and is dated to the reign of Ptolemy II.

25 P. Montet *Psousennes* (Paris, 1951) p. 184.

26 Ibid. p. 20.

is described as the son of King Osorkon and his wife Makare, daughter of King Psusennes. Again, we could mention a son of Herihor named Osorkon, as well as Amenemope (interred next to Psusennes in Tanis), who set up an Apis stele in the 23rd year of Osorkon II. Thus there is no doubt that these Osorkons were contemporary with the Twenty-First Dynasty.

It is of interest to note here that David Rohl (*A Test of Time*, 1995) proved in some detail that Psusennes, placed around 200 years before the Libyan era, actually lived shortly after the Libyan pharaohs next to whom he was interred.

It is instructive also to note that in the famous Genealogy of Memphite Priests a King Akheperre (believed to be this same Psusennes, i.e., Psusennes I), is placed immediately after the last Nineteenth Dynasty pharaoh, Amenmeses. Two further kings named Psusennes follow, and then comes a Sosenk, after two further entries which do not mention the reigning monarch's name. Thus the Memphite Genealogy apparently jumps straight from the Nineteenth Dynasty to the Twenty-First, with none of the great pharaohs of the Twentieth having reigned long enough to be mentioned. Clearly this is impossible, and strongly supports our belief that the "Libyan" Twenty-Second Dynasty, as well as most of the Twenty-First, actually come before the Twentieth Dynasty, whose greatest pharaoh, Ramses III, is equated by us (in accordance with the reconstruction outlined by Velikovsky) with Nectanebo I.

Yet the King Akheperre who followed Amenmeses cannot have been Akheperre Psusennes I, who clearly lived closer to the end of the Persian epoch. Evidently the name Akheperre was also used by some of the earlier "Libyans" or Ethiopians. And this brings us to another point worth stressing. The order in which the kings of this chaotic period reigned is by no means certain. Great confusion exists in all areas, a confusion generated to no small degree by the use of the same names by more than one king. In this way, Akheperre is a prenomen also employed by Osorkon the Elder (Twenty-First Dynasty), as well as Sosenk V and Osorkon IV (Twenty-Second Dynasty). Again, both Osorkon II and III are also called Usermaatre-setepenamun, which is bad enough in itself, but is made even worse by the evidence (highlighted by David Rohl) that Osorkon II actually lived before Osorkon I.[27] In short, it could well be that the king we know as Osorkon III was the first pharaoh of that name. This may seem strange, but is supported by evidence of more than one variety, and enables us to begin to make sense of the entire "Libyan" epoch. The king Osorkon who was placed in power by the intervention of Piankhy the Ethiopian (supposedly circa 730 BC) would

---

27 The inner hall of the temple at Bubastis was built by Usermaatre Osorkon II, whilst the outer court surrounding it was constructed by Sekhemkheperre Osorkon I — precisely the opposite of what we would expect. See D. Rohl, *A Test of Time* (London, 1995) p. 377.

not therefore have been Osorkon III, but Osorkon I. Tefnakht, against whom Pi-ankhy marched, would have been an Assyrian (Persian) vassal loyal to King Gau-mata, murdered by the usurping Sargon II (whom we shall argue was Darius I Hystaspes). Osorkon was thus probably an ally of Sargon II/Darius I, and would have called in the aid of the Nubian — no doubt with a promise of rich rewards to come from the Great King in the east.

Sure enough, Sargon II records the "tribute" he received from Shilkanni (rec-ognized as a transliteration of Osorkon) of Egypt.

But loyalty to the Assyrian/Persian Great King was at best an unreliable fac-tor, and in a very short time the Ethiopians, now under the leadership of Shabaka, would seek to overthrow the power of the Great King in the land of the Nile.

Ramessides and Ethiopians

We have stated that the Ethiopian (Twenty-Fifth) Dynasty immediately fol-lows the reign of Amenmeses, last important pharaoh of the Nineteenth. We must therefore expect the Nineteenth and Twenty-Fifth Dynasties, separated in the textbooks by over five centuries, to display striking affinities in terms of art, architecture, literature and culture in general. Is this the case?

As a matter of fact, historians have long been struck by the very clear cul-tural parallels observed in the two epochs. Since conventional chronology places such an enormous span of time between them, the similarities are viewed as most mysterious, and attempts to explain them have generally centered upon a hy-pothesis that the Nubian kings were descended from a branch of the Tanite royal family. Certainly there is much evidence to suggest a direct link between the two lines. Horemheb, the founder of the Nineteenth Dynasty, or at least a personage who shares his name, is honored repeatedly by the Nubian kings. Royal titles from the two epochs reinforce the impression of a dynastic connection. Thus for example the Golden Horus name of Horemheb (Aa-khepresh) and Mernep-tah (Aa-khepresh-hu-Sati) are recalled in the Golden Horus name of the Nubian Shabataka (Aa-khepresh-h ... -nebu).

A well-known relief, carved on the wall of a small Nubian temple at Kar-nak, shows Tirhaka the Ethiopian together with a character named Horemheb. Whilst we do not suggest that this Horemheb is the same person as the founder of the Nineteenth Dynasty, he nevertheless shares his name, and the accompany-ing inscription is most interesting. In his 1873 study of the monuments of Tirha-ka, the French scholar De Rouge describes the relief:

> Tirhaka is standing and takes part in a panegyric. An important per-
> sonage, named Hor-em-heb, a priest and hereditary governor, addresses to
> the people the following discourse in the name of the two forms of Amon:

"Hear Amon-ra, Lord of the Thrones of the World and Amon-ra, the husband of his mother, residing in Thebes! This is what they say to their son, the king of Upper and Lower Egypt [Neferatmukhure] son of the sun, Tirhaka, given life forever: 'You are our son whom we love, in whom we repose, to whom we have given Upper and Lower Egypt; we do not like the kings of Asia ...'"[28]

The priests of Amon, the tutelary god of Egypt, were normally chosen from the royal family; and it is evident that the priest Horemheb must have carried in his veins the blood of the royal house of Tanis. This suggests very strongly that no great stretch of time elapsed between the end of the Nineteenth Dynasty and the rise of the Twenty-Fifth.

Fig. 1. Unnamed Egyptian queen, reign of Ramses II

There is evidence that this same Horemheb briefly sat on the throne, for an otherwise enigmatic tomb in the Theban necropolis, that of a dignitary named Petamenophis (which clearly dates from the Ethiopian epoch), nevertheless bears the name of Horemheb.[29] But here Horemheb is not the High Priest of Amon; his name is surrounded by a royal cartouche. The same pharaoh Horemheb also appears in the tomb of a prince Sosenk, son of Osorkon II and his wife Karoma. The tomb, discovered in 1942 and excavated by Ahmed Badawi, contained on the lintel of the doorway an incised relief of Horemheb kneeling in front of a table bedecked with offerings. Behind Horemheb can be seen the deceased prince, also kneeling. Although his cartouche was damaged and a deliberate attempt had evidently been made to erase it, the name was clearly read as Horemheb.[30] Here then is additional proof that the Ethiopian and "Libyan" dynasties commenced simulta-

28 M. le Vicomte de Rouge, «Étude sur quelques monuments du règne de Taharka,» *Mélanges d'Archéologie* Vol. 1 (1873). Also in *Bibliotheque egyptologique* 28 (1918) p. 268.

29 C. R. Lepsius, *Denkmäler aus Aegypten und Aethiopien* Vol. 1 (1897) Text 245 middle.

30 A. Badawi, "Das Grab des Krönenprinzen Scheschonk, Sohnes Osorkon's II, und Hohenpriesters von Memphis," *Annales du Service des Antiquites*, Vol. 54 (1956) p. 159 and pl. IV.

neously and reigned concurrently. Tirhaka was evidently a contemporary of Osorkon II, which can only mean that the first "Libyan" king reigned around the same time as Tirhaka's recent predecessors, Piankhy and Shabaka.

We shall meet this second Horemheb again; he played a significant role in the struggles that rent Egypt during the Ethiopian and Neo-Assyrian (Persian) invasions.

Fig. 2. Alabaster statue of Amenardis, wife of Shabataka, Dynasty 25. Note the striking similarities with the 19th Dynasty queen, especially with regard to the headdress. Yet five centuries supposedly separate the two portrayals

The evidence of art and cult-practices agrees in placing the Ethiopian epoch beside the Ramesside. Thus during the time of Shabaka and Tirhaka the Aton-city built by Akhnaton in Nubia, Gem-Aton, continued to be a major center, with its Aton-temple simply being redesigned as the temple of "Amon, Lord of Gem-Aton."[31] Early in the 20th century Breasted drew attention to this strange anomaly, remarking that the Nubian city bore the same name as the major Aton temple erected by Akhnaton in Thebes: "The name of the Theban temple of Aton therefore furnished the name of the Nubian city, and there can be no doubt that Ikhenaton was its founder, and that he named it after the Theban temple of his god ... We have here the remarkable fact that this Nubian city of Ikhenaton survived and still bore the name he gave it nearly a thousand years after his death and the destruction of the new city of his god in Egypt (Amarna)."[32]

31 J. H. Breasted, "A City of Ikhenaton in Nubia," *Zeitschrift für Aegyptische Sprache* 40 (1902/1903) p. 107.
32 Ibid.

Strange then that this shrine carried, through the great period of time that supposedly elapsed between the Amarna epoch and the Ethiopian conquest, a name recalling a heretical cult, which had supposedly been suppressed almost seven hundred years earlier. Stranger still, in all this time the name remained unnoticed in contemporary documents. After the time of Akhnaton, the Gem-Aton is first referred to by Tirhaka in one of the side-chambers of his temple at Gebel-Barkal, but "its earlier history is totally unknown."[33]

The art of the Ethiopian age shows striking affinities with the art of the late Eighteenth and Nineteenth Dynasties. This is illustrated for example in the decoration of the tomb of Mentuemhet, High Priest of Amon at Thebes in the time of Tirhaka and Ashurbanipal. In 1947, "a fragment of limestone relief of exceptional quality" from the tomb was purchased by the Brooklyn Museum. Ignorant of the relief's origin, the Museum's Egyptian Department evaluated it as a product of the late Eighteenth Dynasty. The work contained scenes of peasant life already known from paintings of the Eighteenth Dynasty tomb of Menna in the Theban necropolis. However, "only a few months later two other fragmentary reliefs were offered to the Museum," and these were assessed by Professor Cooney of the Museum to the late 7th century.[34] At first the museum did not suspect a link between the two pieces. In the words of Professor Cooney, "I was so convinced of the early date of the relief with the peasant scenes that I failed even to consider a relationship between it and the Saite pieces."[35] Yet, to the astonishment of the Museum authorities, it was subsequently discovered that all three reliefs were from the tomb of Mentuemhet.

Because of the close similarities between the scenes in the tombs of Menna and Mentuemhet, Professor Cooney assumed that the artists of the Ethiopian epoch must have had access to the tomb of Menna and its paintings, to serve as models, after more than seven hundred years had elapsed. In Cooney's words, "The lucky preservation of the Eighteenth Dynasty original, which served as a model to the Sai'te sculptor provides an ideal chance to grasp the basic differences between the art of these periods separated by a span of almost eight centuries."

But the artists of the Ethiopian epoch had no need to break into ancient tombs to find inspiration for their work. Between the end of the Eighteenth Dynasty and the beginning of the Ethiopian epoch there were not seven centuries,

---

33 Ibid. p. 106.
34 John D. Cooney, "Three Early Saite Tomb Reliefs," *Journal of Near Eastern Studies* 9 (1950) p. 193.
35 Ibid. p. 194.

only one, and between the end of the Nineteenth Dynasty and the Ethiopian age only a decade.

Ethiopian Rule

Shortly after the time of Tiglath-Pileser III, Hosea, the king of Israel, sought to free himself from the yoke of the Great King in the east and approached the king of Egypt, with whom he had a secret correspondence. The Scriptures give the name of this Egyptian monarch as So.

Historians are fairly unanimous in the opinion that pharaoh So of 2 Kings 17:4 was Shabaka, generally recalled as the first Ethiopian king of Egypt. The reconstruction of history formulated in the present volume can concur with this identification, though it must be stressed that the circumstances under which the Nubian kings first became involved in the affairs of Egypt are not understood by historians, and need to be explained in the light of what we have discovered in the foregoing pages.

The Scriptures name Shalmaneser (V) as the Neo-Assyrian king on the throne at the time of pharaoh So, though it is generally agreed that these events must be dated to the time of Sargon II. The latter king, we shall argue, was an alter-ego of Darius the Great, who seized the throne of Persia after murdering the brother of Cambyses, whom he claimed was a Mede impostor. It is known that Darius' usurpation shook the Achaemenid Empire to its foundations. Rebellion erupted in the satrapies, and Egypt, along with many other provinces, was temporarily lost. In the scheme outlined here, it was at this point that the Ethiopians first gained control of Egypt. The kings of Nubia, utilizing the chaos and dissension in Egypt, marched northwards, and, posing as peacemakers, gained a foothold in the country. It was in this context that Piankhy campaigned in support of prince Osorkon, who can only have been Osorkon I. The latter may have been loyal to Sargon I (Darius), but that did not prevent Piankhy's successor Shabaka from shortly afterwards invading Egypt with an entirely different object in mind. Now the Nubians, fomenting rebellious discontent among the Egyptians, occupied the country and made war on the Persian garrison. This was the Ethiopian invasion well-remembered by all the ancient chroniclers, from Herodotus through to Diodorus and beyond.

For a while Shabaka was successful, and an independent Egypt under its Nubian king briefly began to jockey for position and influence in Palestine/Syria. Israel and Judah, traditional allies of Egypt, joined the rebellion and looked to Shabaka for assistance in defending their new-found freedom. But Egypt, as Sennacherib's general was shortly to say, was a "broken reed" incapable of defending her friends. Israel in particular paid a heavy price for this final display of loyalty to Egypt. The remainder of the Ten Tribes, who had not been deported by Tiglath-Pileser III and Shalmaneser V, were soon to be uprooted once and for all from their homeland and transported to the Iranian Plateau, where they were lost to posterity.

Although it is not generally admitted that Sargon conquered Egypt, a very clear hint that he did control the country is found in an inscription of his in which he records how a character named Jaman (probably a Greek) stirred up trouble in Philistia, then fled to Egypt when the Great King's troops approached. We are told that the rebel was put in chains by the Egyptian authorities and deported to Assyria.

After the reconquest of Egypt, Sargon (Darius), must have realized that the brutal oppression experienced under Shalmaneser V (Cambyses) had contributed to the revolt. He thus initiated a more lenient and less oppressive regime. The kings of Persia were to discover that the independent power of Nubia in the south, which Cambyses had been unable to subdue, would always remain a focus of Egyptian hopes so long as there was no line of native Egyptian rulers to act as a counterbalance. It is possible to date very precisely the lives and careers of the client monarchy of Tewosret, Siptah and Seti II, as well as of the Great Chancellor Bey. We shall argue that Sargon appointed a member of a minor branch of the old royal family, who was to go down in the records as Ramses Siptah, as a vassal king. This latter character legitimized his rule by marrying Merneptah's grand-daughter Tewosret, and he was to become the father of the child-pharaoh Merneptah-Siptah, who reigned briefly during the time of Sennacherib.

Queen Tewosret and the Three Brothers

The queen, or princess, Tewosret (also Twosre) is regarded as one of the most outstanding characters in Egyptian history. Jewellery found in a cache in the Valley of the Kings shows her to have been the principal wife of Seti II. Tewosret is regarded as "remarkable" because of the various baffling circumstances under which she appears. She possessed, for example, a separate tomb in the same valley as her husband. The honour of having her own tomb in the Valley of the Kings was a distinction previously accorded to "only one other royalty of female sex, namely Hatshepsowe [Hatshepsut]."[36]

Besides having her own tomb, the actual contents of the sepulcher proved to be "even more intriguing."[37] Whilst Tewosret is named "King's Great Wife" by virtue of her marriage to Seti II, one scene shows her standing behind another king who is making an offering; the name of this king, Merneptah-Siptah, has

36 A. H. Gardiner, *Egypt of the Pharaohs* (Oxford, 1966) pp. 277f.
37 Ibid.

been plastered over and that of Seti II cut into the same place. This presented a puzzle: "Since there are excellent reasons for believing that Sethos [Seti II] was the earlier of the two kings, this replacement must have been due to Twosre's later preference to be depicted with the king who had been her actual husband."[38] But this is a somewhat strained explanation, and has failed to gain widespread acceptance. Indeed the various marital relationships of Tewosret, as well as her actual identity, have long intrigued historians. She was called "King's great Wife," but also "Lady of the Two Lands," as well as "Mistress of Upper and Lower Egypt" — tantamount to being pharaoh herself. Another of her titles was "Hereditary Princess," a name which clearly identifies her as having a fairly unique royal pedigree. In Egypt, inheritance was through the female line, and marriage of a royal prince to the heiress, his sister, legalized his succession. The consort of the royal heiress, whatever his origin, would be elevated to kingship.

Bey, we have seen, established Tewosret's son, the boy Siptah, upon his father's throne. But who was his father? It is normally assumed that he must have been Seti II, since no other royal personage is known (so it is claimed) from the time. Yet other royal personages there were, though their existence is usually ignored in textbooks. A shadowy character known as Ramses Siptah seems to have briefly worn the royal diadem, whilst Horemheb the High Priest of Amon, who was allied to Tirhaka and Osorkon II, also appears to have mounted the throne for a short period, as the inscriptions in the tombs of Petamenophis and the crown prince Sosenk make abundantly clear.

These three, Horemheb, Ramses Siptah and Seti II seem to have been closely related. But how closely? And which of these, if any, was the father of Tewosret's son Merneptah Siptah?

It would appear that the three were brothers and that their story is preserved in Josephus, who lifted it from the pages of Manetho's lost work. The three characters mentioned here, Harmais, Ramesses and Sethosis, are normally believed to represent the characters of these names who established the Nineteenth Dynasty (i.e., Horemheb, Ramses I and Seti I), yet the story of how the Nineteenth Dynasty came to power is recounted by Manetho in quite a different place, where we hear of the rebellion of Osarsiph against pharaoh Amenophis and the wars of the "polluted wretches."[39] Nor does Manetho's account of the lives of Sethosis and Harmais accord in any way with the life-stories of the first Horemheb and Seti I. Thus we shall argue that the story of the three brothers Harmais, Ramesses and Sethosis belongs to the end of the Nineteenth Dynasty, not its beginning; and the Harmais mentioned here is the second Horemheb, the High Priest of Amon

---

38 Ibid.
39 I have dealt with this episode at some length in my *Empire of Thebes* (New York, 2007).

who lived and schemed during the reigns of Tirhaka and Sennacherib. The story is preserved thus in Josephus:

> The last-named king [Sethosis], who possessed an army of cavalry and a strong fleet, made his brother Harmais viceroy of Egypt and conferred upon him all the royal prerogatives, except that he enjoined upon him not to wear the diadem [and] not to wrong the queen.... He then departed on a campaign against Cyprus and Phoenicia, and later against the Assyrians and the Medes ... meanwhile, sometime after his departure, Harmais, whom he had left in Egypt, unscrupulously defied all his brother's injunctions. He violated the queen ... put on a diadem, and rose in revolt against his brother.... Sethosis instantly returned to Pelusium and recovered his kingdom.[40]

Evidently Sethosis of Manetho is Sethos of Herodotus, and the expedition of Sethosis against the Medes and Assyrians is the expedition of Sethos recounted by Herodotus against Sennacherib. This should have prompted the question: Was Sennacherib a Mede or Persian?

If we are on the right track, Ramesses of the above story is one and the same as Ramses Siptah. It must have been he who was the first husband of Tewosret and father of the boy pharaoh, Merneptah Siptah. In the earliest copy of Josephus, the medieval "Laurentian" manuscript (so named after the monastery of St Lawrence, where it is preserved), there is an interpolation in the form of a marginal note put there by the scribe: "In another copy [of Josephus] was found this reading: 'After him [a king named Amenophis] Sethosis and Ramesses, two brothers. The former [Sethosis] ... slew Ramesses and appointed Harmais, another of his brothers, viceroy of Egypt.'"

It would appear then that Ramses Siptah was a puppet ruler of Egypt appointed by the Great King's satrap Bey (whom we shall argue was Achaemenes, the satrap appointed by Xerxes). Ramses' brother Seti, the High Priest of Ptah at Memphis, at some stage rebelled; and during an engagement between rebels and troops loyal to the Great King, Ramses Siptah was slain. Bey (Achaemenes) then appointed the child heir Merneptah Siptah to his father's throne. In the meantime much of Egypt, with Tirhaka's assistance, was liberated. The Great King Sennacherib (Xerxes) approached the borders of the Nile kingdom with a mighty army, intending to bring the rebel province to heel, and Seti II, with a motley band of patriots, went to meet him. At this point, fate took an unexpected turn.

---

40 Josephus, *Against Apion* (Thackeray trans. pp. 201ff).

Seti II

One of the most enigmatic passages of Herodotus describes how the Assyrian King Sanacharib was overcome at the borders of Egypt when thousands of field mice overran the Assyrian camp, devouring quivers, bowstrings, and shield handles.[41] Herodotus informs us that the Egyptians had little hope of success against the mighty Assyrian host, and that, failing to persuade any of the country's warrior class to risk battle, a weak army composed of craftsmen was led against the invaders by Sethos, the priest of Hephaestus (i.e., Ptah).

Historians regard it as strange that Herodotus should make a leader by the name of Sethos (i.e., Seti) contemporary with Sennacherib, since it is believed that the last pharaoh of that name, Seti II, died over five centuries before Sennacherib was born: "In the popular tradition preserved by Herodotus the name of the Egyptian king is given as 'Sethos' ... the true appellation of the monarch has disappeared in favor of the great Seti."[42] Yet according to the reconstruction proposed in these pages, Seti II would indeed have been a contemporary of Sennacherib, and there is no need to postulate a mistake by either Herodotus or his informants. Since we shall identify Sennacherib as the alter-ego of Xerxes, it is clear that Seti II must have led a rebellion near the end of Xerxes' reign, a rebellion which continued into the time of Artaxerxes I. As such, he is almost certainly an alter-ego of Inaros, son of Psamtek, the rebel leader who enlisted the aid of Greek warriors in his prolonged war with the Great King. Herodotus informs us that no man ever did more mischief to the Persians than Inaros.[43]

One thing is certain. Seti himself enlisted the aid of northern troops, a fact proved by the existence of a leaf-shaped bronze broadsword, of European manufacture, inscribed with his name.

Whilst Herodotus' Egyptian informants made a native Egyptian lead her army against Sennacherib, we know from other sources, including the Bible, that the Nubian King Tirhaka was the real power in the land at the time. Thus in 2 Kings 19:9 we read:

> Word reached the Assyrians that the Egyptian army, led by King Tirhakah of Ethiopia, was coming to attack him.

Clearly Seti II was an ally, and very probably a vassal, of Tirhaka, and it was as an ally of Tirhaka that he moved against the Assyrians. How then are we to

---

41 Herodotus, ii, 141.

42 H. R. Hall, *The Ancient History of the Near East* (London, 1913) p. 492.

43 If Seti II was Inaros, then he suffered a terrible fate. After surrendering to Esarhaddon/Artaxerxes I, he was kept prisoner in Mesopotamia for five years, only to be finally impaled at the behest of the Great King's mother.

reconstruct the evidently momentous events of the period? It would appear that Egypt was firmly under the control of Assyria/Persia during most of the reign of Sargon, who, after securing his authority throughout the Iranian Plateau and Mesopotamia, marched into Egypt and sent Shabaka fleeing southwards into the Sudan. These events are obliquely referred to in 2 Kings 17:4. Four years before the death of Sargon, however (if we are right in identifying him with Darius I), Egypt again rebelled; and once more the Ethiopians, this time led by Shabaka's son Shabataka, marched north as liberators. But the new King Sennacherib (Xerxes) proved himself equal to the task of keeping the empire together and the Nubian army was routed for a second time.

It was at this stage that Tirhaka entered the scene. Manetho tells us that he became king after slaying "Sebichos." Certainly his rise to the throne is mysterious, and he was not a son of Shabaka. All we know is that he had gone north "as a youth of only twenty years with a king whose name is unfortunately lost, who nevertheless must have been Shabaka."[44] It is believed that he was entrusted with the command of the army in the second campaign against Sennacherib. "We know nothing of the circumstances which brought about his advent to the throne, but Manetho states, that leading an army from Ethiopia he slew Sebichos (who must be Shabataka), and seized the crown."[45] He is then abruptly pictured at Tanis as king, summoning his mother, whom he has not seen for many years, from Napata to Tanis that she might assume her proper station as queen-mother there. Interestingly, "it is not improbable that the Ethiopians at this time maintained Tanis as their Egyptian residence."[46] Tanis was Egypt's capital during the time of the Nineteenth Dynasty, supposedly five centuries earlier, and had enjoyed no comparable status in the intervening years. Once again, we see the Ethiopians display, an altogether mysterious (for conventional scholarship) connection with the Ramesside era.

In reality, however, this was the epoch of the latter Nineteenth Dynasty monarchs, of Tewosret, Siptah, and Seti II. In the years following Sennacherib's first and successful expedition against Egypt, Tewosret, acting as regent for her young son Siptah, effectively ruled the country as a vassal of the Great King in Asia.

Half way through the reign of Sennacherib, Egypt, spurred on by the intrigues of Tirhaka, rose again. The leader of the patriots, the High Priest of Ptah at Memphis, was Seti Merneptah (soon to be pharaoh Seti II). This man, with Tirhaka's support, inaugurated a guerrilla war against the Persian garrison and slew the

---

44 Breasted, *A History of Egypt* (1951) p. 554.
45 Ibid.
46 Ibid.

Persian puppet, his brother Ramses Siptah, as well as the Persian satrap Bey (Xerxes' brother Achaemenes). When Ramses Siptah's young son Merneptah Siptah died, probably of natural causes, Seti married the widowed queen Tewosret and claimed the throne for himself. With the assistance of Tirhaka, and the much more powerful support of Greek hoplites, Seti now prepared to meet the advancing host of Sennacherib. Encouraged by the example of Egypt, the tiny kingdom of Judah, Egypt's ancient ally, rebelled.

Meanwhile Seti II, who had made his brother Horemheb viceroy, marched in the direction of Palestine with whatever troops he could muster. It was at this juncture, when Assyrian/Persian victory seemed certain, that Horemheb, no doubt with the assistance of a surviving Persian garrison, betrayed his brother. He crowned himself pharaoh, legitimizing his position by marrying the royal heiress Tewosret. This was the meaning of Manetho's statement that Harmais had "violated the queen" in his brother's absence. But the reign of this second Horemheb was to be short-lived. The army of his ally Sennacherib was unexpectedly and dramatically destroyed in southern Palestine. What exactly happened on that fateful night, when the Great King's host died in their sleep, is anyone's guess. Certainly something did happen. The Egyptians explained it in terms of field mice; the Bible attributed the destruction to the Angel of the Lord.

Whatever the truth, Egypt was granted a prolonged period of independence and peace. Seti "instantly returned to Pelusium and recovered his kingdom," as Manetho puts it. The fate of the treacherous Harmais may be easily imagined. Sennacherib was to fare no better. By this stage probably a broken man, he was murdered by two of his sons while worshipping in the temple of Nergal. Another son, Esarhaddon, pursued the killers, but they escaped over the mountains to the north.

Esarhaddon at the Gates of "Sethosville"

After establishing his authority throughout Mesopotamia and the Iranian Plateau, Esarhaddon set out to regain control of Syria and Egypt. He wrote "I besieged, I captured, I plundered, I destroyed, I devastated, I burned with fire."[47] Various rebellious kings were executed. He threatened Tyre, whose king had "put his trust in his friend Tirhakah (Tarku), king of Ethiopia." He "threw up earthworks against the city," captured it, and made a vassal of its King Ba'lu.[48]

Having reduced Syria and the Phoenician coast, Esarhaddon's troops entered Egypt, only to experience a major reversal; in the "Esarhaddon Chronicle," writ-

---

47 R. Campbell-Thompson, *The Prisms of Esarhaddon and Ashurbanipal* (London, British Museum, 1931) p. 18.
48 D. D. Luckenbill, *ARAB* ii, 528.

ten over a hundred years after his death, we read: "In the sixth year the troops of Assyria went to Egypt; they fled before a storm."[49] What manner of "storm" could put the battle-hardened troops of the Great King to flight we can only guess. What is certain is that the campaign was a failure, for thereafter we hear, "in the tenth year, the troops of Assyria went to Egypt."[50] In this second campaign Esarhaddon marched along the military road running across Syria and along the Palestinian coast. He took the city of Sidon and "tore up and cast into the sea its walls and its foundations." Its King Abdimilkute tried to escape by ship but "was pulled out of the sea like a fish."[51] Esarhaddon cut off the head of the unfortunate king and sent rich booty from the plundered city to Assyria: "gold, silver, precious stones, elephant hides, ivory, maple and boxwood, garments of brightly colored wool and linen."[52] He carried off Abdimilkute's wife, his children, and his servants: "His people from far and near, which were countless.... I deported to Assyria."[53]

After the fall of Sidon, Esarhaddon summoned "twenty-two kings of Hatti, the seashore [i.e., Syria/Palestine], and the islands." Among the kings of the sea-coast were Manasseh (Me-na-si-i), king of Judah (Ia-u-di) and various princes of Edom, Moab, Gaza, Ashkelon, Ekron, Byblos, Arvad, Beth-Ammon and Ashdod — all referred to by name. He also summoned ten kings of Cyprus (Iadnana), mostly Greeks, if their names are anything to go by.

The route to Egypt and the flanks having been secured, Esarhaddon wrote: "I trod upon Arzani [to] the Brook of Egypt."[54] The "Brook of Egypt," Nahel Musur in the Assyrian texts, is Nahel Mizraim of the Hebrew texts, i.e., Wadi el-Arish, the historical frontier of Egypt and Palestine.

Esarhaddon entered Egypt and marched only a short distance before meeting his adversary, Tirhaka. This encounter occurred at a city named Ishupri. From here on his progress was slow: we are told that it took fifteen days to advance from Ishupri to Memphis, near the southern apex of the Nile Delta, close to modern-day Cairo.

> From the town of Ishupri as far as Memphis, his royal residence, a distance of fifteen days' march, I fought daily, without interruption, very bloody battles against Tirhakah, king of Egypt and Ethiopia, the one accursed by all the great gods. Five times I hit him with the point of my arrows, inflicting wounds from which he should not recover, and then I laid

49 "The Esarhaddon Chronicle" in Sidney Smith, *Babylonian Historical Texts Relating to the Capture and Downfall of Babylon* (London, 1924) p. 14.
50 Ibid.
51 Luckenbill, loc cit. ii, 527.
52 Ibid.
53 Ibid.
54 Ibid. ii, 710.

siege to Memphis, his royal residence, and conquered it in half a day by means of mines, breaches, and assault ladders; I destroyed it, tore down its walls, and burned it down.[55]

Scholars were puzzled by the mention in these accounts of Ishupri, the settlement at the starting-point in Esarhaddon's confrontation with Tirhaka. Its name was previously unknown, and it did not appear to occur on any of the hieroglyphic texts of the imperial age of Egypt. Eventually it was realized that Ishupri (or Ishhupri) had to be an Assyrian transcription of the throne-name of Seti II (Usikheprure), meaning "Sethosville" or "Sethosburg." Albrecht Alt, the leading German orientalist, was the first to reach this conclusion, and the solution was accepted by other scholars.[56] The problem raised by this identification, however, was the enormous span of time separating Seti II from Esarhaddon in the conventional timescale: over five centuries. The survival of the name Ishupri/Sethosville was regarded by Alt as "remarkable," and even more strange was the fact that for these five centuries the town remained unmentioned in the hieroglyphic texts, appearing for the first time in the annals of Esarhaddon. How, it was asked, could an Assyrian king of the seventh century come to call a town or fortress of the eastern Delta by the name of an obscure pharaoh of an age long past? And how did this settlement, referred to no fewer than three times by Esarhaddon, escape mention in all other texts, Egyptian or otherwise, prior to 671 BC?

But of course there was no gap of five centuries between Seti II and Esarhaddon; they were contemporaries. Seti II is the Sethos of Herodotus, and almost certainly is the same person as Inaros, who led the Egyptians against Sennacherib/Xerxes just twelve or thirteen years earlier. (Seti II's Golden Horus name was Aaneruemtawnebu, or Ineru-emtawnebu, vowels being conjectural.) He was a national hero and a savior of the country, and it is only natural that a city or fortress guarding the Asiatic frontier should bear his name. If this identification is correct, it seems likely that Esarhaddon (whom we shall argue was identical to Artaxerxes I) personally led the initial campaign and left the "mopping-up" operation, including the defeat of Seti II/Inaros and his Greek allies, to his general Megabyzus.

Seizing Memphis, Esarhaddon captured Tirhaka's family, his queen, his children, and the women of his palace "as well as horses and cattle beyond counting" and all this he sent to Assyria. "All Ethiopians I deported from Egypt, leaving not even one to do homage to me. Everywhere in Egypt I appointed new kings,

---

55 Ibid. ii, 580.
56 "Ishupri," *Orientalistische Literarzeitung* (1925) Nr. 9/10.

governors, officers." The fact that here he refers to "new" kings and governors, suggests that kings and governors had earlier been appointed by his father Sennacherib, something not generally accepted by scholarship. Among these earlier appointments, of course, were Tewosret and Siptah.

After the capture of Memphis, Esarhaddon pushed south to Nubia. "From Egypt I departed, to Melukha (Ethiopia) I marched straightaway."[57] The journey south lasted thirty days. Summing up this campaign, Esarhaddon wrote: "I conquered Egypt, Upper Egypt, and Ethiopia (Musur, Patursi, and Kush). Tirhakah, its king, five times I fought with him with my javelin, and I brought all of his land under my sway, I ruled it."[58] On his way back to Assyria, Esarhaddon carved a record of his achievement onto a rock at Nahr el-Kelb, the Dog River. The story of his conquest is placed, with obvious ironic intent, next to an inscription of Ramses II, the latter commemorating the great pharaoh's victories in Asia. Scholars are forced by the logic of accepted chronology to assume that Esarhaddon placed his record next to that of a pharaoh who lived almost six centuries earlier. But there is no gap of many centuries between the two. The record of Ramses' victories against the peoples of Asia was carved less than a hundred years before the Asiatic Great King responded with a record of his victories against the peoples of Egypt and Ethiopia. The Nahr el-Kelb reliefs are just one more vital clue to the true chronology of the period.

Upon his return to Mesopotamia, Esarhaddon must have assumed that the kingdom of the Nile would give him no more trouble. Yet after just a few years Tirhaka again moved north out of Nubia and took possession of Egypt.

Wenamon

"In the twelfth year the king of Assyria went to Egypt, fell sick on the road, and died on the tenth day of the month of Marcheswan."[59] These words, from the "Esarhaddon Chronicle," record the death of the Great King on his way to Egypt. With very little delay, the crown prince Ashurbanipal asserted his claim to the throne and assembled a new army for the reconquest. In his account of events leading up to the campaign, Ashurbanipal narrates that:

> In my first campaign I marched against Egypt [Magan] and Ethiopia [Meluhha]. Tirhakah [*Tarqu*], king of Egypt [*Musur*] and Nubia [*Kusu*], whom Esarhaddon, king of Assyria, my own father, had defeated and in whose country he [Esarhaddon] had ruled, this [same] Tirhakah forgot the might of Ashur, Ishtar and the [other] great gods, my lords, and put his

---

57 Luckenbill, loc cit. ii, 557ff.

58 Ibid. ii, 580.

59 S. Smith, "The Esarhaddon Chronicle," *Babylonian Historical Texts Relating to the Capture and Downfall of Babylon* (London, 1924) p. 15.

trust in his own power. He turned against the kings [and] regents whom my father had appointed in Egypt. He entered and took residence in Memphis [Me-im-pi], the city which my own father had conquered and incorporated into Assyrian territory.[60]

No mention is made of any resistance on the part of the Assyrian-appointed kings and governors. When Tirhaka "sent his army to kill, to plunder, to despoil" Egypt, he says ,they appealed to Assyria for help. "I was walking round in the midst of Nineveh," he recounts, "when a swift courier came and reported to me," and "my heart was bitter and much afflicted." There and then Ashurbanipal vowed to "make the greatest haste to aid the kings and governors, my vassals."

Within a year of his father's death, then, a great army was assembled and set out on the road to Egypt. Ashurbanipal did not personally participate in the campaign, entrusting the task to his generals. Outside Memphis, Tirhaka's forces met the army of the Great King. Ashurbanipal records the outcome laconically: "On the wide battlefield I accomplished the overthrow of his [Tirhaka's] army." When news of the defeat reached Tirhaka in his palace in Memphis, "terrible fear struck him." He decided to flee: "To save his life in a ship he sailed; his camp he abandoned and fled alone." The Nubian king retreated up the Nile to Thebes (No), whilst the Assyrian army captured Memphis, along with the ships of the Ethiopian fleet. Ashurbanipal's generals now quickly pressed their attack southward, and were joined by the local kings who claimed they had been unwilling hosts to Tirhaka and his forces.

Within only ten days the army of the Great King reached Thebes, but Tirhaka was no longer there. He had forsaken the city and established himself in a fortified position on the opposite bank of the Nile. For the time being, the Assyrian troops were content to leave him be.

At this stage, Ashurbanipal recorded a list of twenty Egyptian princes and potentates whom he appointed or reappointed as his local agents. The list contains the names of many of the rulers earlier named as client kings of Esarhaddon. There is a Pedubast (Butubisti) of Tanis, as well as a Sosenk (Shushinqu) of Busiris, contemporaries who share the same names as Pedubast I and Sosenk III, two other contemporaries who are however in the conventional chronology supposed to have lived many years earlier. There is in addition a very interesting newcomer: one Unamon (Wenamon), a prince of Natkhu (perhaps Buto in Lower Egypt).[61] Now, a potentate of the same name is famous for the record he left of a fraught journey he made to Byblos at the request of the High Priest Heri-

---

60 J. Prichard, *ANET* p. 294 (trans. Luckenbill).
61 F. Petrie, *A History of Egypt* Vol. 3 (London, 1905) p. 299

hor, in order to procure cedar wood for the building of a sacred barge of Amon. The humiliation suffered by Wenamon, and the open contempt with which he was treated on his travels, vividly illustrates the state of abject subjugation into which the land of Egypt had fallen. Surely, we might imagine, a very apt description of the Nile kingdom during the years of conquest and subsequent exploitation inflicted by Esarhaddon and Ashurbanipal. But here we encounter a grave problem. The Wenamon who journeyed to Byblos is not regarded as the same person as the Wenamon mentioned in the list of Ashurbanipal. On the contrary, this man is placed in what is called the Twenty-First Dynasty, during the time of the later Ramessides, and therefore almost five centuries before his namesake, the contemporary of Ashurbanipal. Yet again, that gap of five centuries!

It should of course be recalled that Velikovsky has already identified the Twenty-First Dynasty as a line of priest-kings who "reigned" during the latter years of the Persian epoch and the early years of the Ptolemaic age.[62] For other reasons, quite unconnected to the arguments presented in this volume, Velikovsky had come to the conclusion that Wenamon, as well as Herihor, the High Priest for whom he labored, were contemporaries of Darius II, and that the Twenty-First Dynasty Wenamon was identical to yet another man of the same name who flourished under Darius II and erected a shrine at the Siwa Oasis. Thus we know of a Wenamon of the 12th century, one of the 7th century, and one of the 5th. Note the two hiatuses which we earlier promised to close.

Like Velikovsky, we too place Wenamon in the reign of Darius II, for the latter king and Ashurbanipal were one and the same man.

Ethiopia Defeated

From Ashurbanipal's records we know that scarcely had Assyrian control been re-established than the native princes of Egypt once again began communicating with Tirhaka. In the words of Ashurbanipal, "their hearts plotted evil." But their secret correspondence was discovered by Assyrian officials: "An officer of mine heard of these matters and met their cunning with cunning. He captured their mounted messengers, together with their messages, which they had dispatched to Tirhaka, king of Ethiopia."[63] The governors implicated were sent to Nineveh in chains.

Ashurbanipal took savage vengeance upon the civilian population of Egypt's cities. The soldiers "put to the sword the inhabitants, young and old — they

---

62 In his Peoples of the Sea (1977).
63 A. C. Piepkorn, *Historical Prism Inscriptions of Assurbanipal* (Chicago, 1933) pp. 13-15.

did not spare anybody among them. They hung their corpses from stakes, flayed their skins, and covered with them the walls of the towns."[64]

When the twenty conspirators reached Nineveh, all save one were put to death. Only Necho (Nikuu), king of Sais, was allowed to live. No doubt mindful of the need for a reliable ally in Egypt to keep it safe from the Ethiopians, Ashurbanipal sent Necho back to the country as its sole king: "And I, Assurbanipal, inclined towards friendliness, had mercy upon Necho, my own servant, whom Esarhaddon, my own father, had made king in Kar-bel-matate [Sais]." The Great King secured Necho's allegiance by "an oath more severe than the former. I inspired his heart with confidence, clothed him in splendid garments, laid upon him a golden chain as the emblem of his royalty — Chariots, horses, mules, I presented to him for his royal riding. My officials I sent with him at his request."[65] In addition to all this, Necho's son Psamtek was appointed to rule Athribis.

It is of interest to note that in reinstating Necho and Psamtek Ashurbanipal was employing a policy which Herodotus claims was peculiar to the Persians:

> And had it not been suspected that he [Psammenitus] was planning innovations, he would probably have recovered Egypt, so as to have the government intrusted to him. For the Persians are accustomed to honour the sons of kings, and even if they have revolted from them, nevertheless bestow the government upon their children; that such is their custom may be proved from many other examples, and amongst them by that of Thannyras, the son of Inarus the Libyan, who recovered the government which his father had; and by that of Pausiris, son of Amyrtaeus, for he also recovered his father's government: yet none ever did more mischief to the Persians than Inarus and Amyrtaeus.[66]

Strangely enough, it is quite possible that one of the two examples provided by Herodotus has a direct bearing on the events of Ashurbanipal's reign — for according to the reconstruction of history proposed here, the rebellion of Amyrtaeus (in the time of Artaxerxes I) would have coincided with the reigns of Esarhaddon and Ashurbanipal. It may even be that Amyrtaeus and Pausiris are identical to Necho and Psamtek.

Tirhaka made no further attempts on Egypt, and we are told that in his 25th year he accepted a son of Shabaka named Tanutamen as co-regent. A few months later he died at Napata.

With the optimism and naivety of youth, Tanutamen once more, in the fourth year of Ashurbanipal, led an Ethiopian army north into Egypt. He fortified Thebes and Heliopolis, and besieged the Assyrian/Persian garrison at Mem-

---

64 Luckenbill, loc cit. ii, 876.
65 Ibid. ii, 905.
66 Herodotus, iii, 15.

phis. Necho, who remained loyal to Ashurbanipal, was slain.[67] His son Psamtek, Herodotus tells us, escaped to Palestine and lived there in exile. But "when the Ethiopian departed by reason of what he saw in a dream, the Egyptians of the province of Sais brought him back from Syria."

It was no dream that persuaded the Ethiopian to quit Egypt but the very real threat of Assyrian arms. Ashurbanipal's response to the new crisis was characteristically swift. "Against Egypt and Ethiopia I waged bitter warfare and established my might." Routing the Nubians in Lower Egypt, the Assyrian/Persian forces moved south to Thebes. "Tandamane [Tanutamen] heard of the approach of my expedition (only when) I had (already) set foot in Egyptian territory." The Assyrian army "defeated him in a great open battle and scattered his (armed) might." Tanutamen "fled alone and entered Thebes, his royal residence." Ashurbanipal's army followed. "They marched after him, covering a distance of one month in ten days on difficult roads as far as Thebes." The Ethiopian did not risk another battle: "He saw my mighty battle array approaching, left Thebes, and fled to Kipkipi."

The ancient and revered capital of Upper Egypt now lay prostrate before Ashurbanipal's troops and was "smashed (as if by) a floodstorm." A great slaughter of the population took place and its chief citizens were led into captivity. Besides, wrote Ashurbanipal, "I carried off from Thebes heavy booty, beyond counting," The Assyrian king listed some of the truly fabulous wealth looted from the ancient city, mentioning in particular an enormous obelisk of electrum, weighing 2,500 talents.[68] "I made Egypt and Nubia feel my weapons bitterly and celebrated my triumph. With full hands and safely I returned to Nineveh." The ferocity of Ashurbanipal's treatment resounded throughout the whole Mediterranean world, and a few years later we find the prophet Nahum, in a famous passage, reminding the people of Nineveh of Thebes' fate, as a timely warning of what the future held in store for them: "Art thou better than populous No [Thebes] that was situate among the rivers.... Ethiopia and Egypt were her strength and it was infinite.... Yet was she carried away, she went into captivity: her young children were dashed into pieces at the top of all her streets: and they cast lots for her honourable men, and her great men were bound in chains."

Psamtek and the 'Saite' Dynasty

With the departure of Tanutamen, Ashurbanipal appointed Psamtek, the son of Necho, in his father's place. Information about this rather enigmatic character

---

67 Ibid. ii, 152. Herodotus was actually mistaken on one detail, for he says that it was Sabakos (Shabaka) who killed Necho — whereas in reality it was Shabaka's son, Tanutamen.
68 H. R. Hall "The Ethiopians and Assyrians in Egypt" in *CAH* Vol. 3 (1ˢᵗ ed. 1929) p. 285.

is derived from a number of quite separate sources. He is referred to by Herodotus, who names him Psammetichos; he describes him as having enlisted the aid of Ionian and Carian mercenaries.[69] Ashurbanipal of course also has much to say about him. Yet he occurs again, strangely enough, in documents of supposedly two hundred years later, from the time of Artaxerxes I and Darius II.

Psamtek is a mystery man in more ways than one. Even his name is an enigma. Since the discovery of the key to Egypt's ancient language by Young and Champollion, scholars have sought to make sense of this important figure's origin. It was concluded that the name was indeed Egyptian, and meant "the negus-vendor" (i.e., the lemonade-seller). Now, as Immanuel Velikovsky noted, kings of Egypt were regarded as incarnations of the deity and their names reflected their exalted status. Thus we have "son of Ra," "Amen is content" etc. But "the lemonade-seller"! We can only agree with Velikovsky that such a translation suggests that the name is not Egyptian at all — and sure enough, a prominent linguist advised Velikovsky that the ending -ek was strongly suggestive of a Persian origin.[70] But this of course then begs the question: How could a vassal king of Egypt, supposedly under Assyrian domination in the 7th century, bear a name of Persian origin?

Yet Psamtek, we noted, was also the name borne by a vassal king of Egypt in the 5th century, when the country was indeed under the domination of Persia — and at this point we need explain a point of confusion that has bedeviled Egyptian historiography for many years.

Historians speak of a dynasty of kings named "Saites" (after the city of Sais in the Delta), designated as the Twenty-Sixth in the Manethoan system. These rulers, listed as Necho I, Psammetichus, Necho II and Amasis, are normally placed in the 7th and 6th centuries BC, and it is not doubted that the kings Necho (Nikuu) and Psammetich (Psamtek) mentioned in the annals of Esarhaddon and Ashurbanipal are identical to the Saites of Manetho. Yet, as we said, kings, or more properly priest-kings, of the same names occur in the time of Artaxerxes I and Darius II, supposedly two centuries later. Indeed, in many ways the situation in Egypt during the reigns of these two Persian monarchs looks like a mirror-image of Egypt in the time of the Neo-Assyrians. Thus for example a tomb at Sheikh Fadl, reliably dated to the time of Artaxerxes I, names, as apparently contemporary rulers, a man called Tirhaka, as well as "some Saite Pharaohs,"[71] whilst we are told that the "Egyptians of the Achaemenid period consciously revive the

---

69 Herodotus, ii, 152.
70 In a personal communication between Velikovsky and Professor Martin Dickson of Princeton University. See Velikovsky, *Peoples of the Sea* (1977) p. 97.
71 J. D. Ray, "Egypt 525-404 BC" in *The Cambridge Ancient History* Vol. 4 (2nd ed, 1988) p. 280.

grandiose names involving those of Saite kings, including even the unpopular Necho."[72]

Yet this is clearly much more than a simple "reviving" of names two centuries old. We might imagine Egyptian princes reviving the names of other Egyptians, such as Necho or Psamtek (even though the latter was probably Persian). But why, in all seriousness, would they simultaneously revive the names of Ethiopian kings like Tirhaka?

The fact is, all of the "Saite" kings belong in the Persian period. The priest-king Psamtek, who sent grain to the Athenians in 445 BC, and who was mentioned by the satrap Arsames in the famous Cairo parchment texts,[73] was identical to the Psamtek appointed by Ashurbanipal. When we come to reconstruct the political history of Egypt during this time, we must therefore use simultaneously the material that is recognized as Persian Age along with the material recognized as Neo-Assyrian Age.

From what can be gleaned from Neo-Assyrian documentation, it has been surmised that for a while Psamtek played the part of a loyal puppet and ally of the Great King; yet all the while, displaying the same guile as his father, he worked to increase his own authority. Thus in Ashurbanipal's fourteenth year it is believed that Psamtek apparently contrived to have the Great King's garrison quit Egypt. The problem here is that Ashurbanipal's records do not name Psamtek, but refer to one Tushimilki as the leader of the insurrection. Historians merely assume that Tushimilki must be an alter-ego of Psamtek because they derive their ideas from Herodotus, who described Psammetichus as a mighty ruler who re-established Egypt as a great power in the 7th century, following the period of Assyrian domination. The confused chronology of Herodotus is a topic we shall return to at a later stage.

Psamtek was in fact no heroic liberator of Egypt. We know from the Cairo Aramaic parchments that throughout his apparently long period in office he acted as a loyal servant to the Persian satrap Arsames, a man resident in Babylon who systematically plundered the wealth of Egypt. One of the latter of these parchments, written to Psamtek's successor Nekht-hor, describes the long and faithful tenure of Psamtek in the position of Arsames' plenipotentiary.

From Ashurbanipal's records, which are of course the records of Darius II, it would seem that the rebel Tushimilki achieved some measure of independence for Egypt with the assistance of troops from across the sea sent by a King "Guggu of Sparda." With this aid, said Ashurbanipal, Egypt had "thrown off the yoke of

---

72 Ibid. p. 276.
73 These documents are discussed in some detail by Velikovsky in *Peoples of the Sea* (1977).

my sovereignty." Since these documents are believed to date from the 7th century, the latter character is normally identified as Gyges of Lydia (Sparda being the normal name for Lydia in the cuneiform writings of Achaemenid times). However, from the point of view of the reconstruction proposed here, we shall identify this Guggu of Sparda as a king of Sparta, who went to the assistance of Egypt in the latter part of the 5th century. That Sparda could not in any case be Lydia is confirmed by the fact that Ashurbanipal describes it as "a district of the other side of the sea, a distant place, whose name the kings, my fathers, had not heard."[74] By no stretch of the imagination could we describe Lydia as on the "other side of the sea" from Mesopotamia.

Thus Guggu of Sparda was in all probability a king of Sparta. It is known that throughout the 5th century both Athens and Sparta periodically intervened in Egypt against the authority of the Great King. And sure enough, a Spartan king named Aegeus was indeed active against the Persians and their interests towards the end of the 5th century.

We must therefore now look at the question of a precise chronology.

The withdrawal of the Assyrian garrison is normally placed in the year 654 BC, a date which, of course, if we are correct, is about 200 years too early. These events really took place during the reign of Darius II, in the second half of the 5th century BC.

In the scheme of things proposed here, Esarhaddon was the same man as Artaxerxes I, and we know that he became Great King in the year 465 BC. Whilst Artaxerxes I is normally accorded a reign of 40 years, the Neo-Assyrian monuments seem to give Esarhaddon a reign of 12 years (though, as we shall see later, there are some grounds for believing this should be more like 18 years). The 40 (or 41) year reign really belonged to his successor Darius II/Ashurbanipal. Thus, in the present scheme, Artaxerxes I must have died in 446 BC, which date must mark the true starting point of Darius II's reign. Fourteen years after this, then, in 432 BC, the rebel leader Tushimilki apparently threw out the occupying army of the Great King.

Yet we know from other sources that a truly independent Egypt was only achieved around 401 BC, at the earliest. Such being the case, it is clear that Tushimilki's rebellion was ultimately a failure.

With the death of Ashurbanipal, the "Neo-Assyrian" Empire was rent by the most serious wars of succession it had ever experienced. These, which we shall refer to again at a later stage, were of course the same wars as marked the death of Darius II, when the Empire was rocked by a civil war between two of the

---

74 Luckenbill, loc cit. ii, 784.

Great King's sons, Cyrus the Younger and Artaxerxes II. It was then that Egypt finally threw off the Persian yoke.

Egypt Regains Her Freedom

Let us recapitulate briefly. History says that during the reign of the Neo-Assyrian King Ashurbanipal, Egypt was administered by a native potentate named Psamtek, son of Necho, and that sometime near the end of Psamtek's reign, the kingdom of the Nile regained its independence.

History also says that two centuries later, in the time of Darius II, Egypt was again administered by a native potentate named Psamtek (also apparently a son of Necho), and that shortly after this man's time the kingdom of the Nile regained its independence.

If these two epochs are one and the same, then it is incumbent upon us to reconstruct the course of events which led to Egyptian independence.

According to conventional ideas (which are derived both from the Bible and from classical authors such as Herodotus), after the death of the 7th century Psamtek, the new king, known as Necho II, set out to re-establish Egypt's Asiatic Empire. He led a great army northwards to the Euphrates, apparently as an ally of the last Neo-Assyrian King Ashuruballit II but actually intent on sharing in the spoils from the corpse of the Assyrian state. After some initial successes, Necho II was defeated at a great battle near Carchemish with the Babylonians, who were commanded by the crown-prince Nebuchadrezzar (II).

This conflict is normally dated around 605 BC. However, since, as we state, Necho I, Psamtek, and Necho II actually belonged to the Persian period, we must see in these events (almost all of the knowledge of which is derived from the Bible) the wars which rent the Persian Empire following the death of Darius II, in 404 BC. According to the classical writers, who are the main source for the story of Egypt during the 5th and 4th century, the freedom struggle was initiated by a leader named Amyrtaeus II, who, taking advantage of the civil war then raging between Cyrus the Younger and Artaxerxes II, managed to liberate large areas of the country. When Amyrtaeus died, around 400 BC, the cause was taken up by Nepherites, who succeeded in establishing complete independence from the Persian crown and even sought to re-establish Egyptian control in Palestine and Syria.

Classical sources report that after only a short reign Nepherites died and was replaced not by a son, but by a pro-Persian potentate named Acoris. Yet the disintegration of Persian authority continued unabated, and after little more than two or three years of pretended loyalty to Artaxerxes II, Acoris too (probably inspired by Evagoras of Cyprus) rebelled. Acoris died in 379 or 378 BC, and the throne was seized by Nectanebo I, who claimed to be a son of Nepherites.

For us, this Nepherites must have been one and the same as Setnakht, founder of the Twentieth Dynasty, whom the Harris Papyrus names as the liberator of the country after the years of exploitation endured under Arsa/Arsames the Asiatic. We have already referred to the extensive collection of parchment correspondences between Arsames and his Egyptian agents Psamtek and Nekht-hor. The latter of these, Nekht-hor, is identical (as Velikovsky so ably argued in *Peoples of the Sea*) to Nekht-hor-heb, the "king" normally identified by historians as the hieroglyphic version of Nectanebo I. Yet Velikovsky presented manifold proofs that Nekht-hor-heb could by no means be identified with Nectanebo I, the mighty pharaoh who repulsed the Persian attempt at reconquest in the time of Artaxerxes II. Nevertheless, it is just possible that Nekht-hor, or Nekht-hor-heb, was indeed a fighter for Egyptian freedom; for in view of the strong tradition, found both in the Bible and in Herodotus, that Necho II (who battled against a great Asiatic power at Carchemish) was the son of Psamtek, it seems highly likely that Nekht-hor, the Persian Age Psamtek's successor, was also identical (simultaneously) to the Persian Age freedom-fighter Nepherites and the "Saite" freedom-fighter Necho II.

We know from the classical authors that the re-establishment of Egypt's independence near the year 400 BC was a rather complicated and by no means straightforward affair. A system of alliances existed by which Egyptian rulers and potentates affiliated themselves with different power-brokers in the Achaemenid state. The final break with Persia may well have occurred when Artaxerxes II, victor in the war against his half-brother Cyrus the Younger, turned against the Egyptian allies of Cyrus the Younger. The latter's Egyptian confederate, namely Nepherites/Setnakht, would then have had no option but to proclaim the country's independence.

If, as we say, Nekht-hor-heb was the same person as the freedom-fighter Nepherites, we might expect some echo of this in his dealings with his Persian master Arsames. This latter exploited Egypt ruthlessly, and the last of his letters from the Cairo collection are actually to Nekht-hor-heb. What is remarkable about these documents is the disrespect with which Arsames addresses Nekht-hor-heb.[75]

Now it is known that Arsames died before the end of Darius II's reign, after a public career of fifty-three years. Although dates are unclear, it is quite probable that his passing preceded that of Darius II by no great span. We do not know

---

75 See *Peoples of the Sea* p. 25 "Arsames' letters to Nekht-hor have no introductory salute, showing the satrap's haughty attitude toward his plenipotentiaries of Egyptian extraction."

who succeeded Arsames, but we can be fairly sure that Nekht-hor-heb would have been anxious to find any means of obtaining a less severe taskmaster in Persia.

Nekht-hor-heb, we know, was initially a Persian client, as was Nepherites. Yet the defeat of Cyrus the Younger did not end Artaxerxes II's problems. Other rebels arose to challenge him, and his weakness soon became apparent to the long-suffering inhabitants of Egypt. As we shall see at a later stage,[76] by his tenth year Artaxerxes II was involved in another round of civil war, this time with the satrap of Assyria. Now the Egyptian ruler — whether Nekht-hor-heb/Nepherites or Acoris — his confidence boosted by a decade of Persian non-interference, marched northwards towards the Euphrates with the intention of offering assistance to the Assyrian rebel. Arriving too late however to affect the outcome of the war, the Egyptians encountered the Great King's forces (commanded by the crown-prince Nebuchadrezzar) near the city of Carchemish, where they were routed.

Our only knowledge of this battle comes from the Old Testament. Here it is portrayed as a major defeat for the Egyptians and a preliminary to the reconquest of the country which occurred during the reign of Nebuchadrezzar himself, after his father Nabopolasser had died. The Bible however fails to mention that an earlier attempt by the "Babylonians" to invade Egypt — shortly after the clash at Carchemish — was repulsed by the Egyptians.

In his much-maligned *Ramses II and his Time*, Velikovsky argued that the biblical battle of Carchemish was identical to Ramses II's famous battle at Kadesh. This of course cannot have been the case, since the Battle of Kadesh occurred around 580 BC and the Battle of Carchemish around 395 BC. Nevertheless, in view of the striking parallels between the biblical description of the conflict at Carchemish and the Egyptian description of Kadesh (in both encounters, for example, the Wood of Bab or Baw is mentioned), it would appear that certain traditions about the earlier Egyptian defeat at Kadesh were incorporated by the biblical scribes into their description of the Battle of Carchemish. This could have happened because of the close geographical proximity of Kadesh to Carchemish. Indeed, as Velikovsky argued, they may even have been identical since the word *kadesh* implies "holy" and was a name applied to many cult-center cities in Syria/Palestine.

---

76 In Chapter 6.

CHAPTER 3. *PEOPLES OF THE SEA* REVISITED

A NEGLECTED VOLUME

We have already mentioned the evidence of *Peoples of the Sea*, a volume devoted by Velikovsky towards reconstructing the latter years of pharaohnic history. In *Peoples of the Sea*, Velikovsky argued, as we do, that the Nineteenth Dynasty came to an end with the Persian Conquest in 525 BC, and that the Twentieth Dynasty did not immediately follow the Nineteenth but commenced around 400 BC, and was identical to the so-called Thirtieth Dynasty, which saw the re-emergence of an independent Egypt under pharaohs Nepherites and Nectanebo I.

The present author was taken to task for his support of this work by British writer John Bimson at a conference held in London in 2002. In his paper, Bimson argued that no great lapse of time could have existed between the Nineteenth and Twentieth Dynasties, and this theme was taken up again in the *Proceedings* published a few months later.[77] The major evidence cited was that of the genealogies of the workmen of Deir el-Medina. These genealogies shall be examined presently.

Before looking at these however it should be remarked that whilst Velikovsky's critics have tended to concentrate on such things as the Deir el-Medina genealogies, which appear to pose a problem for him, they have tended to completely ignore the veritable mountain of other evidence in his favor which he pre-

---

77 John Bimson, "Finding the Limits of Chronological Revision" *Proceedings of Society for Interdisciplinary Studies, Conference: Ages Still in Chaos?* (London, September, 2002).

sented in the various volumes of the *Ages in Chaos* series, as well as in numerous articles and lectures.

As mentioned in Chapter 2, the sheer quantity of evidence presented in *Peoples of the Sea* would require a book in itself to examine properly. This is not our purpose here. Nevertheless, since the argument presented in *Peoples of the Sea* is fully supported in these pages, it behoves us to take a brief look at some of the material found therein. This is due to the fact that, whilst our reconstruction has tended to look at the Egyptian Twenty-Second to Twenty-Sixth Dynasties, as well as the Neo-Assyrian and Neo-Babylonian histories, we have not dealt at all with the Twentieth or Twenty-First Dynasties, which were the major focus of Velikovsky's investigations. In fact, the Twenty-Second to Twenty-Eighth Dynasties were actually contemporary with the Twenty-First Dynasty. Both the latter and the former belong in the Persian Age, though some of the Twenty-First Dynasty rulers flourished even later, in the period of Egyptian independence in the Thirtieth Dynasty and even into the early Ptolemaic epoch.

Whilst we have presented abundant proof that the kings and potentates of the Twenty-Second to Twenty-Sixth Dynasties were contemporaries of the Persians, we shall find exactly the same is true of the Twenty-First Dynasty, a line of "rulers" who were not actually kings at all, but priest-princes appointed by the Persians themselves. In their tombs and monuments, in their inscriptions and documents, these men left a wealth of evidence showing quite clearly that they were contemporaries of the Achaemenid Great Kings.

But before looking at these men, let us summarize, as briefly as possible, the main thesis of *Peoples of the Sea*, which was, essentially, that the great pharaoh Ramses III, of the Twentieth Dynasty, was an alter-ego Nectanebo I, the king who, in the middle of the 4th century BC, won a famous victory over the Persian general Pharnabazus as he sought to reincorporate Egypt into the Achaemenid state. The story, as outlined in *Peoples of the Sea*, is recounted in Velikovsky's inimitable fashion, and it must be stated that any reader wishing to acquaint himself properly with the evidence needs to read the original.

Ramses III Repulses the Persians

In *Peoples of the Sea* Velikovsky brought forward a huge body of evidence for making the Twentieth Dynasty equivalent to the Thirtieth, which, under its pharaohs Nectanebo I and Nectanebo II, reasserted Egyptian independence during the first half of the 4th century. Thus in his (and my own) scenario the Twentieth Dynasty, beginning around 400 BC, comes about seventy years after the last pharaoh of the Nineteenth, Seti II, who must have died in 470 BC, or thereabouts.

Some of the most important evidence of the book may be summarized thus.

First and foremost, the Pereset against whom Ramses III waged war bear a name identical to that (Peresett) by which the Persians are known in monuments of the Ptolemaic Age.[78] Secondly, Velikovsky noted that the Pereset wear a distinctive "feathered crown," classic symbol of Persian royalty and divinity. Both the Pereset and their "Sea Peoples" allies wear sophisticated "lobster-shell" armor, reminiscent of the Roman legionaries' *lorica segmentata*. Such armor was not developed by the Romans until the first century BC.[79] Then there is Ramses III's Horus name, part of which reads "Nekht-a-neb" (Nectanebo).

Another crucial piece of the jigsaw was formed by the Greek letters on tiles from the palace of Ramses III at Tell el-Yahudiya. Quoting a number of authorities, Velikovsky showed that the letters, clearly signatures of the craftsmen who manufactured them, were without question Greek letters of a late period, close to the time of the Ptolemies.[80] Anticipating the objections that might be raised, Velikovsky demonstrated how a concerted and prolonged attempt to interpret these letters as Egyptian hieratic symbols had produced no good equivalents, and he made the telling point that even the few approximate similarities observed were far from convincing. Furthermore, asked Velikovsky, how was it that out of the thousands of hieratic symbols that Egyptian craftsmen might have used, they only employed a very few which almost all looked exactly Greek?

This point was never answered by the critics.

Velikovsky could even refer to one art historian who noted the peculiarly Persian look of the glazing on the colored side of the same tiles.[81]

Artwork of the Twentieth Dynasty, Velikovsky proved, has its closest parallels in that of the Persian and Ptolemaic Ages. This evidence too was ignored by the critics.

---

78 On the Canopus Decree, from the time of Ptolemy III they are described as the "vile P-r-s-tt" who had carried away the statues of the gods from Egypt. The Greek version of the same part of the text reads: "And the sacred images which had been carried off from the country by the Persians".

79 One point missed by Velikovsky, but which should be mentioned here, is that on the bas-reliefs at Medinet-Habu traces of blue paint can still be seen indicating the original colour of the swords carried by the Pereset and Sea Peoples. These were evidently of iron. Yet according to Greek tradition (in Pausanias, iii, 7, 8 and iii, 11, 8) the Hellenes did not begin to use iron swords until the time of the Spartan king Anaxandrides (ie around 575 BC). We should remember here too that a steel (not iron) dagger was found in the tomb of Tutankhamun; utterly impossible in the 14th century BC, but to be expected near the end of the 7th.

80 See *Peoples of the Sea* pp. 6-12. Velikovsky quotes Emil Brugsch, who noted that "The Greek letters, and especially the alpha, found on fragments and disks leave no room for doubt that the work was executed during the last centuries of the Egyptian Empire and probably in the time of the Ptolemies."

81 According to Naville, "This work strikingly reminds us of Persian art, both modern and antique. In Persia, it seems to have been made on a larger scale than in Egypt." E. Naville, *The Mound of the Jew* p. 6.

The great war in which Ramses III repulsed the attacks of the Pereset and Sea Peoples offers, as Velikovsky demonstrated, very precise parallels with the war waged by Artaxerxes II in his attempted reconquest of the Nile kingdom. These parallels too were given no serious consideration by the critics.

Then there was the Harris Papyrus (already alluded to in Chapter 2), a document of the Twentieth Dynasty, apparently composed during the reign of Ramses III or his son, which mentioned a foreign invasion and prolonged period of oppression, during which Egypt was under the rule of an Asiatic potentate named Arsa.

Yet some of the strongest evidence brought forward in *Peoples of the Sea* was not concerned with Ramses III at all, but with a number of characters from the time of the so-called Twenty-First Dynasty a line of priest-kings who "reigned" both before, during and after time of the Twentieth Dynasty. This evidence, especially concerning Ourmai, Wenamon, Psusennes and Si-Amon, was of primary importance and should not have been dismissed in the perfunctory manner it was. It was of such importance that I propose to devote considerable space here to a simple reiteration of what was said.

The Dynasty of Priests

Historians are agreed that a character named Ourmai, who left a letter lamenting the catastrophic state that Egypt had fallen into in his time, marks the beginning of what has come to be known as the Twenty-First Dynasty. From Ourmai onwards, who was evidently a member of the aristocracy, the genealogy of the Twenty-First Dynasty rulers can be traced with a fair degree of accuracy through to a certain Si-Amon, a man who was responsible for the rewrapping and reburial of a large cache of royal mummies at Deir el-Bahri.

We shall deal with the most important of these in turn, and highlight the virtually irrefutable evidence brought forward by Velikovsky for placing all of them in the Persian and early Ptolemaic ages.

In his letter, which is regarded as the first document known from the Twenty-First Dynasty, Ourmai complains how foreign invaders had plundered the entire land, had thrown him from his home and had carried off servants and members of his own household. The letter, first translated in 1961, paints a truly terrifying picture of the state of the country:

> I was carried away unjustly, I am bereft of all, I am speechless [to protest], I am robbed, though I did no wrong; I am thrown out of my city, the property is seized, nothing is left [to me]. I am [defenseless] before the mighty wrongdoers.

As Velikovsky remarked, Ourmai is only one of many victims. In the next sentence he seems to refer to his colleagues and employees:

> They are taken away from me; their wives are killed [before them]; their children are dispersed, some thrown into prison, others seized as prey.
> I am thrown out of my yesterday's domicile, compelled to roam in harsh wanderings. The land is engulfed in enemy's fire. South, north, west and east belong to him.

Conventional scholarship claims to know of no foreign conquest of Egypt during the time of the Twenty-First Dynasty, so the mention by Ourmai of such an event is regarded as most mysterious.[82] On the other hand, Egyptologists claim that no contemporary Egyptian account of Cambyses' invasion has survived: yet, as Velikovsky demonstrated, important details in Ourmai's letter call the Persian Invasion, as described by Herodotus, very forcefully to mind. Thus for example, at one stage, Ourmai complains about the bodies of the dead having been exposed and left without anyone to rebury them. This sounds precisely like Herodotus' account of Cambyses, whom he describes as opening the royal sepulchers and examining their contents.[83] He also slaughtered an Apis bull in addition to other sacrilegious acts.

Again, as above, Ourmai complains of children being "seized as prey." This sounds very like the complaint that Herodotus puts into the mouth of the captive King Croesus, who accused Cambyses of killing children.[84] Herodotus reports that shortly after completing the subjugation of Egypt, Cambyses permitted the Greek mercenaries to return home.[85] Once again, this seems to find a reflection in the statement of Ourmai that "the marines" have gone home.

Most strikingly of all, however, the statement of Ourmai that he is compelled to beg bread from the occupying soldiers is strikingly similar to an incident mentioned by Herodotus, where the captive King Psammenitus sits impassively as all his family and friends are butchered by Cambyses. Only when he sees an old friend, a formerly wealthy and powerful man, begging bread from the Persian troops, does he burst into tears.[86] Velikovsky argued that it may well even have been the real experiences of Ourmai that inspired this account in Herodotus, a proposition that the present writer also regards as highly plausible.

*

---

82 G. Fecht, "Der Moskauer 'literarische Brief' als historisches Dokument," *Zeitschrift für Aegyptische Sprache* 87 (1962).

83 Herodotus, iii, 16.

84 Ibid. iii, 36.

85 Ibid. iii, 25.

86 Ibid. iii, 14.

Wenamon has already been mentioned. He was an important official of the Twenty-First Dynasty, whose account of an expedition to Byblos to obtain wood for a barque of Amon is one of the best-known documents of ancient Egyptian literature. We have noted also that a priest-prince named Wenamon built a shrine at the Siwa oasis during the reign of Darius II. No one denies that the latter Wenamon was of the Persian Age, though it is said that he was not the same man as the servant of Herihor in the Twenty-First Dynasty.

The existence of a third Wenamon has also been mentioned, one who was active in the time of Ashurbanipal, a man whom we have identified with Darius II. Velikovsky of course did not realize that the Neo-Assyrian kings were identical to the Persians, though he did note the peculiar reoccurrence of characters and individuals in the Neo-Assyrian period (supposedly 7th century) and the Persian period of the 5th. Thus in *Peoples of the Sea* he argued quite forcefully that the Psamtek, or Psamshek, who interred a number of Apis bulls and whose monuments are found throughout Egypt, was not a man of the 7th century but of the 5th.[87] In addition, he cited evidence showing that a character named Amasis, generally believed to be the 6th century king of that name, was actually a contemporary of Darius II.[88]

Any attempt to dissociate the Twenty-First Dynasty Wenamon with his Persian Age namesake has to answer the somewhat awkward fact that the Wenamon of Dynasty 21 was a servant of the High Priest of Amon, Herihor,[89] whilst the Persian Age Wenamon built his shrine to Amon at Siwa, one of the greatest of all centers of Amon-worship in the later period.[90] The lives of both Wenamons are intimately connected to the cult of Amon.

On the walls of the Siwa shrine Wenamon boasts that he is the "true master of foreign lands." Now, as Velikovsky observed, no commoner such as Wenamon could dare claim to be a ruler of foreign countries. Evidently "master of foreign lands" means an authority on foreign lands, one knowledgeable about foreign lands. And of course the Wenamon of the Twenty-First Dynasty, by virtue of his long sojourn in Byblos, could indeed rightly claim to be an authority on foreign countries. Yet more proof that the two Wenamons are the same.

---

87 Velikovsky, *Peoples of the Sea* pp. 23-5 and 93-8.

88 A. H. Gardiner, *Egypt of the Pharaohs* p. 366: "a general, whose business it was to summon all the mayors of the country to bring gifts for the embalmment of the Apis bull, bore the same name as King Amasis and wrote it in a cartouche, although his stela alludes to the Persian invasion [occupation]."

89 Herihor had a son called Piankhy. Yet Piankhy was a name associated with the Nubian kings of the 25th Dynasty, supposedly of the 8th-7th century. Again, a strange echo after five centuries of cultural features belonging to the Late Bronze Age of the 12th-11th centuries.

90 The earliest monuments of Siwa, it should be noted, are of the Persian period, so no one denies that the Wenamon buried at the oasis was a contemporary of the Persian Empire. The only question is: Which king of the Persians was he contemporary with?

As described in Chapter 2, Wenamon was appointed by Ashurbanipal/Darius II as governor of Natkhu in Lower Egypt just one year into the latter's reign. The man appointed by Ashurbanipal must have been the same person as the Wenamon who set out on his journey to Byblos in year 5 of an unnamed ruler. However, since Darius II and Ashurbanipal are one and the same person, this would imply that Darius II had a much longer reign than is conventionally believed. Nevertheless, there are excellent reasons to suppose that Wenamon died near the end of the period of Persian dominance (i.e., around 410 BC).

Thus Wenamon must have survived for perhaps as long as forty years as governor of Natkhu and servant of the High Priest of Amon.

After the time of Wenamon and Herihor, there arose in Lower Egypt a prince named Psusennes (Pesibkhenno). Psusennes was the son of Nesubanebded, who is mentioned in the travels of Wenamon as the prince with a residence in Tanis. Psusennes inherited from his father the residence and title, and added to it those of high priest and first prophet of Amon, the titles of his father-in-law Herihor. On some occasions he also used the title "king."

Psusennes' tomb, virtually intact, was discovered at Tanis by Montet. Many wonderful items, including a coffin of solid silver and a face-mask of gold, were found therein. These items, however, Psusennes had appropriated from another king, Osorkon II, of the Twenty-Second Dynasty, who, in conventional chronology, should actually have come *after* Psusennes. More on this presently.

Montet's team also uncovered, among a veritable Alladin's Cave of wonders, twenty-eight bracelets of gold and silver. On one of these was written the words: "The king, master of the two lands [Upper and Lower Egypt], master of the sword, first prophet of Amon-re-souter (Psousennes Miamoun), given life." What drew the excavator's attention here was the spelling of "king" (n-s-w): it was written in a very peculiar way. It was spelled by designing a baboon (cynocephalus) holding an eye (oudja). "The word n-s-w or 'king' is written here as in the Ptolemaic period...."[91] The baboon and the eye between its hands was a sophisticated way, a pun or play on words, to express the word king, and appeared only very late in Egyptian texts.[92]

There was another peculiarity in the same sentence; the word "god" (accompanying the name of Amon-re) "is written with a hawk as often found in the Ptolemaic period."

---

91 P. Montet, *Psousennes* p. 149 Cf. Emile Chassinat "Le Mot seten 'Roi', *Revue de l'Egypte Ancienne* II (Paris, 1929) 5f.
92 Montet, loc cit.

As noted, Psusennes, of the so-called Twenty-First Dynasty, actually reused the grave and materials of a "Libyan" or Twenty-Second Dynasty pharaoh. In the words of Velikovsky:

> Osorkon II, who placed foundation deposits under two corners of the temple enclave, also built himself a tomb inside the enclosure. Very little was found of funerary equipment — the tomb had already been violated by tomb robbers and left rather empty in antiquity. The laborers who worked for Montet in clearing this tomb passed "without noticing" ... to the tomb of Psusennes, thus making a discovery. This tomb had not been emptied of its treasures: violators had not discovered it. Montet wrote: "The thieves who pillaged the tomb of Osorkon II, adjacent to that of Psusennes, having made numerous trial diggings all around and having found nothing, abandoned their search."
>
> How could it happen that with many trial diggings the tomb thieves of antiquity missed the adjacent tomb whereas the fellahin working for Montet, even without perception of a discovery, moved from one subterranean tomb to the other? Yet signs of search and tunneling around the tomb of Osorkon were still in evidence.
>
> Apparently Osorkon's tomb was pillaged before Psusennes was put to rest and possibly by Psusennes himself. Furthermore, as shall be discussed shortly, Psusennes' tomb was originally built for a king of the Libyan Dynasty. Psusennes appropriated it for himself.[93]

Velikovsky rightly perceived that Psusennes had violated and plundered, for his own use, the tombs of his "Libyan" predecessors. However, believing as he did that the Libyans had flourished in the 8th century BC, he could find no rationale for Psusennes' actions. But the rationale has been provided in the present volume. The "Libyan" kings were in fact a line of Asiatic overlords placed in power by the Persian invaders. By the time of Psusennes, however, who must, according to Velikovsky, have flourished during the reign of Ramses III — thus during the period of Egyptian independence which began around 400 BC — the "Libyan" rulers had been expelled or killed. Psusennes' looting of these kings' tombs thus makes perfect sense, and begins to look as much like an act of vengeance as one of simple opportunism.

The Twenty-First Dynasty is generally ended with a character named Si-Amon. He it was who closed and sealed the royal cache at Deir el-Bahri, where, along with some of the important rulers of the Eighteenth and Nineteenth Dynasties, he also placed the remains of his immediate predecessor, Peinuzem II. Si-Amon, who never claimed the title of king, was apparently active all over Egypt, for evidence of his presence is also found in the royal burials at Tanis in the Delta, where he seems to have replaced the remains of Psusennes' queen with those of

---

93 *Peoples of the Sea*, pp. 154-5.

Amenemope. A scarab of Si-Amon was found in the tomb's vestibule, an artifact that "amounts to a signature," in the words of Montet.

So there is little doubt that Si-Amon belongs to the Twenty-First Dynasty, and indeed he is normally dated to the first half of the 10th century BC. Yet here there arises a problem, for there existed another Si-Amon, also a priestly ruler who never claimed royal titles; but this Si-Amon belonged to the age of the Ptolemies.

It was in 1940, at the height of World War II, that the tomb of this second Si-Amon was discovered, dug into a hillside in the Siwa Oasis. The sepulcher was found to contain beautiful examples of the Egyptian painter's art, and was much visited. Shortly after its discovery, a local Arab moved in with his family and for a small fee allowed tourists of every kind to come and take what they wanted. Much was destroyed.

After this initial destruction, the site was examined by Ahmed Fakhri, who performed a thorough survey.

Fakhri found that Si-Amon himself, as well as family members, was much in evidence. In most scenes he is portrayed in traditional Egyptian garb. In a few murals however he is shown with a mane of black hair and a curly black beard. In another picture, where he is shown with his younger son, the boy "wears a short cloak of Greek style."[94] Indeed, even a glance at the boy leaves not the slightest doubt that he wears a chiton, described by Fakhri as "a cloak of pure Greek style."

As noted, this Ptolemaic-age Si-Amon, like his Twenty-First Dynasty namesake, makes no claims to royal tutelary. Nevertheless, like his predecessor, he goes apparently as far as he dares, with a succession of empty cartouches painted around the tomb walls.

Now in view of the rather obvious similarities between the two Si-Amons, we might expect Egyptologists to have considered the possibility that they might be identical. They did not do so, because it would have meant overturning the whole of ancient history. Instead, reasons were sought to differentiate between them. It was said, for example, that the Si-Amon of the Siwa Oasis had his name spelled in a slightly different fashion to that of the Twenty-First Dynasty prince. Yet in anticipation of such objections, Velikovsky demonstrated in great detail how the art and culture of the Ptolemaic Si-Amon's time permitted no differentiation at all. Thus for example Twenty-First Dynasty Si-Amon placed a magnificent decorated leather canopy in the long passage leading to the cache of royal burials at Deir el-Bahri. This artifact was adorned in a manner strikingly

---

94 A. Fakhri, *Siwa Oasis* (1940).

similar to the paintings on Si-Amon's own tomb at Siwa; both the canopy and the tomb showed lines of vultures, whose portrayal was identical in both cases. Other features of the canopy and the tomb displayed similar precise parallels. So much so, indeed, that the observer is left with the impression that canopy and tomb must have been executed by the same artist.[95] Yet the Si-Amon buried at Siwa was unquestionably of the Ptolemaic period, as the various illustrations of himself and his son show only too well.

Scholars are left then with not one but a veritable host of conundrums when they look at the Twenty-First Dynasty. The art and culture of the time seems late. So too does the language, with numerous expressions and words otherwise attested only in the Persian and Ptolemaic periods. Persian words, even, such as Shahedet, appear. And characters duplicate themselves. Thus there must be postulated two Wenamons: one in the late Persian period, and one in the 11th century. Thus also must be postulated two Si-Amons: one in the early Ptolemaic period and one in the 10th century. Even the number of generations separating the two namesakes appear to repeat themselves. Thus the Twenty-First Dynasty Wenamon is separated from the Twenty-First Dynasty Si-Amon by about five generations, whilst the Twenty-First Dynasty Si-Amon is separated from the Ptolemaic Si-Amon by about five generations.

Surely we must, with Velikovsky, reach a point where we must call a halt and declare that the emperor has no clothes.

The Deir El-Medina Genealogies

In the present work I have argued that the last Nineteenth Dynasty rulers, Siptah, Tewosre and Seti II, are actually to be placed within the Persian period itself, with the "king maker" Bey, who raised Siptah to the throne, identified with the Persian satrap of Darius I or Xerxes. Thus I said that Seti II (identical to Sethos of Herodotus) was to be identified with Inaros, the Egyptian enemy of Xerxes/Sennacherib and Artaxerxes I/Esarhaddon and must have flourished roughly between 475 and 465 BC. In this scheme then, from the absolute end of the Nineteenth Dynasty to the beginning of the Twentieth, there is a gap of about 70 years.

In 2002, John Bimson suggested that the genealogies of the workmen at Deir el Medina permitted no gap at all, not even of 70 years. I'll return to this question presently. For the moment, however, I want to emphasize one thing. Whether or not we place the end of the Nineteenth Dynasty at the start of the Persian epoch, there is no question whatsoever that it was followed by an Asiatic occupation. This is put beyond doubt by the material relating to Bey as well as that concern-

---

95 A conclusion arrived at by Velikovsky himself. *Peoples of the Sea*, pp. 186-7.

ing Arsa the Asiatic, in the Harris Papyrus. So leaving aside for one minute the length of the interlude and its absolute date, there is no doubt of its reality — and this is denied by no one.

All very well, but still we must face the thorny question of duration. Bimson argued that these Asiatic invaders could not have been Persians because the duration of the occupation was too brief. But was it? Another crucial piece of evidence, as discussed in Chapter 2 of the present work, comes in the well-known Genealogy of Memphite priests. In this document a King Akheperre (believed to be Psusennes I of Dynasty 21) is placed immediately after the last pharaoh of Dynasty 19, Amenmesses. Two further kings named Psusennes follow, and then comes a Sosenk, after two further entries which do not mention the reigning monarch's name. Thus the Memphite genealogy apparently jumps straight from the Nineteenth Dynasty to the Twenty-First, with none of the great pharaohs of the Twentieth Dynasty having reigned long enough to be mentioned (thus the conventional explanation). Yet this is utterly impossible, because Ramses III alone had an extremely long reign.

Clearly then the evidence of the Memphite Genealogy strongly supports the contention that the Twentieth Dynasty did not immediately follow the Nineteenth, and that the so-called Twenty-First Dynasty (of Psusennes kings) was a client dynasty under the Persians, which actually came *before* the Twentieth Dynasty.[96]

Yet this entire scheme, along with the evidence presented for it in the foregoing pages, is challenged and overturned by the Deir el-Medina genealogies, or so it is claimed by John Bimson.

The workmen of Deir el Medina, who constructed the royal tombs at Thebes, left a great deal of written information (usually in the form of short inscriptions carved on ostraca) about themselves and their families. Bimson referred to the very "dense information" available from here, proving no great lapse of time between the Nineteenth and Twentieth Dynasties. In fact, in his conference paper Bimson mentioned only one character who is said to bridge the gap, this being a "son of Paneb" around in the 29th year of Ramses III. Paneb himself was a contemporary of Amenmesses/Mose. If this "son of Paneb" really was a contemporary of Ramses III, it does then appear to create a problem for me.

What is the answer?

---

96 Though some were contemporary with the 20th Dynasty and one or two even with the Ptolemies. The Memphite Genealogy's placing of kings named Psusennes before the Osorkons and Sosenks might appear to be problematical, since we have made the "Libyans" actually, in general, earlier than the 21st Dynasty. It should be noted however that the Psusennes buried at Tanis very definitely came after the "Libyans," so he cannot be identical to the so-called 21st Dynasty rulers named on the Memphite Genealogy.

To begin with, it has to be admitted that a "son of Paneb" was active at the time of Ramses III, and that Paneb himself was a well-known criminal and hoodlum of the latter years of the Nineteenth Dynasty. Yet it is entirely possible that the "son of Paneb" active in the time of Ramses III was actually a descendant of the Paneb who lived during the Nineteenth Dynasty. Amongst many ancient societies the term "son of" was regularly used to mean "descendant." But if the "son of Paneb" was a real son and not a great-grandson or great, great-grandson, then his father cannot have been the Paneb condemned in the last years of the Nineteenth Dynasty for his criminal activities. It strikes me as rather odd that someone would wish to be known as the son of such a notorious miscreant, though I do concede that, given the peculiarities of human nature, this is not impossible. Nevertheless, the evidence indicates that the name Paneb was not confined to a single individual but was a family title passed down through the generations and borne by many people.

In his paper Bimson referred to an article by Egyptologist Michael Jones, which went into much more detail regarding the Deir el Medina genealogies. And I must admit that on first looking into this article it did appear that he had provided as strong evidence as Bimson claimed. But a more careful reading of the paper revealed deep flaws in Jones' thinking.

The "son of Paneb" mentioned by Bimson is also mentioned by Jones. To the "son of Paneb" Jones also adds Paneb himself, who is said to be traced from the 66th year of Ramses II right through to the 6th year of Ramses III. Jones also claims a vizier Hori, said to have held office from the first year of Siptah to the early part of Ramses III's reign.[97] All of this sounds impressive enough, but closer inspection raises serious questions about Jones' methods. The claim for example that Paneb is traced from the 66th year of Ramses II to the 6th year of Ramses III sounds suspicious. And whilst the data putting him in the 66th year of Ramses II is first hand (from an ostracon), that putting him in the 6th year of Ramses III is revealed by Jones, at a later stage, to be based on pure speculation.[98] Thus he tells us that, "Since Paneb is named as Chief Workman in an inscription dated in the 8th

---

97 In fact, this same Hori (supposedly) is said to have held office much longer than Jones admitted: actually from the time of Merneptah right through to Ramses III — an impossibly long period. This is all the more so when we remember that viziers were normally appointed in mid to late life. Obviously there was more than one Hori — a fact confirmed by the monuments which speak of a Hori, son of Hori.

98 Ironically enough, in his own conference paper Bimson suggests that some characters spanning the 19th and 20th Dynasties seem to have too long a life-span and that, if anything, their lives should be shortened. Confusingly, he did not make it plain that it was commoners, and not kings, whose lives were "too long." The elongation of the lives of these commoners of Deir el Medina is a result of trying to force fit their lives into a preconceived chronology. Generations of families used the same names, but this has not been taken into account by Egyptologists.

year of Queen Tawosret, the last ruler of the XIXth Dynasty ... the king whose 6th year has just been mentioned *must in all probability be Ramesses III*"[99] (my italics). In other words, since conventional chronology places Ramses III immediately after the end of the Nineteenth Dynasty, he must be the king referred to.

This tendency to circular reasoning is confirmed by other statements of Jones. Thus another character named Amennakht is said by him to be dated to "the reigns of Seti II, Amenmesse, Siptah and *possibly* Ramesses III."[100]

Thinking of similar type is revealed throughout the paper. Thus the Chief Workman from Ramses III's 11th year is named Nekhemmut. According to Jones, Nekhemmut "is first attested as a workman in the first year of the reign of King Amenmesse, and he is seen again in the reign of Siptah."[101] Thus Jones has Nekhemmut as a prime example of a character spanning the Nineteenth-Twentieth Dynasty interchange. But in the genealogical table accompanying the text there is information which calls his confident assertion into serious doubt. Here we find a Nekhemmut (in addition of course to the man who lived in the time of Amenmesse and Siptah) in the time of Ramses II (19th Dyn.), a Nekhemmut in the time of Ramses III (20th Dyn.), and a Nekhemmut apparently spanning the reigns of Ramses IV to Ramses IX (late 20th Dyn.). No attempt is made by Jones to explain this recurrence of Nekhemmut over a period which even he must concede covers many generations. The obvious solution is that there was not one Nekhemmut (as in the article Jones nevertheless tries to imply) but many.

The same scenario is repeated with regard to a character named Khons. Thus Jones states that "Nekhemmut was old enough to have had a son, Khons, who is mentioned among the offenders in the Salt Papyrus. But Khons must have been cleared of all charges, since he followed his father in office as Chief Workman in the 16th year of Ramesses III."[102] In other words, another prime example of someone spanning the 19th and 20th Dynasties. Yet once again the accompanying genealogical table casts doubts on this interpretation. Here there is a Khons in the early reign of Ramses II, a Khons in the late reign of Ramses II or the early reign of Amenmesse, a Khons in the time of Ramses III, and a Khons in the reigns of Ramses X and XI. In other words, there were a number of characters bearing the name. Yet, as with Nekhemmut, this was a factor neither considered nor even mentioned in the article.

The evidence taken as a whole suggests that the Deir el Medina material is very much open to interpretation, given that the same names recurred in families

99 Michael Jones, "Some Detailed Evidence from Egypt against Velikovsky's Revised Chronology," *SIS Review*, Vol. VI p. 29.
100 Ibid.
101 Ibid.
102 Ibid.

over many generations. That writers such as Michael Jones see in these documents proof of a continuity from the Nineteenth to the Twentieth Dynasties is evidence of circular reasoning. In order to "tie in" the two dynasties, Jones is even prepared to fly in the face of logic. Thus common sense alone would suggest it to be highly unlikely that a man (Khons) named as a criminal on the Salt Papyrus would later be appointed Chief Workman under Ramses III. If Jones had been following reason rather than trying to make the data fit preconceived notions of chronology, it would have been obvious that the Khons of Ramses III was an entirely different person.

Before leaving this topic, let me reiterate: If the Deir el Medina material means what Michael Jones and John Bimson claim it means, then it stands in total contradiction to the Harris Papyrus and the Memphite Genealogy. And whilst the evidence from Deir el Medina is confused and open to many interpretations, the evidence of the Harris Papyrus and the Memphite Genealogy is crystal clear in its meaning.[103]

Tomb Robbers and Craftsmen of Deir el-Medina

Is it possible to make sense of the Deir el-Medina material along the lines of the reconstruction presented in the foregoing pages? I believe that it is.

The world of the Deir el-Medina community, in its later years (from the latter period of the Nineteenth Dynasty onwards) was a world of disturbance and instability. Tomb robbery, apparently, was a major problem, as was criminality of other kinds. A general disintegration of this variety is normally a sign of political unrest.

For Velikovsky of course (and for us) the Twentieth and Twenty-First Dynasties, from which time many of the Deir el-Medina characters are dated, corresponded to the Persian epoch; and during this period, particularly in the Twenty-First Dynasty, tomb robbery became a major problem in Egypt. Many of the Twenty-First Dynasty "rulers" themselves were little more than plunderers who, under the pretext of "rewrapping" royal mummies, actually relieved them of jewels and other valuables. For Velikovsky, it was the Persian Invasion itself which led to this situation, with the conqueror Cambyses giving the lead.[104]

---

103 This of course raises question: Why then do scholars trust the Deir el Medina material against the Harris Papyrus and the Memphite genealogy? The answer is the inertia and ossification normally associated with what might be called the conventional view. Long before the discovery of the Harris Papyrus or the Memphite Genealogy it had already been "established" that Ramses III came immediately after the 19th Dynasty. No new discoveries have been able to uproot this dogma.

104 Velikovsky quotes Herodotus iii, 37-38, who speaks of Cambyses opening the royal burials and examining the contents.

In *Peoples of the Sea* Velikovsky refers to a tomb robbery episode of the late Twentieth Dynasty very similar to that described in the Salt Papyrus, from the time immediately following Seti II. According to the reconstruction outlined in the present volume, Seti II was himself a contemporary of the Persian King Xerxes and would therefore also have been contemporary with the priest-kings of the late Twentieth and Twenty-First Dynasties.

The tomb robbery mentioned by Velikovsky is recounted in the famous Papyrus Mayer A, now in the Liverpool Museum. The papyrus, from Year 1 of an unnamed king, speaks of an investigation concerning the plunder of the royal tombs of the Eighteenth and Nineteenth Dynasties. The document is reliably dated to the time of Ramses IX, regarded as belonging to the final years of the Twentieth Dynasty. It is worth pointing out here that Velikovsky regarded the last of the Ramessides, from Ramses IX onwards, as actually coming before Ramses III and his immediate successors. He had excellent grounds for making this adjustment, as the reader of *Peoples of the Sea* will readily understand, and it is a position fully supported by the present writer. In this scheme then Ramses IX, X, and XI were priest-kings who "reigned" in the mid to late 5th century, during the times of Artaxerxes I and Darius II. Actually, it was Ramses IX who appointed Herihor as High Priest of Amon, the same Herihor who sent Wenamon to Byblos early in the reign of Darius II. From our point of view then the tomb violations of this epoch are to be placed little more than a decade after the crimes referred to on the Salt Papyrus, from the time of Seti II.

At a hearing before a commission appointed to investigate the crime, a certain porter called Ahautinofer, as well as various other witnesses and accused, was interrogated. The testimony of Ahautinofer relates that a group of "barbarians" (i.e., foreigners), led by one Peheti, had come and seized a temple, presumably one of the Theban shrines. Ahautinofer also mentions the suppression of Amenhotep, "who used to be High Priest of Amon."[105] Several inscriptions of this High Priest Amenhotep are known; one bas-relief shows him offering homage of flowers to King Neferkere-setpenre, designated by modern historians as Ramses IX.

Since it was Ramses IX who appointed Herihor as High Priest, we conclude — to repeat what we said above — that the tomb violations, the seizure of the temple of Amon and the removal of the High Priest Amenhotep, all occurred little more than a decade after the time of Seti II and the similar tomb robbery described in the Salt Papyrus.

At least two characters mentioned at Deir el-Medina were contemporaries of Ahautinofer and must have been aware of the trial mentioned in Mayer Papyrus A. Thus one of the Nekhemmuts was alive in the time of Siptah (late Nineteenth

---

105 Papyrus Mayer A, 6, published in T. E. Peet, *The Mayer Papyri A and B* (London, 1920).

Dynasty — around 475-465 BC) and in the time of Ramses IX (around 450 BC). It is therefore likely that the Nekhemmuts of Siptah's and Ramses IX's time were one and the same person. The Nekhemmut of Ramses III's time (circa 380-340 BC) was however probably a grandson or great-grandson.

Nekhemmut's son Khons must also have witnessed the trial recounted in Mayer A, for he too was a contemporary of the late Ramessides, Ramses X and XI.

Those convicted of theft in the wake of the trial were put to death by Pinhasi (or Pinehas), a commander, apparently, of the "barbarians" who had earlier seized the temple and deposed Amenhotep. We might imagine, as Velikovsky said, that a man who thus restored order would be highly regarded by the population, but this was not the case. "The name Pinhasi is written in such a way as to make it certain that he was an enemy of the loyalists at Thebes, and the absence of any title shows that he was a very well-known personage."[106] Why should a man who punished criminals and established order be regarded as "an enemy of the loyalists" or nationalists? Pinhasi is known also to have imposed or collected taxes in towns south of Thebes and at times made the population scatter in fear of some people who are described in hieroglyphic texts by a foreign word, *mdwt-'n*. No other occurrence of this name is found in Egyptian literature, but we can conclude, with Velikovsky, that *mdwt-'n* in all probability refers to the Medes.

Thus the evidence of Deir el-Medina, contrary to the assertions of some, in no way contradicts the scheme presented here. If the interlude between the Nineteenth and Twentieth Dynasties was brief and peaceful, why would tomb robbery have been such a problem? Why too would "barbarian" troops be responsible for keeping order at the time? Why also would these foreigners, even though they restored order, still be regarded as enemies by the "loyalists" or "nationalists" at Thebes? Why even the existence of "nationalists" at all, if Egypt were an independent country? And to recapitulate: Why would a foreigner such as Bey have the ability to appoint Egyptian kings in the final years of the Nineteenth Dynasty? And why should Ramses III of the Twentieth Dynasty speak of "long years" and "empty years" of anarchy even *before* Egypt came to be exploited by Arsa the Asiatic?

Taken together, the evidence powerfully supports our contention that the Twenty-First Dynasty of Priest Kings, as well as the late Ramessides of the Twentieth Dynasty (i.e., Ramses IX, X, and XI), came between the Nineteenth and Twentieth Dynasties, and that these "rulers" presided over a land occupied, oppressed and exploited by the mighty power of Achaemenid Persia.

---

106 A. H. Gardiner, *Egypt of the Pharaohs* (Oxford, 1966) p. 302.

PART 2

Having thus completed the reconstruction of the Persian Period of Egypt's history, it behoves us now to complete the second task we set ourselves at the beginning of the book, namely to reconstruct Neo-Assyrian (or more accurately Persian) history.

The pages to follow will reveal that the Neo-Assyrian and Neo-Babylonian kings are in fact alter-egos of the Achaemenid Persians — a group of monarchs who, though ruling Mesopotamia at one of the most prosperous periods of its history, left (apparently) little or no trace of their stay in the Land of the Two Rivers. We shall note how archaeologists have remained puzzled and perplexed by this Persian disappearing act for over a century and how the various attempts made to explain it away have all proved unsatisfactory. We shall see how in site after site throughout Mesopotamia, the Neo-Assyrian (and Neo-Babylonian) archaeology is found directly underneath that of the Hellenists — without any Persian Age material intervening. According to the normal rules of stratigraphy, that would and should have automatically meant the identification of the Neo-Assyrians and Neo-Babylonians with the Persians. But in Mesopotamia the normal rules of stratigraphy were not followed, and a false history entered the textbooks where it has heaped problem after problem on the heads of historians ever since.

As a first step then in reconstructing the history of the Fertile Crescent, we need to examine how the present chronology was formulated and how it came to achieve the status, quite literally, of divine revelation.

Chapter 4. Archaeology's "Centuries of Darkness"

Puzzles and Anomalies

The history and archaeology of the Fertile Crescent presents scholars with problems of perhaps far greater magnitude than those facing Egyptologists. How the histories of the great nations of Mesopotamia and Syria/Palestine were reconstructed by archaeologists in the 19th century, and how dubious were some of the methods used, is a story we shall examine presently. We can be content at the moment to state that it has become increasingly evident that scholars committed major errors in the compilation of the region's chronology, and that rather than face up to the problems and re-examine the fundamentals, they resorted first of all to convoluted explanations of anomalous facts, and then quite simply to ignoring them.

Yet, as demonstrated in Part 1 of the present work, the habit of brushing things under the carpet has begun to trip us up. Increasingly the uncomfortable facts are raising their ugly heads and re-emerging from the footnotes of the obscure academic journals to which they had been banished.

In the past fifteen years alone there has been a rush of publications highlighting some of the problems. The wider public has now been made familiar (thanks to Peter James, et al.) with the "centuries of darkness" that shroud the histories of the Near Eastern civilizations between the end of the Bronze Age and the beginning of the Iron. In *Centuries of Darkness* (1991), James and his co-authors presented fairly compelling evidence to show that at least a couple of centuries in the history of the region are unaccounted for archaeologically. More recently, David Rohl (*A Test of Time*) has argued that this gap is closer to three centuries. The evidence presented by these and others can now be added to the enormous body of material brought forward by Immanuel Velikovsky in his various publications, which demonstrated fairly conclusively that there are actually around five centuries unaccounted for between the Middle Eastern Bronze and Iron Ages. The remainder of the present work will examine a substantial volume of evidence corroborating Velikovsky's initial findings. We shall find that the nations and civilizations of the Near East disappear, leaving not a trace, around 1300 BC, only to re-emerge, completely unchanged, around 800 BC. This holds good for Hittites, Assyrians, Babylonians, and Greeks.

Yet even greater question-marks have now emerged. In Germany Gunnar Heinsohn has shown that the problems are by no means confined to the Bronze Age/Iron Age interchange. In various publications, especially *Die Sumerer gab es nicht* (1987) and *Wann lebten die Pharaonen?* (1990), Heinsohn has demonstrated that the problems of ancient chronology are not to be solved by simply closing down the gap (of three or five centuries) between the Bronze and Iron epochs. Something much more fundamental is amiss.

Consider the facts.

In the earliest known chronology of Egypt, that of Herodotus, the pyramid-building pharaohs, Cheops, Chephren and Mycerinus (currently dated around 2,500 BC), are placed almost immediately before the Ethiopian pharaoh Shabaka (currently dated around 720 BC). Only one other king, a man named Anysis, is placed by Herodotus between Mycerinus and Shabaka, which in effect means that the Father of History made the pyramid-builders reign sometime in the 8th century BC — almost 2,000 years after the date provided by modern authorities.

Over the years, as might be expected, Herodotus' chronology has caused no small debate among Egyptologists. One solution has been to suggest that the order of his history is corrupt, and that the pyramid-builders were misplaced by a later editor. Yet an honest appraisal of the evidence, much of which is now simply ignored in the textbooks, would suggest that Herodotus was not far from the truth and that Egyptian chronology needs to be shortened dramatically.

Note, to begin with, the actual architecture. Quite apart from the stunning achievement of the builders of Cheops' and Chephren's great monuments, which apparently display an intimate knowledge of Pythagorean geometry, there is the simple fact, repeatedly ignored, that the Egyptians of this time employed the arch.[107] Yet the arch, it is held (and so it is stated in textbook after textbook),

---

107 F. Petrie, *Egyptian Architecture* (London, 1938) pp. 71-2.

was not known before the 7th century BC. We are therefore required to believe that the Egyptians of the third millennium (along incidentally with the Mesopotamian Akkadians and Sumerians of the same epoch) discovered the use of the arch, which was then forgotten for almost two thousand years, only to be reinvented by the peoples of the Near East in the 7th century BC.

This altogether strange phenomenon of discovery in the third millennium, followed by a loss and then a rediscovery in the first millennium, is something that can be observed in many areas of Near Eastern history.

Take as another example the use of iron. The Egyptians of the Pyramid Age were quite familiar with iron (another fact ignored in textbooks), which was used for both ceremonial purposes and for ordinary tools. The iron used in religious ritual was generally of meteoric origin, as revealed by its high nickel content, but the material used in tools had little or no nickel, and thus was presumably smelted from ore.[108] So plentiful were iron artifacts at this time that one specialist was moved to suggest that in Egypt the Iron Age "may yet be proved to have even preceded the Bronze Age."[109] Yet iron, too, after having been widely used in the Pyramid Age, was virtually forgotten for almost 2,000 years, only to be rediscovered again in the 7th century.

It is precisely the same story with glassmaking and glazing techniques. In his seminal work *Minerals, Metals, Glazing and Man* (1978), the mineralogist John Dayton traces the development of glazing techniques throughout the Near East and concludes that a whole class of glazing technologies employed during the Pyramid Age could not have been understood as early as the third millennium BC. Once again, glazes used by the pyramid-builders were forgotten for almost two millennia, only to re-emerge in the first millennium.

As an answer to the problem Dayton, although not an historian, suggested a radical shortening of Egyptian chronology.

In terms of relationships with other nations, a similar phenomenon is at work. The Egyptians of the Pyramid Age were well acquainted with the Phoenicians, and indeed trade with the cities of Tyre and Byblos was of great importance to the pharaohs of the time. So familiar were the peoples of this region to the Egyptians that their name for a seagoing vessel was *kbnwt* ("Byblos boat").[110] This strongly suggests that the Phoenicians of the Pyramid Age were already established as a great seafaring nation. Yet once again, this anticipates by 2,000 years the very real expansion of Phoenician commercial enterprise in the 9th and 8th centuries BC.

---

108 H. Garland and C. Bannister, *Ancient Egyptian Metallurgy* (London, 1927).
109 Ibid. p. 5.
110 Margaret S. Drower, "Syria Before 2200 BC." in *CAH* Vol. 1 part 2 (3rd ed.) p. 384.

How is all this to be explained? Could it be that there is indeed something dramatically wrong with the chronologies of the Egyptians and the other ancient nations of the region? Browsing through the many Egyptology volumes typically stocked in modern libraries, the casual reader is left with the impression that the dates of Egyptian history are firmly established. But just how secure are they?

Duplicating and Triplicating History

It is an astonishing fact that the chronologies still used for Mesopotamia and Egypt are essentially the same as (and ultimately based upon) the system devised by the early Christian chroniclers, most especially Eusebius, in the fourth century AD. Using the histories of Egypt and Mesopotamia, as found in Manetho and Berossus, Eusebius sought to "prove" the truth of the Old Testament against Greek and Roman critics who held the Book of Genesis to be pure myth. In this way these writers made Menes, the first pharaoh, the same as Adam, and therefore dated him to between 3,700 BC (the Creation date favored by Jewish tradition). All the rulers of Egypt whom Manetho placed between Menes and the Ptolemies, were positioned in the intervening centuries. Most especially, the pharaohs of Manetho's Nineteenth Dynasty, some of whom bore the name "Ramesses," were linked to Moses and the Exodus (the Hebrew slaves were said to have built a city called Ramesses), and were therefore following biblical chronology, placed around the 14th century BC.

The history of Mesopotamia was harnessed by Eusebius towards the same end. Here however he did not go back as far as Adam, but contented himself with proving the historical existence of Abraham, whom the Bible decreed to be a native of southern Mesopotamia. Placing Abraham in the city of Ur around 2000 BC (following the chronology provided in Genesis), Eusebius therefore had a fixed date for this ancient settlement. Further equating Berossus' Ninos with the biblical Nimrud — who lived just a few generations before Abraham — Eusebius reached a date of roughly 2300 BC for the first Assyrian (Semitic-speaking) Empire in Mesopotamia.

Over the centuries this chronology gained, in Christian Europe, the status almost of revealed truth. So established were his dates, dates ultimately dependant on a fundamentalist interpretation of the Old Testament, that the science and archaeology of the 19th century could not uproot them. On the contrary, new dating methods, held at that time to be the last word in scholarly technique, were used, almost unconsciously, to uphold Eusebius. Thus for example in 1798, over twenty years before Young and Champollion had found the key to unlocking the secrets of the hieroglyphs, Napoleon could point to the Great Pyramid and exhort his troops with the words, "forty centuries look down on you." In fact,

Napoleon's estimate in not far removed from that still found in the textbooks. Thus too, in a book by a Scottish psychiatrist, J.C. Prichard, published in 1819, two years before the translation of the hieroglyphs, the date of 1147 BC is given for the start of the reign of Ramses III. Neither Napoleon nor Prichard provided any source for their Egyptian dates, though they were evidently derived one way or another from Eusebius' working of Manetho.

Strange as it may seem, Prichard's date for Ramses III is within fifty years of that still provided for this pharaoh in the textbooks!

The first serious challenge to textbook chronology was launched in the 1950s by Immanuel Velikovsky. In *Worlds in Collision* (1950) Velikovsky argued that the Israelite Exodus from Egypt had taken place amidst a violent and world-wide upheaval of nature. In *Worlds in Collision* he collected an enormous body of traditions from every corner of the globe which described events virtually identical to those recounted in the Book of Exodus. Peoples as far apart as the Aztecs and Chinese told of a darkness enveloping the earth, of rivers and seas turning red as with blood, of a terrible tempest, of devastating plagues, of mighty tidal waves.

The problem for Velikovsky was that Egyptologists claimed to know the very coronation-date of the pharaoh who sat on the throne at the time of the Exodus (supposedly around 1425 BC), and neither this pharaoh, nor any others of the epoch, had mentioned anything remotely resembling the events of the Exodus. (For this very reason scholars were now beginning to deny that such an event had ever happened.) Nevertheless, a search of Egyptian documents did reveal references to catastrophic disturbances of nature corresponding closely to those described in the Exodus. Yet these were dated many centuries earlier than the traditional date of the Exodus. Velikovsky soon came to realize that these papyri (as for example the Lamentations of Ipuwer and the Prophecy of Neferty) did refer to the catastrophe of the Exodus, and that as a consequence there was something dramatically wrong with the way ancient history had been put together.

From this premise, Velikovsky began work on *Ages in Chaos*, a series of books aimed at correcting the errors. In *Ages in Chaos* Vol.1 (1952) he argued that Egyptian history was too long by five centuries, and that removing those five centuries could reveal some dramatic correspondences between the histories of Egypt and Israel. Very briefly, Velikovsky made Egypt's glorious Eighteenth Dynasty (with pharaohs such as Thutmose III and Amenhotep III) contemporary with the early monarchy period of Israel (thus with David, Solomon, Asa, etc.), and the picture he painted brought the two histories to life in spectacular fashion.

Yet problems were soon to arise. Placing the Eighteenth Dynasty roughly between 1000 and 800 BC, it was expected by one and all that the Nineteenth

Dynasty should be brought forward by the same amount of time and therefore take its place in the century between 800 and 700 BC. But in *Ramses II and his Time* (1978) Velikovsky shocked his supporters by suggesting that Ramses II and the rest of the Nineteenth Dynasty belonged in the 7th and 6th centuries BC — 200 years after the demise of the Eighteenth Dynasty. Velikovsky thus wished to re-duce the antiquity of the Eighteenth Dynasty by five centuries and that of the Nineteenth Dynasty by seven! Why the discrepancy?

For over a decade the debate raged. Many who had been won over by Velik-ovsky's work in *Ages in Chaos* Vol. 1 were dismayed by the contents of *Ramses II and his Time* (and *Peoples of the Sea*, which placed Ramses III in the Persian epoch). The present writer was more inclined to accept the latter two volumes, but was unable to square this with the 10th/9th century date for the Eighteenth Dynasty proposed in *Ages in Chaos* Vol.1.

The mystery, I shall argue, was finally resolved in the latter 1980s when Gun-nar Heinsohn proposed bringing the Eighteenth Dynasty down into the 7th cen-tury, rather than pushing the Nineteenth Dynasty back into the 8th.

Heinsohn's work on Mesopotamia made him realize that a contraction of ancient timescales much more dramatic than anything even Velikovsky had en-visaged was called for. Above all, by 1987 he became convinced that the Mitanni, the Indo-European-speaking people who controlled most of Mesopotamia dur-ing the time of the Eighteenth Dynasty, had to be one and the same as the Medes, the great conquerors of the Assyrian Empire, who, according to the classical au-thors, had ruled much of the Near East during the 7th and early 6th centuries BC. If the Mitanni were not the Medes, then no trace of this great people and kingdom could be found anywhere in the region.

Heinsohn found that in every north Mesopotamian historical site the Mitan-ni were immediately preceded by the so-called Akkadians, a Semitic-speaking people whose greatest king was named Sharru-kin (Sargon). Yet according to the textbooks the Akkadians had flourished seven centuries before the Mitanni, so that in all the excavated sites (as for example Tell Hamadiyah, Munbaqa, Ba-rak, Balawat and Nimrud) the archaeologists spoke of a "hiatus" or gap during which these cities had been abandoned, only to be reoccupied in the Mitanni epoch.

It became evident to Heinsohn that this hiatus was non-existent, a textbook construct, and that the "Akkadians" whom they had replaced were none other than the Imperial Assyrians of the 8th century, whose conquest by the Medes was recounted in many ancient authors.[111] As a matter of fact, the Mitanni kings

---

111 See Heinsohn's *Die Sumerer gab es nicht* (Frankfurt, 1988); also *Wann lebten die Pharaonen?* (1990).

were famous for their conquest of the Assyrian cities, a feat they obviously took great pride in.

But the occupation-gap between Akkadians (23rd century BC) and Mitanni (16th century BC) was only one of three discovered by Heinsohn. Immediately above the Mitanni, after a gap of five centuries, excavators come across the Neo-Assyrians of the 9th and 8th centuries. (Occasionally between these are found so-called Middle Assyrian remains — but the Middle Assyrian kings bore the same names as those of the early Neo-Assyrians, so these are not Middle Assyrians but early Neo-Assyrians). Then, immediately above the Neo-Assyrians, just where excavators expected to find Medes and Persians, they invariably found Hellenistic remains. This then constituted a further occupation gap of two centuries, a third hiatus during which the cities of northern Mesopotamia were apparently abandoned and for which no archaeology exists.

Of all the problems encountered by Near Eastern archaeologists this final hiatus is perhaps the most acute. The Persians, we know, ruled the whole of Mesopotamia for over two centuries, two hundred years of prosperity and high civilization. Yet scholars now have to assert that the Persians left virtually no evidence of their stay in the region at all.[112] This is an incredible state of affairs, a fact which has now had the inevitable result of prompting some historians to begin asking some fundamental questions about the nature of the Persian Empire.[113] The solution, Heinsohn suggested, was simply to remove the hiatuses. Thus the so-called "Neo-Assyrians," who occupy the first pre-Hellenic strata — exactly where we should expect the Persians — are in fact the Persians in the guise of rulers of Assyria. The Mitanni, who lie immediately underneath the Neo-Assyrians (with a five-century gap intervening) are of course the Medes, the immediate predecessors of the Persians. And last but not least the Akkadians, who lie immediately underneath the Mitanni (with a seven-century gap intervening) are the Assyrians, the immediate predecessors of the Medes.

Heinsohn came to the conclusion that the three hiatuses are the result of applying three entirely separate dating systems. Not only was world history duplicated in the second millennium, as Velikovsky believed, but also triplicated in

---

112 See e.g., A. L. Oppenheim's, "The Babylonian Evidence of the Achaemenian Rule in Mesopotamia" in *The Cambridge History of Iran* Vol. 1 (Cambridge, 1985) p. 530." The encounter between the Achaemenian Empire and Babylonia [Mesopotamia] seems to have left surprisingly little impact on the latter." Also A. Kuhrt's "Babylonia to Xerxes" in *CAH* Vol. 4 (2nd ed.) p. 135 "It should be clear from the foregoing that the evidence for Persian rule of Babylonia from 539 to 465 presents major problems and that a reconstruction of the political history of the area is an almost impossible task."

113 See e.g., Dr Heleen Sancisi-Weerdenburg and H. Kuhrt (eds.), "The quest for an elusive empire," *Achaemenid History IV: Centre and Periphery* (Leiden, 1990). Sancisi-Weerdenburg does not question the existence of an Achaemenid Imperium, but argues, as we do, that the Persians in Mesopotamia need to be found in the guise of local rulers.

the third millennium. Yet this veritable comedy of errors had a rationale and followed its own internal logic. It was, as Heinsohn has demonstrated, constructed upon three quite separate dating blueprints. Thus the history of the first millennium, which is in fact the true history of the region, is known solely through the classical and Hellenistic sources and is dated according to these sources. A "history" of the second millennium, however, is supplied by cross-referencing with Egyptian material, and this chronology is based solely on these sources, which are dated via Eusebius/Manetho and the so-called Sothic Calendar. The final part of the triplication, the ghost-kingdoms of the third millennium, is supplied by cross-referencing with Mesopotamian cuneiform documents, and this chronology is based solely on these sources, which are ultimately dated on the basis of biblical history.

In this way the Imperial Assyrians of the 8th century BC, who are known from the classical writers, are identical to the Hyksos of the 16th century (who also supply the date for the Mitanni), who are known from the Egyptian sources, and are also identical to the Akkadians of the 24th century, who are known from the Mesopotamian sources.

The Akkadian-Empire Assyrian (or Old Assyrian) equation has already been dealt with in some detail, both by the present author and Professor Heinsohn.[114] This represents the closing of the first hiatus, in some ways the easiest task. The others are more complex. With regard to the second hiatus, we must be very clear in determining its length. Velikovsky argued that it was over five centuries long, a proposition we agree with. If this is correct, we must be able to show that Neo-Assyrians, of supposedly the 9th century, come immediately after the Mitanni, of supposedly the 14th. We must also, with regard to the final hiatus, be able to show that the Neo-Assyrians themselves are not separated from the Hellenic Seleucids by two or three centuries, but are their Persian predecessors. The closing of these two artificial gaps in the history of Mesopotamia will be accomplished in the chapters to follow.

Biblical Synchronisms

The fall of the Assyrian/Hyksos empire saw the emergence from its ruins of a number of regional powers. Amongst these were the Eighteenth Dynasty of Egypt, the Mitanni (Median) Empire, and the Hittite (Lydian) Empire. Alongside these newly emergent states the present writer also places the Hebrew monarchies, whose early kings, Saul and David, actually participated in the destruction of Hyksos/Assyrian power in Palestine and Syria. Yet Saul and David are normally placed near the start of the 10th century BC, not the 7th. This is because,

---

114 In Heinsohn's *Die Sumerer gab es nicht* (1988) and in my *Pyramid Age* (1999).

as we have seen, the chronology of the Bible itself is no more reliable than that of Egypt, and it too needs to be shortened — not by the seven to eight centuries needed for Egypt, but by well over two centuries. Thus, as mentioned in Chapter 1, we hold broadly by the chronology outlined by Immanuel Velikovsky in *Ages in Chaos* (1952), except that we would place the events described in the above volume in the late 8th and 7th centuries BC, not the 10th and 9th, as Velikovsky did.

In accordance with this scheme of things, Ahmose of the Eighteenth Dynasty, who defeats the Hyksos King Apopi, is contemporary with Saul of Israel who defeats the Amalekite King Agog. These events are to be dated around 720 BC, and describe the death-throes of the Assyrian Empire in the south and west.

Two generations later Solomon is visited in Jerusalem by the fabulous Queen of Sheba (or Queen of the South), who is none other than Hatshepsut of Egypt, the queen who left an account of her glorious expedition to Punt and the Divine (Holy) Land in her magnificent temple at Deir El Bahri. Josephus describes this woman as the queen of Egypt and Ethiopia, and as Lisa Liel of Israel has pointed out, her capital city, Thebes, is apparently a mispronunciation of Sheba, by which name Josephus knew the capital of Ethiopia. The swapping of "s" for "t" or "th" (lisping) follows a normal linguistic pattern characteristic of many Semitic dialects. The Egyptian hieroglyphic name for Thebes, reconstructed as Waset, should apparently be spelled She(t)wa, with the "t" being unpronounced. Another great center of the god Amon, the oasis of Siwa, bears the same name.

The Bible relates that after the death of Solomon, the temple of Jerusalem was plundered by a pharaoh named Shishak, who carried off vast quantities of treasure to Egypt. Similarly, Egyptian sources say that after the death of Hatshepsut, her ambitious young nephew Thutmose III launched a series of devastating invasions of Palestine and Syria, scoring some of the greatest military triumphs in Egypt's history. In his first campaign, directed against Palestine, he plundered the treasures of the great temple in the city of Kadesh, which is named as the region's most important center. These treasures Thutmose displayed on the walls of his temple at Karnak. Kadesh, as Velikovsky demonstrated, can be little other than Jerusalem, the Holy (*Kadesh*) mountain, by which name (*Al Kuds*) the city is still known in modern Arabic.

One of Thutmose's numerous titles (his Golden Horus name) was Djeser-kau, which was probably pronounced something like Shesy-ka, very close indeed to the biblical Shishak.

In accordance with these synchronisms it is incumbent upon us to place the latter Eighteenth Dynasty, in the time of Amenhotep III and Akhnaton, contemporary with Asa of Judah and Baasha of Israel, all of whom should be dated to the second half of the 7th century. These latter characters are of course also near-contemporaries of the early Neo-Assyrian kings Ashurnasirpal II and Shalmaneser III, so it is clear that this epoch of Assyrian history must be made to square with the history of the Near East as revealed in the Amarna letters, the documents of Boghaz-koi, and the various monuments of the Nineteenth Dynasty.

As stated above, we are involved in a double adjustment of ancient chronology. The Late Bronze Age, contemporary with New Kingdom Egypt and dated in accordance with Egyptian Sothic chronology, must be brought forward by just over five centuries, to bring it in line with the early Iron Age, contemporary with the Neo-Assyrian kingdom, which was dated in accordance with Biblical chronology. But this chronology is also unnaturally lengthened, and it too must be brought forward by over two centuries, to make it contemporary with the Medes and Persians. Thus the Late Bronze material must be down dated by a total of around seven and a half centuries.

Ramessides and Neo-Assyrians

If the Egyptian Eighteenth Dynasty should rightfully be placed in the 7th century BC, as we claim, this means that the early Neo-Assyrian kings (Ashurnasirpal II and Shalmaneser III) must also belong there — at the end of the century, as a matter of fact. However, it is held that the end of the Eighteenth Dynasty corresponds with the rise of the so-called Middle Assyrian state, whose first important king was Ashuruballit I. Such being the case, it is clear that the "Middle Assyrian" rulers who follow Ashuruballit I must be alter-egos of the early Neo-Assyrian rulers, and that most probably Ashuruballit I, who virtually founds the revived "Middle Assyrian" kingdom, is an alter-ego of Ashurnasirpal II, who more or less founds the "revived" Neo-Assyrian kingdom.

That conclusion is supported by the evidence of art and culture in general — for the material and technological culture of the early Neo-Assyrians, beginning with Ashurnasirpal II, matches closely that of the latter Eighteenth and Nineteenth Dynasties in Egypt. In addition, it is a simple fact that the Nineteenth Dynasty is stratigraphically contemporary with these early Neo-Assyrians. Excavations have repeatedly shown that directly above the Mitanni layers (which everyone agrees are contemporary with the Eighteenth Dynasty) archaeologists invariably find either "Middle" or early Neo-Assyrian remains. In fact, I would suggest that all the material located immediately above the Mitanni belongs to the early Neo-Assyrians, because the throne-names used by these kings — Shalmaneser, Shamshi-Adad, Adad-Nirari etc. — are indistinguishable from the real Middle Assyrians, who are, I will argue, little more than alter-egos of the Mitanni themselves.

The point is that nowhere does the depth of strata separating the Mitanni from the late Neo-Assyrians (beginning with Tiglath-Pileser III) indicate the existence of a span of five centuries, which, according to the textbooks, separate these two lines of kings. On the contrary, if the depth of strata is used as a time gauge, no more than a century would be indicated between Tushratta, last of the "Mitannian" kings, and Tiglath-Pileser III.

The contemporaneous nature of the early Neo-Assyrians and the late Eighteenth and Nineteenth Dynasties is further confirmed by the discovery of countless artifacts belonging to these pharaohs in the ruins of the Neo-Assyrian cities. A particularly large number of late Eighteenth Dynasty scarabs were found at Nimrud (Calah), the city built by Ashurnasirpal II. These were mainly of Thutmose III and Amenhotep III. According to Layard, "... most of the Egyptian relics discovered in the Assyrian ruins are of the time of the Eighteenth Egyptian dynasty, or of the 15th century before Christ — a period when, as we learn from the Egyptian monuments, there was a close connection between Assyria and Egypt."[115] But Layard's statement strikes as somewhat disingenuous when we remember that these artifacts were found in Neo-Assyrian cities, some of which, such as Nimrud/Calah and Khorsabad/Dur-Sharrukin, didn't even exist, according to the textbooks, until five to six centuries after the end of the Eighteenth Dynasty.

Among the most celebrated Egyptian art-work discovered in Assyria were the famous Nimrud Ivories. These exquisite artifacts were discovered in three large rooms at the fortress erected in Calah by Shalmaneser III, and many of them were clearly made in Egypt during the Amarna period — the end of the Eighteenth Dynasty. As with so many archaeological anomalies, the Nimrud Ivories were explained away as being the result of an ancient passion for collecting antiquities and heirlooms. But when the art and culture of the early Neo-Assyrians is compared with that of the New Kingdom Egyptians, we are repeatedly struck by the close stylistic parallels — parallels rendered most mysterious by the five centuries which supposedly intervene between the two epochs. This is most clear perhaps in the field of military technology, where the usage of the late Eighteenth and Nineteenth Dynasties is precisely matched by that of the Neo-Assyrians from the time of Ashurnasirpal II and Shalmaneser III onwards.

In this context the deployment of cavalry should be mentioned. The first certain appearance in Egypt of such troops is right at the end of the Eighteenth Dynasty, when a single man on horseback is portrayed in the Memphis tomb of Horemheb. In Mesopotamia, cavalry are mentioned during the reign of Tukulti-

---

115 Austen H. Layard, *Discoveries in the Ruins of Nineveh and Babylon* (London, 1853) p. 282.

Ninurta II, the father of Ashurnasirpal II, but are first portrayed in the latter's time, where they appear on the Nimrud bas-reliefs.

In Egypt, Hittite cavalry are shown in action against Seti I, and their deployment displays striking parallels with that of the cavalry belonging to Ashurnasirpal II. Thus for example the Neo-Assyrian horsemen ride bareback, obtaining a firm grip by means of pressing the raised knees against the horse's flanks — exactly the method of riding employed by the Hittites portrayed on the monuments of Seti I and Ramses II. Again, both the early Neo-Assyrian cavalry and those of the Hittites against whom Seti I battled employed the bow as their only weapon. Even more importantly, they are used in an identical way tactically; they are invariably used in conjunction with the chariotry. Describing the cavalry of Ashurnasirpal II, which was believed to be five centuries later than those of the Hittites against whom Seti I fought, Gaston Maspero commented: "The army [of Assyria] ... now possessed a new element, whose appearance in the field of battle was to revolutionize the whole method of warfare; this was the cavalry, properly so called, introduced as an adjunct to the chariotry."[116] More specifically, "This body of cavalry, having little confidence in its own powers, kept in close contact with the main body of the army, and it was not used in independent manoeuvres; it was associated with and formed an escort to the chariotry in expeditions where speed was essential, and where ordinary foot soldiers would have hampered the movements of the charioteers."[117]

But the cavalry of the Hittites, depicted on the monuments of Seti I and Ramses II, are deployed in exactly the same way. How peculiar, that after five centuries the art of horsemanship should have evolved so little! And this at a time when, we might imagine, any tactical innovations would have been quickly seized upon.

Chariot design tells the same story. The earliest Egyptian chariots, dating from the start of the Eighteenth Dynasty, were light machines, designed to carry only one or two persons. Wheels were likewise light, and four-spoked. From the time of Thutmose IV, however, stronger and heavier chariots, with six-spoked wheels, were introduced. These machines, which could carry up to three persons, typically had powerful metal fittings, a wicker body, and crossed quivers at the sides.

The earliest Mesopotamian chariots had four solid wheels, and were obviously very slow-moving, cumbersome contraptions. The Akkadian epoch saw the introduction of the two-wheeled chariot. By the beginning of the early Neo-Assyrian epoch, in the reign of Ashurnasirpal II, chariots are virtually identical

---

116 Gaston Maspero, *History of Egypt* Vol. VII (London, 1906) p. 8.
117 Ibid. pp. 9-10.

to those of latter Eighteenth Dynasty and Nineteenth Dynasty Egypt. Wheels are six-spoked for strength, there is a wicker body with metal fittings, and crossed quivers are attached to the sides. By the time of Tiglath-Pileser III, however, just a few generations later, chariot design had changed completely. The only period during which the machines used in Egypt and Mesopotamia were identical was during the later Egyptian New Kingdom and this early Neo-Assyrian epoch.

Again, it might be mentioned the types of body-armor employed during the second half of the New Kingdom and the early Neo-Assyrian time showed striking parallels. Just as Egyptian soldiers of the Nineteenth Dynasty begin to employ full-length coats of scale armor, so too do the troops of these early Neo-Assyrian kings. This was the only epoch during which soldiers of these two kingdoms wore such mail shirts.

Almost innumerable cultural parallels between these kingdoms and epochs could indeed be listed, but the above should suffice to illustrate that any attempt to date the early Neo-Assyrian kings must be closely related to the date assigned to Egypt's New Kingdom. In short, the early Neo-Assyrians, from Ashurnasirpal II through to Ashur-Nirari V, must in some way be alter-egos of the "Middle Assyrian" monarchs who are recognized as contemporary with the latter Eighteenth and Nineteenth Dynasties. Since, as we saw, these kings really belong near the end of the 7th and the 6th centuries, this too must be where we place the early Neo-Assyrians.

The Stratigraphy of Israel

It has been stated that the stratigraphic record of Mesopotamia allows for no gap of five centuries between the epoch of the Mitanni (supposedly ending in the 14th century BC) and that of the Neo-Assyrians (supposedly commencing in the 9th century BC). Yet the impossibility of such a gap is demonstrated even more clearly by the stratigraphy of the land of the Bible.

The fundamental principle established by Velikovsky in *Ages in Chaos* was that the pharaohs of the Eighteenth Dynasty were contemporaries of the early Israelite monarchies, and that it was one of those pharaohs, Thutmose III (supposedly of the 15th century), who had plundered the temple of Jerusalem immediately after the death of Solomon (late 10th century). It so happens that scarabs and other artifacts of Thutmose III and his successors are extremely common throughout Israel, and these occur at the beginning of strata defined in archaeological terms as Late Bronze. In fact, we can be more specific than that: scarabs of Thutmose III appear at the beginning of the epoch described as Late Bronze IIA. Late Bronze I was therefore contemporary with the first half of the Eighteenth Dynasty, when Egypt exercised no power over the nations of the region. Both Late Bronze I and

II were periods of high civilization in Palestine, and offer, in cultural terms at least, a far better match for the wealthy monarchies of early Israel described in the Bible than the Iron Age settlements conventionally associated with these kingdoms. The Iron Age cities of Palestine, which supposedly date from the 11th and 10th centuries, display great impoverishment, and can in no way (much to the embarrassment of archaeologists) be made to correspond with the mighty and opulent kingdom of David and Solomon described in the Scriptures.

Velikovsky solved the problem by moving the wealthy Late Bronze settlements down from the 15th and 14th centuries into the 10th and 9th, and making them the cities and towns of David and Solomon. If this surmise was correct, it means that the later Iron Age strata, conventionally placed in the 10th and 9th centuries, must also be brought down the timescale, and most likely these towns and villages are the remnants of the Israelite settlements destroyed in the ferocious campaigns of Tiglath-Pileser III and his successors Sargon II and Sennacherib. Is there any evidence to suggest that the first Iron Age towns were really contemporary with these Assyrian kings? There is powerful evidence to that effect.

It is well known that the transition from Late Bronze to Iron Age in Israel was marked by a fairly dramatic deterioration in levels of culture, and by the destruction of a number of important cities, among them Hazor, Gezer, Lachish and Debir. Since the ruin of these settlements is normally dated to the late 13th or early 12th century, the destruction is normally regarded as the work of the invading Israelite tribes. However, it has been demonstrated that the new Iron Age culture, which appears after the destructions, is merely an impoverished form of that of the Late Bronze Age,[118] and that "there is no reason to attribute it to a nation of newly-arrived settlers apart from the *a priori* assumption that the settlement of Israel was taking place at this time."[119]

If the Late Bronze Age really is contemporary with the Israelite kingdoms, then the destruction of these cities can only have been the work of the Assyrian kings Tiglath-Pileser III and his successors Shalmaneser V, Sargon II and Sennacherib; and indeed the cities damaged at this juncture are actually named in the records of these Assyrian kings and in the Bible. Thus II Kings 15:29 reports that Tiglath-Pileser III attacked and reduced Hazor, (conventionally dated to 733 BC) whilst the end of Late Bronze Age Gezer was likely to have been the work of the same campaign, when the Assyrian armies attacked Philistia. The conquest of Gezer is depicted in reliefs from Tiglath-Pileser III's palace at Nim-

118 J. B. Pritchard in J. P. Hyatt (ed.), *The Bible in Modern Scholarship* (1965) pp. 320-1.
119 J. Bimson, "Can There be a Revised Chronology Without a Revised Stratigraphy?," *SIS: Proceedings, Glasgow Conference* (April,1978) p. 18.

rud.[120] The end of Late Bronze Lachish would be the work of Sennacherib (conventionally 701 BC), his conquest of the city being recorded in II Kings 18:14 and in his own reliefs.

Similar correlations could be suggested for a whole series of other sites displaying evidence of destruction at this time, among them Megiddo, Debir, Beth-Shan, Ashdod, Aphek and Beitin. In all these cases the Iron Age culture which followed these destructions was an impoverished form of what had gone before, clearly representing a scattered population's efforts at recovery in the wake of the destruction of the major cities and death and possibly deportation of large numbers of the people. Even more to the point, the new Iron Age culture now displays, for the first time in the region, the unmistakable influence of Assyria. Hitherto the prevailing influence throughout Syria and Palestine had come from Egypt.

The most striking evidence for this was revealed at Timna, an ancient copper-mining site in the Arabah. The predominant pottery at the site, named "Edomite," was decreed to be transitional LBA-Iron Age, and accordingly dated to the 12th century by most archaeologists, including the influential Yohanan Aharoni and Beno Rothenberg. However, the site's excavator, Nelson Glueck, begged to differ. He insisted that the town must date to the Sargonid Age (8th/7th century) because he had already found identical "Edomite" pottery at Tell el-Kheleifeh (possibly ancient Ezion-geber), where it is clearly dated — through inscriptional material and Assyrian pottery — to the 8th-6th centuries BC. A prolonged and acrimonious debate ensued: Aharoni and Rothenberg insisting, on the strength of New Kingdom Egyptian finds at the site, that the Timna material be dated no later than the 12th century; Glueck and his ally William Albright equally insistent (on the strength of the Sargonid material) that the settlement be dated to the 8th and 7th centuries.[121] So great is the prestige of Egyptology that most authorities finally found in favor of Aharoni and Rothenberg, and continued to date Late Bronze Timna to the 12th century. Yet Glueck never capitulated; and on the contrary, pointed to various other transitional LBA/Iron Age sites in Palestine where artifacts, especially pottery, of clearly Sargonid design, was located together with material otherwise dated to the 12th and 11th centuries.

Much of the evidence for dating the first Iron Age towns of Palestine to the Sargonid epoch was brought together by John Bimson. Though Bimson later repudiated the chronological scheme outlined by him in the 1970s, the work he did then was invaluable, and has never been refuted. In the "Ages in Chaos?" Con-

---

120 H. Tadmor, *Biblical Archaeology* 29 (1966) p. 89, n. 15.
121 N. Glueck, *Eretz-Israel* 9 (1969) p. 54 and *The Other Side of the Jordan* (1970) pp. 73, 93-4.

ference at Glasgow in 1978, Bimson pointed to a number of crucial facts about transitional LBA/Iron Age Palestine:

- At Tell Deir Alla, in the Jordan Valley, the final LBA settlement, supposedly destroyed at the start of the 12th century, yielded several plates of scale armor which, according to Bimson, offer a precise match for the scale armor worn by soldiers of Sennacherib at the siege of Lachish.

- At the same site the first Iron Age town (supposedly 11th/12th century) yielded a child's feeding-bowl, of pottery, which was compared by the archaeologist Franken to an almost identical bowl, in metal, from a tomb of 7th century Gordion in Anatolia.

- In many of the rather impoverished Iron Age II cities of Palestine, which Bimson dated to the time of Sennacherib, scarabs of a pharaoh Menkheperre are commonly found. Bimson noted that Menkheperre was one of the names of the Ethiopian King Shabataka, and that the supposedly "Solomonic" cities where these scarabs occurred should be dated to his time (contemporary with Sennacherib).

- A number of architectural features found in the Iron II cities of Hazor, Megiddo, Gezer, and elsewhere, and supposedly dating from the 10th century BC, are strongly reminiscent of designs otherwise found in buildings of the 7th and 6th centuries.

The evidence from Israel then seems to be fairly consistent with that from other regions, which suggests that the demise of the so-called Late Bronze Age (Egyptian New Kingdom) needs to be brought forward by five centuries to make it contemporary with the advent of the major expansion of Neo-Assyrian military power under the Sargonids. The stratigraphy then presents the following picture:

PALESTINIAN STRATIGRAPHY

Stratum	Predominant Cultural Influence
Late Bronze I	Egypt — early 18th Dynasty
Late Bronze IIA	Egypt — late 18th Dynasty
Late Bronze IIB	Egypt — 19th Dynasty
Iron Age I	Sargonid Assyria (circa 750 BC)

The Neo-Hittites of Syria

Towards the end of Egypt's Eighteenth Dynasty the Mitanni kingdom collapsed in face of a series of ferocious campaigns waged by the Hittite King Suppiluliumas I. From then onwards, and continuing throughout much of the Nineteenth Dynasty, the Hatti land was the dominant power throughout Anatolia and northern Syria; and indeed the pharaohs of the Nineteenth Dynasty had to wage a number of campaigns against the Hittites in order to protect their Syrian possessions. But this dominance came to an end, and, according to conventional ideas, the Hittite Empire collapsed in the early part of the 13th century BC, shortly after the reign of Tudkhaliash IV, apparently in the wake of a devastating attack by the mysterious "Sea Peoples," who occur quite prominently in the inscriptions of Ramses III, of the Twentieth Dynasty. The next few centuries are regarded as constituting a "Dark Age" in the history of Anatolia, from which very few remains have survived. Yet around the middle of the 9th century BC, and contemporary with the rise of the early Neo-Assyrian kingdom, Hittite culture and civilization experienced a spectacular "rebirth" in the city-states of northern Syria. These city-states, whose kings had names familiar from the Imperial Age, are commonly regarded as the inheritors of Hittite culture after its destruction in central Anatolia.

Nevertheless, the centers of power during the Neo-Hittite period were also important during the earlier Imperial age. Carchemish, for example, was a major provincial capital of the Empire from the time of Suppiluliumas I to that of Tudkhaliash IV — a span of four generations. Indeed it was Suppiluliumas who made Carchemish part of the Empire and installed its first Hittite king, his own son Sarre-Kushukh, on the throne. But Carchemish was also a major regional power during the Neo-Hittite age, and its name frequently occurs in the annals of Assyrian rulers from the time of Ashurnasirpal II to Tiglath-Pileser III.

Scholars were immediately surprised at how faithfully the Hittites of northern Syria had preserved their native culture after so many centuries. Their surprise grew as excavation after excavation revealed the astonishing parallels between the two cultures. How could mere refugees from the depredations of the Sea Peoples preserve traditions of monumental sculpture and other fine arts so well? This begged the question: What had actually happened to the Hittites during the centuries that separated the fall of the Empire from the rise of the Syrian city-states? It is almost as if they had ceased to exist and then suddenly burst into new life, like seeds regenerating in spring.

But the Neo-Hittite cities had another surprise in store for archaeologists. Given the supposed history of these settlements, scholars had expected to find abundant remains of the Hittite Empire directly underneath strata containing material of the Neo-Hittite epoch. They found nothing of the sort. Invariably they discovered plentiful evidence of Neo-Hittite occupation (9th and 8th centuries) but a strange, indeed incomprehensible, absence of almost all Hittite Em-

pire strata. Where artifacts and other remains of Hittite Empire design and manufacture were discovered, these were invariably found in a Neo-Hittite context.

This fact alone should have caused archaeologists to stop and think. Yet it is
only a single aspect of a vast body of evidence which shows very clearly that the
Anatolian Dark Age never existed, that the four or five centuries which reputedly
separate the demise of the Hittite Empire from the rise of the Neo-Hittites and
Neo-Assyrians is a text-book construct, and that these two epochs are in fact
contemporary.

An examination of just one aspect of Hittite culture should illustrate the
point very clearly.

One of the most characteristic features of Neo-Hittite architecture was the
so-called *bit-hilani*, or hilani-house. It is described as "one of the most remarkable architectural inventions of the ancient Near East."[122] The hilani-house was a
palace-type structure consisting of a vestibule with one to three supports on the
front side, behind which lay a large room with a hearth. Around this room were
grouped smaller rooms. These hilani-buildings were a peculiar feature of the
Neo-Hittite states, and the earliest example from the latter belonged to a prince
named Kilamuwa, of Zincirli, who reigned during the time of Shalmaneser III
and his son Shamshi-Adad IV. However, it seems that Kilamuwa merely revived
an ancient architectural feature, for another hilani house, belonging to Nikmepa
(or Niqmepa) of Ugarit, was already known.[123] Nikmepa was a contemporary of
Mursilis II and Hattusilis III the Hittite Great Kings, and with Tutankhamun
and Horemheb of Egypt. This means that, according to conventional chronology,
Nikmepa's hilani-house was constructed roughly five centuries before that of
Kilamuwa, a situation that defies all reason. The two buildings had to be contemporary. Thus it is clear that Nikmepa, who is indubitably contemporary with
the early 19th Dynasty, must be placed alongside Kilamuwa, who is indubitably
contemporary with Shalmaneser III and Shamshi-Adad IV.

Most of the detailed synchronisms established by Velikovsky in the first volume of *Ages in Chaos* are therefore yet again fully vindicated. The revived Neo-
Assyrian kingdom of Ashurnasirpal II and Shalmaneser III is truly contemporary
with the final years of the Eighteenth Dynasty, and the five centuries separating
these epochs in the textbooks needs to be removed.

As we proceed in our examination of Neo-Hittite culture we shall see the
same process at work again and again. Cultural features belonging to the Hittite Imperial Age reappear in the Neo-Assyrian age without any examples in the
centuries intervening. Thus scholars are forced variously to postulate a "revival"

---

122 E. Akurgal, *The Birth of Greek Art* (Methuen, 1968) p. 69.
123 Ibid. p. 71.

of ancient styles or the "reuse" of ancient artifacts. Alternatively, the appearance of Hittite Empire material in a clearly Neo-Hittite context is explained by the proposal that they are "heirlooms" from the earlier period.

The Hittite Cities: Malatya and Karatepe

The greatest center of Hittite power in eastern Anatolia was the city-state of Malatya, named Milidiya in the Boghazkoi inscriptions, and Milid in the Assyrian records. Excavators discovered an impressive Hittite palace guarded by a monumental Lion Gate, along with a series of orthostat reliefs. This structure lay directly beneath the ruins of an Assyrian palace, which was dated to the period shortly after the Assyrian conquest of the region in the time of Sargon II, supposedly in 713 BC.[124] The Lion Gate and the reliefs were quite naturally therefore dated by their discoverer to the mid-eighth century BC, and this was supported by the appearance, apparently, on several of the sculptures, of the name Sulumeli, an 8th century king of Malatya mentioned in the records of Tiglath-Pileser III.

A serious problem however arose in assigning such a date to the Lion Gate and associated palace, for the architectural style of these remains clearly linked them to the Hittite Empire. Ekrem Akurgal undertook a detailed study of the Malatya sculptures and concluded that they represented "a faithful continuation of the [Imperial Age] sculpture of Hattusa and Alaca."[125] Another scholar, Henri Frankfort, went much further and stated categorically that they belonged to the Hittite Imperial Age.

There arose a heated debate over the monument's interpretation. On the one hand, Akurgal insisted that the palace be dated to the 11th century at the latest, on the grounds of its strong Empire Hittite style and iconography. On the other hand, Frankfort insisted that the palace was of the 8th century, but that the sculptures and reliefs with which it was decorated were heirlooms dating from the Empire. He wrote, "Dating the Malatya sculptures to the empire does not mean that the lions and the reliefs are found where they were placed originally; on the contrary, there is strong evidence that they were reused in a building dating to the eighth century."[126]

Precisely the same problem was encountered at Karatepe in Cilicia, where a number of Hittite monuments were identified by scholars early in the 20th century. A famous inscription, written in hieroglyphic Hittite and alphabetic Phoenician, and associated with a series of bas-reliefs, has caused much scholarly debate over the years.

---

124 L. Delaporte, *Malatya* (Paris, 1940).
125 E. Akurgal, loc cit. p. 95.
126 P. James, *Society for Interdisciplinary Studies Review* Vol. VI p. 43.

The inscription itself was dated to the latter 8th century on philological and historical grounds. Its author, a prince named Azitawatas, claimed descent from a character named Mopsos (Muksh in the Hittite version), and this was hailed as the first example of a personality from Greek legend being attested in the monumental inscriptions of the Levant. Mopsos was reputedly an ally of the Greeks in the campaign against Troy, and upon the sack of that city was said to have led a band of warriors on to further conquests in Cilicia and the Phoenician coast.

Azitawatas himself however was very definitely of the latter 8th century, as demonstrated both by the Phoenician letters on his inscription, and by the mention in the same document of his overlord Awarikus ('Wrks). Scholars immediately identified this man with a king of Cilicia called Urikki, named in the records of Tiglath-Pileser III and Sargon II.[127]

The age of the inscription and associated monuments is thus established beyond question. The problem, of course, is that the artwork is classically Imperial Hittite, showing no signs whatever of any so-called "Assyrianizing" influence which, it is claimed, can be identified in other monuments of the "Neo-Hittite" period. These other monuments, it should be noted, are all closer to Assyria geographically, so it is clear that the appearance of Neo-Assyrian artistic motifs on Hittite work has little to do with date, but a lot to do with location.

Without the accompanying Phoenician inscription and the appearance of the name Awarkus, the Karatepe monuments would unquestionably have been dated to the Hittite Empire.

Carchemish and Its Remains

Carchemish was perhaps the most important of the Hittite city-states during the Imperial epoch, and it was equally important during the Neo-Assyrian era. Yet in common with all the other Hittite centers in northern Syria it could reveal no clearly defined Empire age stratum preceding a Neo-Hittite one. Where artifacts and other artwork of Hittite Empire design and manufacture were discovered, these were always found in a Neo-Hittite context.

One of the great mysteries of Carchemish centered on a series of relief sculptures found on the so-called "Herald's Wall," a structure comprising part of the inner defenses of the fortress. Whilst these buildings clearly dated from "the latest phase of art from Carchemish," in other words, around the 7th century, the style of the reliefs was archaic.[128] The evidence was baffling: "Either the whole wall was a survival from an earlier period incorporated in the late Palace, or the

---

127 J. D. Hawkins, "The Neo-Hittite States in Syria and Anatolia" in *CAH* Vol. 3 part 1 (2nd ed.) pp. 430-1.
128 L. Woolley, *Carchemish III* (1952) p. 190.

individual reliefs had been from an older building and re-used."[129] The nearby King's Gate showed "unmistakable evidence" that the series was of a late date, though "the Herald's Wall and the King's Gate are continuous, and form part of the same building."[130]

The Temple of the Storm-god was dated by Woolley "on grounds of style" to the Empire, though "the Temple complex as we have it was definitely of the Late Hittite ('Syro-Hittite') period."[131] His report on the northern wall of the Temple states: "In the angle there stood undisturbed the basalt stela A.4b bearing a winged disc and an incised inscription which mentions the 'Great King'. It should therefore go back to the time of the late Empire of the Bogazkoy Hittites," and "must therefore be part of the furniture of the original building."[132] However, because it was found in a Neo-Hittite building Woolley had to add: "It is not, of course, in its original position because the north wall of the angle in which it stands was *ex hypothesi* not built when the stela was dedicated."[133]

A tomb underneath the floor of a room (room E) in the North-West Fort of Carchemish contained a great hoard of priceless gold objects. Some of the objects were damaged by fire, since the remains were cremated, and many of the offerings were thrown into the burial pit whilst the ashes, which had been removed from the funeral pyre, were still hot. Nevertheless, thirty-nine small figures were recovered from the ashes and they attracted much attention. According to Woolley, "These little figurines are the jeweller's reproduction in miniature of the great rock-cut reliefs of Yazilikaya. Not only is the general subject the same — a long array of gods, royalties, and soldiers — but the individual figurines are identical in type, in attitude, in attribute, and in dress."[134]

This, however, presented a problem:

> The close relation between the rock carvings [of the Hittite Empire] and the Carchemish jewellery cannot be mistaken. The difficulty is in the first place one of date; the carvings are of the thirteenth century BC and the grave is of the last years of the seventh century. Either then the jewels are themselves much older than the grave in which they were found and had been handed down through very many generations, or they are relatively late in date and of Syrian manufacture (the Hittites of Anatolia having disappeared hundreds of years before) but preserve unbroken the old Hittite tradition. It must be admitted that the "heirloom" theory is far-fetched in

---

129 Ibid.
130 Ibid. p. 191.
131 Ibid. p. 170.
132 Ibid.
133 Ibid.
134 Ibid. pp. 250ff.

view of the fact that Carchemish is far removed from Hattusas and any family continuity bridging that gulf of space and time is most improbable.[135]

But Woolley's interpretation was countered by others. Güterbock for example insisted that the gold objects were indeed of Hittite Empire age, and held that they must, notwithstanding Woolley's objections, have been heirlooms.[136]

But the question: How did carvings of the 13th century get into a tomb of the 7th? is answered by the simple proposition that neither the carvings nor the artwork of Yazilikaya upon which they are modeled date from the 13th century but from the latter 7th and 6th centuries.

Classical Synchronisms

The above archaeological evidence supports in great detail the contention that the chronology of the Egyptian New Kingdom (as well as the Hittite Empire with which it was contemporary) needs to be reduced by over five centuries, in order to make it agree with that of the Bible and Mesopotamian history (Mesopotamia itself being ultimately based on the Bible). It is hardly open to question, therefore, that Ramses II, who fought against the Hittite emperor Hattusilis III, was a contemporary of the Neo-Assyrian Adad-Nirari III, whilst his son Merneptah must have reigned at the time of Tiglath-Pileser III. Both the latter are normally placed in the early to mid-8th century BC.

It is now time however to look at the other great body of archaeological evidence which just as insistently places the pharaohs of the Nineteenth Dynasty in the 6th century BC. This evidence fully supports the largely historical material brought forth in the previous chapter showing that the Nineteenth Dynasty was brought to an end with the Persian Conquest, in 525 BC.

The explanation for this strange anomaly has already been mentioned, but it is worth repeating here.

The fact is, the chronology of the Old Testament, long held to be fairly accurate as far back at least as the start of the kings period, is itself unnaturally lengthened. It is not accurately aligned with that of the classical world, which of course is the true history of the region. Biblical history is in reality stretched by over two centuries (gradually increasing to three centuries by the time of Saul and David). How did this two-century error, the reader may wonder, creep into the Bible? The answer to this extremely important question is supplied in the penultimate chapter of the present volume. Suffice to say here that the Judeans taken captive to Babylon were enslaved by a king who bore both a Persian and

---

135 L. Woolley, op cit.
136 H. G. Güterbock, *Journal of Near Eastern Studies* (1945) pp. 113ff.

a Babylonian name. As a result, the biblical scribes had at their disposal a history which spoke of a Babylonian and therefore pre-Persian captivity, and led inevitably to a duplication of history. Yet the transformation of a late Persian king into a pre-Persian Babylonian left the biblical redactors with a period of two centuries during which nothing, apparently, happened. This creates a two-century "dark age" in Hebrew historiography that is still evident to anyone who reads the Bible.

The Archaeology of Phoenicia

The other regions of the ancient east most closely tied to the Hellenic world, in terms of cultural and artistic links, were Cyprus and Phoenicia. Cyprus was itself largely part of the Greek world, though it formed an important bridge with the civilizations of the east. Phoenicia too formed part of that cultural bridge, though it was of course more closely connected to the worlds of Egypt and Mesopotamia. Nevertheless, both in Cyprus and Phoenicia a wide variety of archaeological material has been discovered which, through clear connections to the Greek world, is dated to the 6th and 5th centuries BC, but which, through Egyptian artifacts of the Nineteenth Dynasty, is also simultaneously dated to the 14th and 13th centuries BC.

As shown in Chapter 1 of the present study, the ancient port of Ugarit, contemporary with the latter Eighteenth and Nineteenth Dynasties, nevertheless produced an abundance of evidence of almost every variety, indicating that the city should really be dated to the 7th and 6th centuries. Thus we recall that the cult of Apollo Didymeus was observed at the settlement, whilst one of its most important kings, Nikmed, bore an Ionian name. The numerous documents, written in alphabetic Hebrew of 6th or 7th century date, also refer more than once to *Jm'an* ("Ionians"). Sepulchral chambers in Ugarit point in the same direction, as they reveal striking resemblances to tombs in Cyprus, just a short distance over the sea, which are there unequivocally dated to the 7th century and later.[137]

And the same phenomenon is seen, right the way through Phoenicia. Wherever the dating of ancient sites has come under the influence of Greek archaeology and history, they have invariably pointed to a Late Bronze Age in the 7th and 6th centuries BC.

---

137 According to E. Gjerstad, the sepulchral chambers of Cyprus, whilst closely resmbling those of Ugarit, "were considerably later and continue down to the 8th and 7th centuries ..." E. Gjerstad et al. *The Swedish Cyprus Expedition, 1927-1931* (Stockholm, 1934-37) Vol. I p. 405.

Another site along the Phoenician coast which should be mentioned again here briefly is Byblos. Just as in Ugarit, discoveries at Byblos called the entire chronology of Egypt into question.

In the royal cemetery located just outside the ancient city there was discovered a tomb belonging to a King Ahiram. Inside the sepulcher archaeologists found a magnificent carved stone sarcophagus, as well as a collection of grave-goods, including pottery and precious objects of various kinds. Among the finds was a Mycenaean ivory plaque, as well as fragments of alabaster vases bearing the cartouches of Ramses II. These finds apparently dated the tomb to the 14th/13th century BC.

Yet here there was a problem. As well as the vases and Mycenaean ivory, excavators also found pottery of Cypriot manufacture. This however looked typical of the 7th or even 6th century. Furthermore, inscriptions at the entrance to the tomb and on the sarcophagus were in alphabetic Phoenician typical of the 6th or 7th century BC at the earliest. A debate, lasting many years, as to the meaning of the archaeology in Ahiram's sepulcher, got underway. Some tried to suggest that the tomb, excavated in the 14th century, was reused in the 7th or 6th — though the inscriptions clearly implied that the sepulcher had been excavated by Ahiram's son as his father's resting place. In addition, although the decoration on the sarcophagus looked typically Phoenician of the Ramesside era, it could equally well have been produced in the 6th or even 5th century BC.

In spite of all this, the question as to the true date of the tomb was never resolved. In the end, it was simply ignored.

Yet in recent years, as knowledge of Phoenician archaeology has grown, even more disturbing facts have come to light. Thus as recently as 1999 Sabatino Moscati, an authority on the Phoenicians, remarked on the fact that "after Ahiram new sarcophagi are only found in the fifth century."[138] He was later to add that "this sarcophagus [of Ahiram] is a unique case since no others have appeared prior to the 6th-5th century."[139]

Barnett, another authority, noted not too many years earlier how the sarcophagus of Ahiram "obviously reproduces in stone a contemporaneous wooden chest decorated with carved panels; it is the earliest example of what later became the established type of Phoenician funerary furniture, continuing with little change through stone sarcophagi such as the late 6th and early 5th century

---

138 S. Moscati et al, *The Phoenicians* (New York, 1999) p. 355; cited by L. Greenberg, "The Lion Gate at Mycenae Revisited," *SIS: Proceedings of Conference 'Ages Still in Chaos'* (14th-15th Sept 2002).
139 Ibid.

pieces from Amathus, Tamassos, and Athienou on to the Satrap of Alexander sarcophagi and that of the 'Mourning Women' at Carthage."[140]

Again and again material from Phoenicia, which is easily compared chronologically with material from the Greek world, shows that the world of the Late Bronze Age, specifically contemporary with the Egyptian Eighteenth and Nineteenth Dynasties, should rightfully be placed in the 7th and 6th centuries BC, rather than the 15th and 14th centuries, to which it is presently assigned.

One more point — Frankfort, interestingly enough, noted that the carved lions which act as supports for the Ahiram sarcophagus "seem to anticipate Syro-Hittite sculpture of the eighth century BC."[141] Syro-Hittite or Neo-Hittite culture is of course dated by its relationship to Assyrian history. On this ground it (and the Ahiram sarcophagus) seems to belong to the 8th century. Thus material which is Egyptologically dated to the 14th century, is at the same time Assyriologically dated to the 8th and classically dated to the 6th centuries.

This same phenomenon is encountered again and again, wherever we look at the art and material culture of the region.

Cypriot Tombs

Towards the end of the 19th century a team from the British Museum conducted excavations at Enkomi in Cyprus, site of an ancient metropolis. A large cemetery, with numerous undisturbed sepulchers, was uncovered. The date of these tombs was quickly established both by the occurrence in them of artifacts of clearly Mycenaean Greek provenance and by the discovery of several Egyptian objects of late Eighteenth and/or early Nineteenth Dynasty origin. Among these were, a scarab bearing the cartouche of Tiy, the wife of Amenhotep III, as well as several gold necklaces of a type typical of the late Eighteenth and Nineteenth Dynasties.[142] Expedition leader, A.S. Murray, was in no doubt that the cemetery was in use for only a relatively short period of time,

> In general there was not apparent in the tombs we opened any wide differences of epoch. For all we could say, the whole burying-ground may have been the work of a century.

Now the Mycenaean, together with Egyptian New Kingdom material, should have settled very quickly the age of the cemetery. Even by 1896, the year of the

140 R. D. Bennett, "Phoenician-Punic Art" in *Encyclopedia of World Art*, XI (New York, 1966) p. 307. Cited from Greenberg. loc cit.

141 H. Frankfort, *The Art and Architecture of the Ancient Orient* (Penguin, New York, 1988) p. 271 Cited from Greenberg, loc cit.

142 All quotations from A. S. Murray, "Excavations at Enkomi" in A. S. Murray, A. H. Smith, H. B. Walters, *Excavations in Cyprus* (London, British Museum, 1900).

excavations, the chronology of the Eighteenth and Nineteenth Dynasties was well established, or so it seemed. There should really have been no doubt as to the placing of the tombs in the 14th century BC. But Murray soon began finding things which made him question the prevailing wisdom. For Cyprus stood at the crossroads between the Greek world and the ancient orient — and many of the artifacts founds in the sepulchers clearly pointed, in Greek terms, to an epoch much more recent than the 14th century BC.

He cited a vase, typical of the burials at Enkomi, as an example. The dark outlines of figures on the vase are accompanied by dotted white lines, making the contours of men and animals appear to be perforated. The feature is very characteristic of Enkomi pottery; and yet,

> The same peculiarity of white dotted lines is found also on a vase from Caere [in Etruria], signed by the potter Aristonothos which, it is argued, cannot be older than the seventh century BC. The same method of dotted lines is to be seen again on a pinax from Cameiros [on Rhodes] in the [British] Museum, representing the combat of Menelaos and Hector over the body of Euphorbos, with their names inscribed. That vase also is assigned to the seventh century BC. Is it possible that the Mycenae and Enkomi vases are seven or eight centuries older?

The connection between a vase of the Mycenaean Age and Aristonothos of the 7th century caused "a remarkable divergence of opinion, even among those who defend systematically the high antiquity of Mycenaean art."

Other features of the vase pointed in the same direction. The workmanship and design of sphinxes or griffins with human forelegs on the object illustrated "its relationship, on the one hand, to the fragmentary vase of Tell el-Amarna (see Petrie, *Tell el-Amarna*, Plate 27) and a fragment of fresco from Tiryns (*Perrot and Chipiez*, VI, 545), and on the other hand to the pattern which occurs on a terra-cotta sarcophagus from Clazomenae [in Ionia], now in Berlin, a work of the early sixth century BC."

It wasn't only pottery that caused problems. Many metal objects, including some of bronze, silver and gold, raised serious questions: "Another surprise among our bronzes is a pair of greaves.... It is contended by Reichel that metal greaves are unknown in Homer. He is satisfied that they were an invention of a later age (about 700 BC)."

One of the Enkomi tombs revealed a collection of gold pins "One of them, ornamented with six discs, is identical in shape with the pin which fastens the chiton [tunic] on the shoulders of the Fates on the Francois vase in Florence (sixth century BC)." A pendant "covered with diagonal patterns consisting of minute globules of gold soldered down on the surface of the pendant" was made by "precisely the same process of soldering down globules of gold and arranging them in the same patterns" that "abounds in a series of gold ornaments in the British Museum which were found at Cameiros in Rhodes" and which were dated to the seventh or eighth century.

Porcelain tells the same story. A porcelain head of a woman "seems to be Greek, not only in her features, but also in the way in which her hair is gathered up at the back in a net, just as in the sixth century vases of this shape." Greek vases of this shape "differ, of course, in being of a more advanced artistic style, and in having a handle. But it may be fairly questioned whether these differences can represent any very long period of time."

Surveying the glass, Murray noted:

> In several tombs, but particularly in one, we found vases of variegated glass, differing but slightly in shape and fabric from the fine series of glass vases obtained from the tombs of Cameiros, and dating from the seventh and sixth centuries, or even later in some cases. It happens, however, that these slight differences of shape and fabric bring our Enkomi glass vases into direct comparison with certain specimens found by Professor Flinders Petrie at Gurob in Egypt, and now in the British Museum. If Professor Petrie is right in assigning his vases to about 1400 BC, our Enkomi specimens must follow suit. It appears that he had found certain fragmentary specimens of this particular glass ware beside a porcelain necklace, to which belonged an amulet stamped with the name of Tutankhamen, that is to say, about 1400 BC.

He came to the conclusion that the "Phoenicians manufactured the glass ware of Gurob and Enkomi at one and the same time." Consequently,

> the question is, what was that time? For the present we must either accept Professor Petrie's date (about 1400 BC) based on scanty observations collected from the poor remains of a foreign settlement in Egypt, or fall back on the ordinary method of comparing the glass vessels of Gurob with those from Greek tombs of the seventh century BC or later, and then allowing a reasonable interval of time for the slight changes of shape or fabric which may have intervened. In matters of chronology it is no new thing for the Egyptians to instruct the Greeks, as we know from the pages of Herodotus.

In his discussion of the Enkomi material, Velikovsky noted that here Murray came close to the real problem, "but shrank from it." He did not dare revise Egyptian chronology, and without taking this bold step he was unable to solve the conundrum. He pleaded for a late date for the Enkomi tombs, but in the face of the apparently unassailable evidence from Egypt, he could put forward no sound argument. His proposal to reduce the time of the Mycenaean Age was rejected by the scholarly world, because this would infallibly also have meant the down-dating of the Eighteenth and Nineteenth Egyptian dynasties by the same margin and into the same period of time — i.e., the 7th and 6th centuries BC. Such a proposition was unthinkable, as Murray's famous contemporary Arthur Evans, the excavator of Knossos in Crete, pointed out. Evans admitted that "nothing is clearer than that Ionian art [of the 7th/6th century] represents the continuity of Mycenaean tradition," and that some objects, such as the porcelain figures "present the most remarkable resemblance, as Dr Murray justly pointed out, to some Greek painted vases of the sixth century BC." Nevertheless, he insisted that the weight of evidence must favor the manifold connections between the Mycenaean Age and Egypt of the Eighteenth and Nineteenth Dynasties. Were not the flasks of the Enkomi tomb almost as numerous in Egyptian tombs of the Eighteenth Dynasty? A gold collar or pectoral inlaid with glass paste, found in Enkomi, had gold pendants in nine different patterns, eight of which are well-known designs of the time of Akhnaton, "but are not found a century later." A metal ring of Enkomi, with cartouches of the heretic Akhnaton, was especially important because, "he was not a pharaoh whose cartouches were imitated in later periods."

There could, then, be no separation of the Enkomi tombs from the late Eighteenth and early Nineteenth Dynasties; but these were unquestionably to be dated to the 14th century BC.

In time, Murray's objections were forgotten, and the Enkomi burials are today confidently dated between the 15th and 14th centuries BC. The flawed measuring-rod of ancient chronology, Egypt, once again did its work.

I should, before moving on, point to the fact that much of the material recovered from the Enkomi tombs, particularly the ivories, bore striking resemblances to artwork from Assyria, which was dated there to the 9th and 8th centuries BC. Thus for example a carving of a man slaying a griffin is remarkable,

> ... for the helmet with chin strap which he [the man] wears. It is a subject which appears frequently on the metal bowls of the Phoenicians, and is found in two instances among the ivories discovered by Layard in the palace at Nimroud. The date of the palace is given as 850-700 BC.

There were numerous artistic indicators pointing in the same direction. Most remarkable, however, was a silver ring engraved on the bezel "with a design of a distinctly Assyrian character — a man dressed in a lion's skin standing before a seated king, to whom he offers an oblation. Two figures in this costume may be seen on an Assyrian sculpture from Nimroud of the time of Assurnazirpal (884-860), and there is no doubt that this fantastic idea spread rapidly westward."

So, the material excavated at Enkomi could be dated Egyptologically to the 14th century BC, Assyriologically (and biblically) to the 9th/8th century BC, and classically (in Greek terms) to the 7th/6th century BC. The tombs demonstrate in a striking way the proposition advanced in the present volume of the need for a double down-dating of Egyptian history. As I have shown elsewhere, Ashurnasirpal II, who built Nimrud (Calah) as his new capital, was one and the same as Ashuruballit I, the king whose letters to Akhnaton were discovered at Tel el-Amarna. Yet Ashurnasirpal II (along with Akhnaton) did not reign in the 9th century, but in the second half of the 7th, just as the archaeology tells us.

Glassmaking

One of the many innovations attributed to the ancient Phoenicians was glassmaking. According to Pliny the Elder (*Natural History II*) the art of making glass was discovered quite by accident. Some sailors, we are told,

> ... had pulled into shore for the night by the beach of the river Belus on the Phoenician coast, and finding no stones on which to support their cooking pot, supported it on blocks of natron (soda) which they fetched from the cargo of their ship. In the morning, in the cold ashes of the fire was found the first glass.

The chronological implications of glass were discussed at some length by John Dayton in his *Minerals, Metals, Glazing and Man* (1978) and further examined by Gunnar Heinsohn in his seminal paper delivered in Toronto, August 1988.

It is generally agreed that Egyptian glassmaking really should be dated only from the Eighteenth Dynasty, though one or two relatively minor occurrences are accepted as predating this period. Nevertheless, it is with the New Kingdom that Egyptian glassmaking flourishes, and over 400 pieces, mostly dating from the Eighteenth and Nineteenth Dynasties, are found in museums and collections around the world. By far the most impressive and numerous examples come from Akhnaton's short-lived capital Akhet-Aton, where "ancient Egyptian glass reached its highest development."[143] In spite of this, around 1200 BC, near the end of the Nineteenth Dynasty, Egyptian glass-making apparently ceases altogether. In the words of B. Nolte, around 1200 BC "the Egyptian production of glass vessels comes to a standstill."[144]

Yet, here is the surprise: around seven centuries later, in the lands of the Phoenician coast, glass makes a sudden and dramatic reappearance, and the forms of vessels produced showed remarkably little difference with regard to those produced in the Egyptian New Kingdom, "About the middle of the VI century, i.e.,

143 P. Fossing, *Glass Vessels before Glass Blowing* (Copenhagen, 1940) p. 1.8
144 B. Nolte, *Die Glasgefässe im alten Aegypten* (Berlin, 1968).

during the long reign of King Amasis [589 to 526 BC], these rare glass objects suddenly became a frequent component of the archaeological material found in Mediterranean coastal countries. Though the forms to some extent are now Greek in style, and for the most part were found together with Greek products, especially Attic vases, there is such a strong likeness between the glass objects of this period and the corresponding products of the New Empire glass industry eight to nine hundred years before, that in all probability the glasses of the VI-V centuries are also Egyptian products."[145]

It should be noted here that the King Amasis (Ahmose) referred to above is not the 6th century king who preceded the Persians (whose real identity we have discovered in Amenmeses of the latter Nineteenth Dynasty) but the 5th century Persian age potentate, whom we have referred to in the previous chapter. Thus the gap referred to above is even apparently longer, from the Twentieth Dynasty (supposedly ending around 1200 BC) right through to circa 450 BC. Yet bringing the Eighteenth and Nineteenth Dynasties down into the 7th and 6th centuries and making the Twentieth Dynasty itself contemporary with the Persians, we can observe that no gap at all exists. Thus we should not be at all surprised by the striking similarities observed in the two sets of glasses, supposedly separated by over seven centuries.

The same gap of seven to eight centuries is observed almost everywhere glass has been found. Thus, Palestine/Israel also produced evidence of glass in the time of the Egyptian New Kingdom,[146] then apparently forgot about it for seven centuries, only to rediscover it in the 7th/6th century.[147]

Specialists are struck not only by the striking similarities between the glasses of the Late Bronze Age and those of the 6th, 5th and 4th centuries, but by the fact that the glassworkers of the later epoch apparently reinvented an incredibly complex technique and technology, which seems to not have existed at all in the interim. After many theories were proposed, a system was tried and tested by F. Schuler, which seemed to work. This is his account of the technique.

> Finally a method was tried (Method 6) which, from earlier work on the mold-casting of bowls, was thought likely to give success. This was the mold-cast the vessel on a core, to cool it, remove the outside mold, clean the outside, then reheat. This would be followed by the thread-decorating steps and by fire-polishing. Such a process seems sophisticated in concept, but the casting step would have been derived from metal-casting, while the re-heating step with thread-decoration and fire-polishing would represent a true invention.

---

145 P. Fossing, loc cit p. 134.
146 H. Weippert, "Glas" in K. Galling, (ed.) *Biblisches Reallexikon* (Tübingen, 1977) 98f.
147 Ibid. 99.

The inner form of a core vessel three inches in height was carved at the end of a seven-inch cylinder of freshly set plaster of Paris and sand mixture. After drying, it was covered by dipping repeatedly in hot wax. An outer form was then cast around this, the cylinder dried at about 90 centigrade and the wax melted out. It was then placed in a furnace, heated to 700 centigrade, and glass added to the top cavity periodically as the temperature was brought to 1000 centigrade. The furnace was then cooled.

Upon removal from the furnace, the outer mold was broken off and the core vessel cleaned up, leaving the core inside. This was then mounted on a rod and preheated to 450 centigrade. The core was then transferred to a hotter region, where the surface was smoothed up by a fire-polishing action. It was then returned to 450 and cooled slowly.

The vessel was taken out of the furnace, the inside core broken out and the surface washed. The completed vessel has a smooth outside surface and a rougher inside one, and closely resembles existing core vessels, except the applied threads.[148]

As Gunnar Heinsohn remarked, "Schuler's conclusion that this casting method 'remained in use for fifteen hundred years' cost him his reputation with glass historians who, after all, had to handle an 800 year gap."

---

148 F. Schuler, "Ancient Glassmaking Techniques. The Egyptian Core Vessel Process" *Archaeology* Vol. 15 (1962) 36f.

Chapter 5. Sargonids and Achaemenids

The Evidence of Art

We have seen how the art and culture of the Egyptian Eighteenth and Nineteenth Dynasties bears, on the one hand, striking resemblances to that of the Neo-Assyrian Age (9th-8th centuries) and on the other to the age of the Medes and Persians, of the 7th and 6th centuries. In follows, naturally, that the art and culture of the Neo-Assyrian Age must be closely related, or identical, to the art and culture of the Medes and Persians. We have already asserted that the Neo-Assyrians are in fact nothing other than the otherwise archaeologically missing Mede and Persian kings as rulers of Mesopotamia. In the pages to follow we shall examine the evidence from Mesopotamia, both cultural and historical, to show that this is indeed the case.

We have already identified the precise point at which the Neo-Assyrian kingdom of the Medes was transformed into the Neo-Assyrian kingdom of the Persians. This was during the reign of Tiglath-Pileser III, a mighty ruler whom we equate with Cyrus the Great. Such being the case, it is clear that the late Neo-Assyrian epoch, beginning with Tiglath-Pileser III and continuing through the Sargonid dynasty, should display detailed cultural comparisons with the Persian Achaemenid epoch. Can such comparisons be shown to exist?

As a matter of fact, the evidence linking the late Neo-Assyrians to the Persians is abundant, and covers virtually every field of knowledge. The achievements of the Sargonids match closely those of the Persians, whilst the religious, artistic, and technological achievements of the Sargonids find their closest parallels in Achaemenid Persia.

It is possible to identify literally scores of very precise parallels between the latter Neo-Assyrians and the Achaemenids. These may be very broadly classified as follows: (a) Identical monumental architecture and sculpture, (b) Identical religious iconography, (c) Identical types of royal insignia and trappings, (d) Identical military equipment and weaponry, (e) Identical domestic utensils, pottery styles etc. Many of these have already been highlighted by Professor Heinsohn, and we shall have occasion to look at some of them as we proceed.

In addition to these, there are varieties of parallels that are very specific. Thus for example the evolution of Neo-Assyrian art precisely matches the evolution of Achaemenid art. Early Sargonid work (beginning with Tiglath-Pileser III) finds its closest parallels in early Achaemenid art, whilst late Sargonid work is precisely matched by that of the late Achaemenid period. Late Sargonid work does not resemble early Achaemenid work, which it should however if textbook chronology is accurate. Both Sargonid and Achaemenid figurative art begins with highly-stylized forms and gradually develops an increasing realism — so much so that much of the later Sargonid and Achaemenid work could almost be Greek. Take for example the lion's head (fig. 3) from the time of Tiglath-Pileser III, and compare with that of the early Achaemenid epoch in fig. 4. It is immediately evident that the parallels are exact and that these two belong to a single artistic style. Now look at the striking realism of the lion's head in fig. 5, from the palace of Ashurbanipal.

It is impossible that the artists of the Near East, after developing a realistic style very comparable to that of classical Greece, should then return, a century later, to a primitive and abstract style long ago abandoned, only to repeat later a second evolution towards Greek-style realism.

We have stated that the religious and royal iconography of the Neo-Assyrians is specifically Persian. The religious material will be examined shortly, but one point relating to royal symbolism needs to be mentioned here. The Persian royal symbol *par excellence* was the feathered crown. This is part of common knowledge and fully accepted by all authorities. Strangely however, and incomprehensibly, the feathered crown also appears in Neo-Assyrian art (see fig. 6), and also in Neo-Assyrian religious iconography. Thus for example from the time of Tiglath-Pileser III onwards the winged bulls who guard the entrances to Neo-Assyrian palaces are shown wearing a tall cylindrical-shaped headdress, of Persian style, surmounted by a feathered crown. Achaemenid royal palaces in Persia proper are guarded by identical beasts.

As Heinsohn has emphasized, such close correspondences can scarcely be explained by simple copying, especially not after a gap of two centuries.

Military Technology

There are almost innumerable parallels in military practice and weaponry between the Sargonids and Achaemenids. Many of these have been highlighted at great length by Heinsohn, who has noted for example identical swords and daggers, identical archery equipment, etc.[149] He has not however looked in too much detail at chariot design, though from this area comes some of the most convincing evidence.

Assyrian chariot design changed radically with the reign of Tiglath-Pileser. These now appear as large square-shaped machines of wickerwork, capable of carrying four persons. In accordance with that purpose the wheels were now strengthened by eight or even sixteen spokes, whilst the outer rims usually had regular stubs or notches, which acted as a tread. Now the chariots of Achaemenid times were virtually identical in every detail. Beginning with Cyrus, Persian chariots appear with a square wickerwork body, large eight-spoked or sixteen-spoked wheels, with tread-notches around the rims. These chariots too could carry up to four persons, and the chariot of Darius I, depicted in Fig. 21, displays very detailed parallels with the chariot of Sargon II (Fig. 20) — even down to the design of tassels hanging from the harness and the pose of the charioteer with the reins.

Whilst many aspects of late Neo-Assyrian military equipment look Persian, other things look suspiciously Greek. Thus for example certain detachments of the Neo-Assyrian army carried large convex-faced shields, very similar to those used by Greek hoplites from the 5th century BC onwards.

Gunnar Heinsohn has in particular highlighted the deployment of Greek peltastes, lightly-armored foot soldiers, in the army of Sennacherib. These are shown, in various bas-reliefs, with typical 5th century Greek equipment, including the plumed helmet and the pelta, the light shield so characteristic of these highly-mobile troops. It is impossible, of course, that peltastes could have been employed in the army of an 8th/7th century Assyrian king, but they are well-attested in the 5th century army of Xerxes. The earliest appearance of Greek-looking soldiers in Neo-Assyrian art is on the monuments of Tiglath-Pileser III. In the scheme proposed here, Tiglath-Pileser represents Cyrus the Great, who first brought the Ionian cities under Persian domination.

---

149 For a detailed examination of the evidence, see Gunnar Heinsohn, *Assyrerkönige gleich Perserherrscher!* (Gräfelfing, 1996).

The Neo-Assyrian kings, beginning with Ashurnasirpal II, armed their troops with iron swords. In my *Pyramid Age* (2nd ed. 2007) I demonstrated in some detail how throughout the Middle East bronze was replaced by iron as the preferred metal for weapons only with improvements in the iron-smelting process, which rendered iron more plentiful and cheaper. Iron (and steel) had been known at a very early period — in fact steel tools had been employed by the builders of the Great Pyramid — but the expense of iron had prevented its widespread use in armies. It so happens that the Greeks recalled very precisely the point at which steel swords were first manufactured in their country. Pausanias reports that during the reign of the Spartan King Anaxandrides an emissary from the city was astonished to see a man in Tegea forging a sword of iron (Pausanias, iii, 3, 7 and 11, 8). Since Anaxandrides reigned around 600 BC at the earliest, the implication is that it was around this time that the Greeks began to abandon the use of bronze for sword manufacture. But this can only have been a gradual process, and there is evidence that some bronze swords were still employed in the country as late as the Persian Wars. Yet from the very beginning of the Neo-Assyrian epoch iron (steel) is the only material used for swords — supposedly from the middle of the 9th century. Could it be that the Greeks were technologically so far behind their Mesopotamian neighbors? This seems highly unlikely, especially when we remember that it was the peoples of Asia Minor and Anatolia — regions the Greeks were very familiar with — who first perfected iron-smelting and steel forging techniques. Far better to assume that the Neo-Assyrians adopted iron weaponry at roughly the same time as the Greeks — some time between 600 and 550 BC.

The Cult of Ahura Mazda

The religious culture of the Neo-Assyrian epoch displays striking correspondences with that of Achaemenid Persia.

In one sense, the Persian Empire can be regarded as the world's first monotheistic state. Around 600 BC the prophet Zoroaster (Zarathustra) proclaimed Ahura Mazda as the one true god. Zoroaster's teachings spread rapidly throughout the Iranian plateau, and by the time of Cyrus the new religion had become dominant. In later years it was to become the official religion of the Great Kings.

Monuments from the Achaemenid epoch reveal that Ahura Mazda was portrayed as a regal figure seated within or above a winged disc. The winged disc was originally a Mitannian, therefore Median, motif which was promulgated throughout the Near East after the conquest of the Old Assyrian Empire. Now it is known that the Achaemenid Persians were monotheists rather than monolatrists, and their worship of Ahura Mazda did not preclude their honoring the gods of other nations, whom they associated with their own supreme deity. Persian religious tolerance is indeed emphasized in the biblical literature. Clearly then, as rulers of Assyria, it might be expected that the Persians would simply have equated the greatest Assyrian god with Ahura Mazda. The supreme and tutelary god of Assyria was Ashur. Does the cult of Ashur, in the Neo-Assyrian epoch, resemble that of Ahura Mazda?

Countless artifacts from Assyria portray Ashur; his image is in fact virtually identical to that of Ahura Mazda: a royal figure inside a winged disc. The precise parallels between these two have of course not gone unnoticed by scholars, yet it is generally assumed that the iconography of Ashur was simply copied by the Persians during the 6th century or so. Thus we read, "It is not too difficult to understand why Ashur never gained willing adherents among other nationalities. It should be remembered, however, that when the Zoroastrian religion prevailed in the land which had once been Ashur's, the symbol of the god still remained to testify to his former glory; for that symbol was adopted to represent the great and good Ahura-mazda, and, together with the symbol, rites and ceremonies once connected with the worship of Ashur, must have passed to the Zoroastrian faith."[150]

In this way the very precise correspondence between Ashur and Ahura-Mazda is explained away.[151] But what is not explained, what is not even mentioned, is that in the whole of Assyria, indeed the whole of Mesopotamia, which was under Persian rule for two centuries, archaeologists have not recovered a single image that could unquestionably be identified with Ahura Mazda. The complete absence of Ahura Mazda is, however, explained if he is one and the same as Ashur.

As we shall shortly see, an overwhelming body of evidence identifies the Neo-Assyrian King Sennacherib with Xerxes. It is well-known that Xerxes was the first Persian monarch to enforce Zoroastrian monotheism, and as part of that project he issued a famous proclamation outlawing what he describes as the "foreign daevas." He also carried off from Babylon the golden image of Bel-Marduk — a blasphemous act long recalled in the latter city.

---

150 S. Smith, "The Age of Ashurbanipal" in *CAH* Vol. 3 (1st ed. 1929) p. 91 It should be noted here that the winged solar disc, used to represent Ahura Mazda, reminds us strongly of the deity of the solar-disc Aton, worshipped by Akhnaton. There is, in addition, a suggestion that Akhnaton may have spent part of his youth in the land of Mitanni (Media).

151 "The supreme god of the Persians, Ahura Mazda, was now represented by the winged disk of Ashur." Proceedings of The Assyrian National Convention (Los Angeles, September 4, 1999) in the *Journal of Assyrian Academic Studies*, Vol. XIII, No. 2, 1999.

In precisely the same way, Sennacherib issued a proclamation outlawing the Babylonian deities, and he too carried off the golden statue of Bel-Marduk, an outrage supposedly repeated two centuries later by Xerxes.

Ahura Mazda's symbol par excellence was fire; and, sure enough, fire altars of a very particular design are found portrayed throughout Iran. How strange then that fire altars of exactly the same type were known in Sargonid Assyria (see fig. 26) supposedly two centuries earlier.

Two Hebrew Prophets

It is universally claimed that the Jews regarded the Persians as their liberators, and that immediately after his conquest of Babylon Cyrus the Great decreed the rebuilding of the Temple in Jerusalem and the repatriation to Israel of those Jews enslaved by the Chaldean under Nebuchadrezzar. Yet according to the reconstruction of history proposed in the present volume, it was the Persians, in their guise of Neo-Assyrians, who enslaved and deported both the Ten Tribes of the northern kingdom and the Two Tribes of Judah. Indeed it was Cyrus, in his Assyrian alter-ego of Tiglath-Pileser, who began the deportation of the Ten Tribes, a process completed by his successors Shalmaneser V, whom we shall argue was an alter-ego of Cambyses, and Sargon II, in whom we see an alter-ego of Darius the Great.

There are numerous clues in the Scriptures which clearly point to these identifications, and which show unequivocally that it was under the Persian kings that the Hebrews experienced captivity in the east. Thus for example the Ten Tribes are deported by Sargon to the "cities of the Medes," whilst the Book of Tobit makes it very clear that the Neo-Assyrian kings Sennacherib and Esarhaddon ruled the entire land of the Medes, including its capital Ecbatana. (Tobit 3:7, 6:6 and 7:1). The Book of Esther describes how the heroine saves her people, who are clearly enslaved, from annihilation by a Persian king named Ahasuerus (in Hebrew, Akhashverosh or Akhshurosh), generally agreed to be Xerxes (Khshayarsha).

The attempt to make the Neo-Assyrian kings precede the Persians has in fact caused all sorts of complications for Hebrew historiography, not least of which is the need to postulate duplications of certain personalities, one belonging to the Neo-Assyrian age and the other belonging to the Persian. This can be illustrated in the lives of two of the best-known Old Testament prophets, Isaiah and Daniel.

Isaiah, it is agreed, received his call from God around 742 BC, just as Assyrian might under Tiglath-Pileser III began to threaten the kingdoms of Judah and Israel. Isaiah issued dire warnings to the people of Israel against any attempt to oppose the Assyrians, who are portrayed as the avenging sword of Yahweh. However, in Chapter 44:28, and again in Chapter 45:1, Isaiah incomprehensibly mentions the name of Cyrus, who is also portrayed as Yahweh's instrument of vengeance and justice:

>Thus says Yahweh to his anointed, to Cyrus whom he grasps by his right hand,
>to subdue the nations before him and strip the loins of kings,
>to force gateways before him that their gates be closed no more.

Because of the mention of both Tiglath-Pileser and Cyrus by the same writer, commentators have been forced to postulate two Isaiahs, or an Isaiah and a pseudo-Isaiah, one living in the 8th century and another in the 6th.

But precisely the same problem is encountered with the prophet Daniel.

It is agreed that Daniel began to prophesy during the time of a Neo-Babylonian king named Nebuchadrezzar, and that he remained active into the reigns of the early Achaemenids. Thus he is thrown into the lions' den by a King Darius, presumably Darius I, who is said to have inherited the kingdom of Belshazzar, Nebuchadrezzar's successor.[152] From this information Daniel is placed squarely in the 6th century BC.

But in contradiction to this date the writings of Daniel are filled with references to the Macedonians, who are mentioned by name (Dan 8:21) and to the early Ptolemies and Seleucids, who are mentioned by implication. He also refers to the Romans, who send their ships to the aid of one of the kings of the region (Dan 11:29-30). But this Roman intervention in the Levant could not possibly precede the alliance with Ptolemy II concluded in 273 BC. In fact, it is now accepted that the Book of Daniel deals with events as recent as the second century BC, which means that the volume covers a range of events lasting four centuries. This of course has forced the complete abandonment of any notion that the book is the work of a historical "Daniel" who lived in the final years of the Neo-Babylonian kingdom.

Thus, it is now said, as well as two Isaiahs there must also have been two (or three or four) Daniels, one in the 6th century and another "pseudo-Daniel" in the 4th/3rd century, with possibly yet another in the 2nd century.

But this flies in the face of common sense. One Daniel, living and prophesying at the end of the Persian epoch, rather than its beginning, eliminates the need for the various "pseudos" postulated by scholarship. The Darius who threw Daniel to the lions was probably Darius III, not Darius I, and the King Nebuchadrezzar who had earlier cast him into the lions' pit could not have been a Babylonian; he

---

152 Daniel 6.

was surely an Achaemenid ruler of Babylon, probably the great conquering king normally known as Artaxerxes III.

The above proposition is put virtually beyond question by Jewish genealogies, a primary example of which is presented at the beginning of Matthew's gospel, where the evangelist seeks to illustrate Jesus' royal pedigree. Beginning with Abraham, Matthew lists fourteen generations to King David. From David to the Babylonian Exile there are enumerated a further fourteen generations, and from the Babylonian Exile to Jesus another fourteen generations.

Now from the time of David at least no one doubts that the characters named by Matthew are real enough. Yet only by contradicting everything we know about history and the historical process can these genealogies be made to square with the "traditional" biblical chronology. Thus for example if we allow 25 years to a generation (a generous figure, given the generally early marriages and deaths of ancient peoples), the Babylonian Exile would have occurred 350 years before the time of Jesus — in other words during the time of the penultimate Achaemenid Great King Artaxerxes III. Only by allowing over 40 years to a generation can the fourteen generations between the Exile and the birth of Jesus be made to agree with the traditional Exile date of c. 585 BC. But 40 years per generation is agreed by all to be an absurdly high figure, and so the genealogy of Matthew remains an enigma and an embarrassment to biblical scholarship.

Thus if we follow Matthew's lead the prophet Daniel would have flourished during the reigns of Artaxerxes III, Darius III, Alexander the Great, and the early Seleucids — precisely where the evidence of the Book of Daniel would place him.

In the same way, the Matthew genealogy would place Isaiah around 530 BC — right in the middle of the reign of Cyrus. Once again, this is a position that agrees entirely with the internal evidence of the Book of Isaiah, and a solution which restores the logic of the text whilst eliminating the necessity of postulating two Isaiahs.

Cyrus and Tiglath-Pileser III

From what has been said so far, it will be obvious that the author views Tiglath-Pileser III, generally regarded as one of the greatest Neo-Assyrian rulers, as the Assyrian alter-ego of Cyrus the Great. This identification, it must be stressed, is not arbitrary — it is forced by the chronology already adopted.

Such an equation by itself is fairly straightforward, but the situation is complicated somewhat by the fact that Cyrus also called himself, for a brief period of time, Tukulti-Ninurta — and a further complication emerges in the fact that

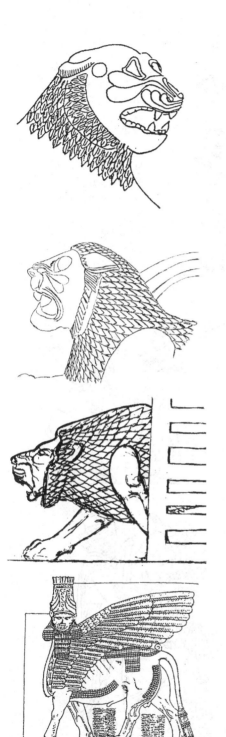

Fig. 3. Neo-Assyrian portrayal of a lion, from the time of Tiglath-Pileser III. (after Akurgal)

Fig. 4. Persian weight in the form of a lion from the time of Darius I. Note the abstract portrayal of the lion, strikingly similar to that of early Neo-Assyrian art

Fig. 5. Realistic late Neo-Assyrian portrayal of a lion, from a bas-relief of Ashurbanipal

Fig. 6. Neo-Assyrian winged bull, with feathered crown. Such crowns appear in Neo-Assyrian art from the time of Tiglath-Pileser III

Left: Fig. 7. Persian winged bull, with feathered crown. The feathered crown was the symbol par excellence of Persian royalty and divinity

Middle: Fig. 8. Late Neo-Assyrian portrayals of the king slaying a lion

Below: Fig. 9. Persian portrayals of the king slaying a lion and a lion-monster

Fig. 10. Neo-Assyrian royal umbrella

Left: Fig. 11. Persian royal umbrella   Right: Fig. 12. Neo-Assyrian human throne

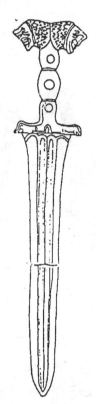

Above: Fig. 13. Persian human throne

Right: Fig. 19. Persian lion-decoration on weapons

Fig. 14. Neo-Assyrian king with scepter and lotus-flower

Above: Fig. 15. Persian kings with scepter and lotus-flower

Below: Fig. 16. Neo-Assyrian goat-armbands

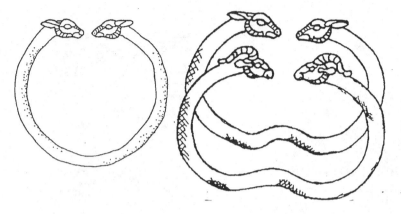

Above: Fig. 17. Persian goat-armbands

Below: Fig. 18. Neo-Assyrian lion-decoration on weapons

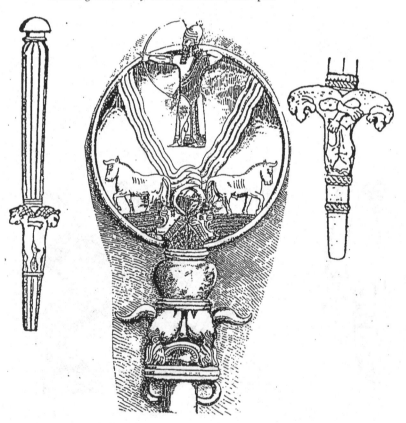

Above: Fig. 20. Chariot from the time of Sargon II, with eight-spoked wheels. Note also tassles on the horses' bridles

Below: Fig. 21. Chariot from the time of Darius I, with eight-spoked wheels and bridle-tassles identical to those on the horses of Sargon II

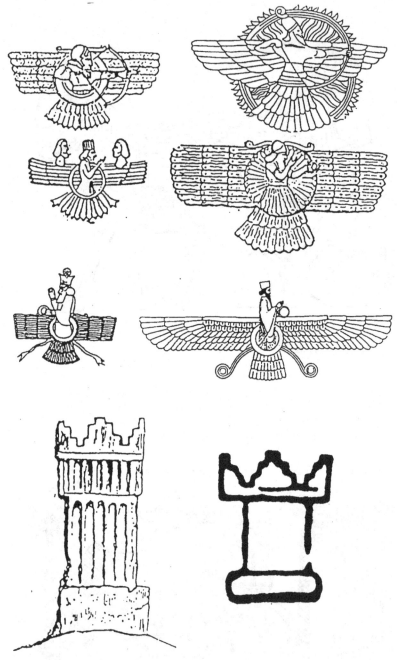

Top: Fig. 23. Neo-Assyrian portrayals of the god Ashur

Middle: Fig. 24. Persian portrayals of the god Ahura Mazda

Down: Fig. 25. Neo-Assyrian fire-altars

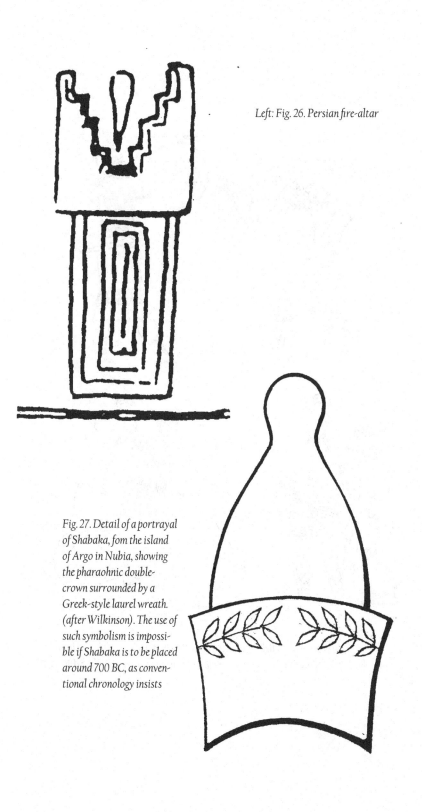

Left: Fig. 26. Persian fire-altar

Fig. 27. Detail of a portrayal of Shabaka, fom the island of Argo in Nubia, showing the pharaohnic double-crown surrounded by a Greek-style laurel wreath. (after Wilkinson). The use of such symbolism is impossible if Shabaka is to be placed around 700 BC, as conventional chronology insists

Fig. 22. Neo-Assyrian portrayals of lightly-armed troops wearing Greek-style plumed helmets.
Such soldiers first appear in Neo-Assyrian monuments from the time of Tiglath-Pileser III

he is also the same person as Tiglath-Pileser I, whom conventional history places five centuries before Tiglath-Pileser III.

Before being diverted into the latter identifications, however, we need to look at some of the evidence linking Tiglath-Pileser III to Cyrus.

Cyrus was one of the most outstanding characters ever to live. Within half a dozen years he had built an empire the likes of which had never been seen before. He reigned from the borders of Egypt to India, and described himself, with some justification, as "king of the world" and "king of the four rims (of the earth)."[153] Such an individual would leave his mark on history irrespective of what name he appeared under. If Tiglath-Pileser is indeed the same man as Cyrus, the parallels between the two should be so clear as to put the matter beyond question. Among the Neo-Assyrian monarchs he should appear as a giant. He should be able to describe himself as "King of the Four Quarters of the World"; his domains should stretch from Egypt to India; he should, above all, be remembered for his conquest of Babylon.

What then do we find? Was Tiglath-Pileser III an outstanding king? Did his realms stretch from Egypt to India? Did he describe himself as king of the world? Did he conquer Babylon?

The answer to all of these questions is in fact a resounding yes.

Tiglath-Pileser III could indeed be described as the greatest Assyrian king who ever lived. The circumstances surrounding his rise to power are shrouded in mystery, though it is generally agreed that he represents a new dynasty. With him, Assyria was to enter a period of massive military expansion and was to become, for the first time, one of the superpowers of the age. It is with Tiglath-Pileser that the might of Assyria reached out to the land of Israel, and we hear how first of all Menahem of Israel and later Ahaz of Judah paid tribute to the Great King from the east. From his time onwards, the actions of Assyrian kings are recorded by the Hebrew chroniclers. Later Assyrian rulers recalled with pride Tiglath-Pileser's awesome achievements, and on his own monuments he described himself as "king of the Four Quarters (of the earth)" as well as "king of Karduniash [Babylonia], king of Sumer and Akkad, king of Sippar and Babylon, king of Tilmun [India] and Meluhha [Egypt/Ethiopia]."[154] Why, it was asked, should a Mesopotamian ruler, supposedly of the 8th century BC, claim to rule from Egypt to India? Unable to answer that question satisfactorily, scholars made repeated attempts to locate Tilmun (or Dilmun) and Meluhha in other areas. However, documents from Persian times and later always translate Tilmun as India and Meluhha as Egypt/Ethiopia, so these attempts remain unconvincing.

---

153 J. Pritchard, *ANET* (1950) p. 316.
154 Ibid.

History says that Cyrus' greatest achievement, aside from his defeat of the Medes and Lydians, was his conquest of Babylon.[155] Certainly he himself, if his inscriptions are anything to go by, regarded it as such. The Persian conquest of Babylon is in fact one of the seminal events of ancient times, a watershed after which all things were different. Persia was now established as ruler of virtually the entire civilized world. Only Egypt and tiny Greece retained some measure of independence.

In the same way, it was from the time of Tiglath-Pileser III that Assyrian domination of all Mesopotamia dates. In his earliest inscriptions, or at least the earliest in which he is named Tiglath-Pileser, the Assyrian king is already master of Babylon. How he came to be ruler of that city is unclear; yet he is certainly the first Neo-Assyrian king to be regarded as such.

We have stated that Tiglath-Pileser III, supposedly of the 8th century BC, was contemporary with the demise of the Hittite Empire, though the Hittite kings against whom he battled are believed to have been weak and degenerate inheritors of the Imperial Hittite mantle. Yet again and again we find that the five centuries which supposedly separate the Neo-Assyrians from the Empire Hittites and Middle Assyrians are illusory. It has already been shown how Hittite art and architecture of Tiglath-Pileser III's reign is indistinguishable from that of the Hittite Empire. In particular, the Hittite prince Sulumeli, ruler of Malatya, who erected a classically Imperial Hittite palace, is named in the inscriptions of Tiglath-Pileser III. Now the same Hittite prince, named Allumari, occurs in the inscriptions of Tiglath-Pileser I, who is generally dated to the 12th/13th century — near the end of the Hittite Empire.[156] Scholars recorded the name Allumari of Malatya without comment, though they well understood that it could, or perhaps should, be read as Ulumeli, a name strangely reminiscent of Tiglath-Pileser III's Sulumeli.

Tiglath-Pileser I is generally dated a few decades after the fall of the Hittite Empire, yet one very important clue points to his direct involvement in its end. In one inscription the Assyrian king records the reception of tribute from Ini-Teshub, "king of Hatti." Now a Hittite prince of that name, a nephew of the last Hittite Great King Tudkhaliash IV, is recorded at Boghaz-koi; and scholars were surprised, indeed shocked, to find the same name recurring supposedly a century after the collapse of Hittite power.[157]

155 Herodotus, i, 178ff.
156 J. D. Hawkins "The Neo-Hittite States in Syria and Anatolia" in *CAH* Vol. 3 part 1(3rd ed.) pp. 380-1.
157 W. F. Albright, "Syria, the Philistines, and Phoenicia" in *CAH* Vol. 2 part 2 (3rd ed.) p. 527.

We should recall here that we have already identified the Hittite Empire as that of the Lydians, and the last Hittite Emperor, Tudkhaliash IV, as identical to Croesus, last of the Lydian monarchs.

Returning to the identification of Tiglath Pileser I and III, we should note that were we to accept them as two different people, then we are involved in not one but numerous character duplications, or even triplications. Thus a Babylonian king named Marduk-apal-iddin (Merodach Baladan I) was active in opposing the Assyrians shortly after the collapse of Hittite power; but in all his activities he merely anticipated by six centuries the life of another Merodach Baladan (III), who opposed the Assyrians during and after the reign of Tiglath-Pileser III.

Again, and this ties both Tiglath-Pileser I and III to Cyrus of Persia — note that a king of Babylon named Nebuchadrezzar I battled against the father of Tiglath-Pileser I, Ashur-resh-ishi; but in this he merely prefigured the struggles of his namesake Nebuchadrezzar, who six centuries later battled against the growing might of the Medes, prior to the loss of Babylonian independence in the time of Nabonidus his son.

We have stated that Tiglath-Pileser III destroyed the Hittite Empire. As such, he must be an alter-ego not only of Tiglath-Pileser I but also of a king named Tukulti-Ninurta. The Hittite records of Boghaz-koi, as well as other contemporary documents, leave no doubt that an Assyrian king named Tukulti-Ninurta corresponded with the last Hittite Emperor Tudkhaliash IV. If our reconstruction of history is correct, this Tukulti-Ninurta cannot be the same man as the father of Ashurnasirpal II, whom elsewhere I have identified as an alter-ego of Tushratta, the Great King of Mitanni/Media.[158] Rather, it seems that immediately upon taking control of the Mede state, the young Cyrus adopted the same Assyrian throne-name as that of Tushratta, whom he evidently believed to be the last legitimate king of the Medes. All who came after Tushratta/Tukulti-Ninurta I were progeny of the murderous Kurtiwaza/Ashurnasirpal II. Thus the youthful Cyrus/Tiglath-Pileser, who was himself of a minor branch of the Mede royal family, sought to establish the legitimacy of his own rule over the Medes.[159]

---

158 In my *Empire of Thebes* (2006), I show that Tushratta, the Mitanni Great King who corresponded with pharaoh Akhnaton, was actually the father of Ashurnasirpal II. These men all belong to the last quarter of the 7th century BC.

159 That Tukulti-Ninurta I did adopt new titles and change old ones is in fact well-known. See *From the Upper Sea to the Lower Sea: Studies on the History of Assyria and Babylonian, in honour of A. K. Grayson* (ed. Grant Frame, London, 2004). Here Cifola discusses changes in the titles used by Tukulti-Ninurta after his Babylonian campaign. Discussion is based on inscriptions found at his new capital of Kar-Tukulti-Ninurta. Apparently he added Babylonian titles after his victory, but then seems to have dropped them when Babylon — apparently — re-established its independence.

It was then this second Tukulti-Ninurta who records the carrying-off of 28,800 Hittite prisoners[160] and is credited with the destruction of the Hittite Empire. He also conquered Babylon, and was universally regarded as the first enemy to capture that mighty metropolis. So memorable was this victory that an epic poem commemorated it. This literary work tells how the Babylonian King Kashtiliash had been spurned by the gods, and how a great battle was fought to the north of the city which resulted in a resounding victory for the Assyrian. Kashtiliash, we are told, fled for protection within the city's walls, but the Assyrian army followed him thither and captured the great capital almost without further resistance. Kashtiliash was carried off in chains and presented before the god Ashur.

All of this sounds remarkably like the conquest of Babylon by Cyrus. According to Herodotus, Cyrus defeated the Babylonian army in a great battle some distance from the city,[161] and that following a siege, the city fell almost without further resistance.[162] Other sources report that after the fall of Babylon Cyrus ordered that its king be carried off in chains to Anshan in Persia.

If we are on the right track, this second Tukulti Ninurta was an alter-ego not only of Cyrus but also of Tiglath-Pileser III. In this regard it is surely significant that all three men conquered Babylon and "took the hand of Bel" (i.e., became king of Babylon officially). After his conquest of Babylon, it would appear that Cyrus changed his Assyrian throne-name from Tukulti Ninurta to Tukulti-apil-esharra (Tiglath-Pileser), and it is perhaps for this reason that we cannot find a record of how Tiglath-Pileser III came to be in control of Babylon, a control attested in his earliest documents.

The king of Babylon at the time of Tiglath-Pileser III is named as Nabonasser (Nabu-natsir), a man who must be the same as Kashtiliash, the Kassite king overthrown by Tukulti-Ninurta. This Nabu-natsir was the Nabonidus who was to go down in history as the last king of an independent Babylon. It should be noted here that the names Nabonasser and Nabonidus have more or less the same meaning (the former "Nebo protects me"; the latter "Nebo is protecting me"), and it is evident that the Babylonian king used both forms of the name.[163] It was only well into the reign of Tiglath-Pileser III that Nabonasser was removed as king and Tiglath-Pileser "took the hand of Bel." Thus it would appear that after his conquest of the city Cyrus allowed Nabonasser/Nabonidus to remain on

---

160 J. M. Munn-Rankin, "Assyrian Military Power 1300-1200 BC." in *CAH* Vol. 2 part 2 (3rd ed.) p. 291.

161 Herodotus, i, 190.

162 Ibid. i, 191.

163 George Rawlinson, *Ancient Monarchies* Vol. 3 (London, 1879) p. 82.

the throne, as a client king, and that his final removal must have been the consequence of an attempted rebellion

The Second Sargon

According to the reconstruction proposed so far, the Neo-Assyrian King
Shalmaneser V, who followed Tiglath-Pileser III, must be the same as Cambyses,
the brutal and semi-insane conqueror of Egypt whose short reign of just seven
and a half years was time enough to destabilize the entire Achaemenid state.
His premature death, which resulted from a self-inflicted wound, left the Empire
reeling. Cambyses' brother Smerdis (Bardiya), or at least a man claiming to be
Smerdis, had mounted the throne whilst Cambyses was still in Syria, on his return journey from Egypt.[164] Yet soon a question-mark arose over the succession.
A rumor spread that the man on the throne was not the brother of Cambyses
(who was said to have been murdered earlier on the king's orders), but a Mede
impostor named Gaumata. It was said that the deception was uncovered and
that Darius Hystaspes, a member of a minor branch of the royal family, then murdered the usurper and declared himself king. Thus Darius was himself a usurper,
and had to fight to secure his position.

Is it not significant then that the man who should follow Shalmaneser V on
the Assyrian throne was also a usurper who named himself Sargon (*Sharru-kin*),
"Legitimate King," almost by way of proclaiming his right to the throne? In a well-
known inscription Sargon justifies his seizure of the royal diadem by asserting
that his predecessor lacked the sanction of the gods. It is normally assumed that
Sargon is here referring to Shalmaneser V; yet his predecessor's name is not giv-
en.[165] If, however, the occupant of the throne was an impostor, as Darius claimed
his predecessor to be, then he would certainly have lacked divine authority.

A great deal is known about the life of Darius I (upon whom has been con-
ferred the title Great), owing chiefly to the wars he waged against the Greeks,
whose writers documented these events in some detail. It was thus with Darius
(Darayavaush) that the world of the Persians impinged on that of the Greeks.
From his time onwards, the histories of the two peoples were to be inextricably
linked.

---

164 Herodotus, iii, 62-5.

165 A. K. Grayson, "Assyria: Tiglath-Pileser III to Sargon II (744-705 BC)" in *CAH* Vol. 3 part
2 (3rd ed.) p. 87 The source of this information is a document named the Ashur Charter,
where Sargon relates how his predecessor had wrongly imposed corvee on the city of
Ashur, for which crime the gods deposed him and appointed Sargon in his stead. It should
be noted that one school of thought sees as one of the major aims of the Magian usurpation
the promotion of Magian deities at the expense of the Zoroastrian Ahura Mazda. If Ashur,
as we claim, was identified completely with Ahura Mazda, then we can see why Gaumata
would have imposed a tribute on his sacred city.

As might be expected, a good deal is known about the personal and private life of this king. His wife Atossa (Persian Hutaosa) was by all accounts a major influence upon him. The daughter of Cyrus, Darius evidently married her to legitimize his own claim to the throne. She remained a major influence on her husband, if Herodotus is to be believed, throughout his life.[166]

Darius, we said, was the first Persian king to clash with the Greeks, and various inscriptions of his refer to some of the events surrounding the wars against the *Yaman* (Ionians). In like manner, Sargon II (who is sometimes also termed the Great) was the first Neo-Assyrian king to record action against the Ionians (*Jamanu*). Describing his victories in the west, Sargon names himself,

> conqueror of Samaria (*Sa-mir-i-na*) and of the entire (country of) Israel ... who despoiled Ashdod (and) Shinuhti, who caught the Greeks who (live on the islands) in the sea, like fish, who exterminated Kasku, all Tabali and Cilicia, who chased away Midas (*Mi-ta-a*) king of Musku, who defeated Musur (*Mu-su-ri*) in Rapihu, who declared Hanno, king of Gaza, as booty, who subdued the seven kings of the country of Ia', a district on Cyprus...[167]

What, we might ask, was an Assyrian king of supposedly the 8th century doing referring to war against the Greeks? The only Greeks believed to have come under the authority of Sargon were those of Cyprus, but the Greeks here referred to were not Cypriots, they were the Greeks of the islands, in the plural, i.e., the Aegean islands. Yet it is believed that Assyria's authority did not come anywhere near the Aegean. However, if Sargon is identical to Darius, a conflict with the Aegean Greeks is entirely to be expected. After the Ionic Revolt, Darius cleared the Aegean islands closest to Asia Minor of their Greek populations.

In the midst of the general rebellion which broke out early in the reign of Darius, it would appear that Egypt too had to be brought to book. The Governor of the Nile Kingdom, Aryandes, was put to death on suspicion of rebellious intent.[168]

Sargon's campaigns in the west, particularly his conquest of Samaria, were likewise part of a much wider action against Egypt and iys allies. After the deportation of Samaria's population, Sargon records how,

> Hanno, king of Gaza and also Sib'e, the *turtan* of Egypt (*Mu-su-ri*), set out from Rapihu against me to deliver a decisive battle. I defeated them; Sib'e ran away, afraid when he (only) heard the noise of my (approaching)

---

166 In 1987 a series of royal tombs belonging to the queens of some of Assyria's greatest rulers were found at Calah. Among the royal burials was that of Atalia, wife of Sargon II and, apparently, daughter of Tiglath-Pileser III. It would appear that Atossa and Atalia were one and the same person.

167 Pritchard, *ANET* p. 284.

168 Herodotus, iv, 166.

army, and has not been seen again. Hanno, I captured personally. I received the tribute from Pir'u of Musuru ...[169]

In another place we are told how an Ionian (i.e., *Iamani*) had raised rebellion against the Great King in the Philistine city of Ashdod, how he was defeated and fled to the territory of Egypt "which belongs (now) to Ethiopia," whence he was eventually delivered in chains to Assyria.[170] It would appear that this event took place before the conquest of Samaria and the defeat of the combined Ethiopian and Egyptian armies at Rapihu. Upper Egypt was apparently occupied by Shabaka shortly after Darius/Sargon's seizure of the throne, and whilst the Great King was content to leave those regions to the Nubians, the situation changed when the Ethiopian pharaoh began to conspire with Persia's vassals in Lower Egypt and Palestine.

Other evidence, of an entirely different nature, shows Sargon to have gained control of Egypt, for it was during his reign that artwork of Egyptian manufacture and influence makes its first appearance in Mesopotamia. Rawlinson mused on the fact that artistic links between Egypt and Assyria "do not appear until we come to the monuments which belong to the time of Sargon," suggesting that it was in his reign that "direct connexion between Egypt and Assyria seems to have begun," a reflection, Rawlinson believed, of the transportation into Mesopotamia of "large numbers" of Egyptian captives.[171]

It seems inherently unlikely that Sargon could have imported "large numbers" of Egyptian captives, especially captives with artistic skills, into Mesopotamia unless he had conquered and subdued the country.

Yet even in his royal titles Sargon claimed mastery over Egypt. Thus he described himself as "King of the Four Quarters (literally edges)" of the earth. Now, ever since the time of Sargon's namesake, Sargon of Akkad, the title King of the Four Quarters had implied world-wide domination: And Sargon of Akkad had actually named Magan/Meluhha as one of the "quarters" over which he ruled. In spite of some attempts to suggest otherwise, it has become increasingly obvious that even in Sargon of Akkad's time Magan and Meluhha meant Egypt and Ethiopia (or, more probably, Lower and Upper Egypt), just as they did in Neo-Assyrian times.[172] Thus Egypt/Ethiopia was every bit as much the western "edge" of the world in the time of Sargon II. He could not have claimed the title King

169 Pritchard, loc cit. p. 285.
170 Ibid. p. 286.
171 George Rawlinson, *Ancient Monarchies* Vol. 1 (1879) p. 370.
172 See e.g., Samuel Noah Kramer, *The Sumerians* (Chicago, 1963).

of the Four Quarters unless he had ruled Egypt, precisely as did Darius I two centuries later.

On the subject of Sargon's relationship with Egyptians and Greeks I would like at this point to call the reader's attention to a little-known statue of the Ethiopian pharaoh Shabaka, located on the isle of Argo, just upstream from the Nubian capital Kerma. The unusual feature of this statue is that it portrays Shabaka wearing the Double Crown of Egypt decorated with a laurel-wreath.[173] The laurel-wreath was *par excellence* the Greek symbol of royalty and divine authority, and this is the only known appearance of the symbol in native Egyptian/Nubian iconography. Yet the occurrence of such a motif on the royal insignia of a pharaoh who is supposed to have reigned circa 700 BC is a major embarrassment for textbook chronology, as such Hellenic influence upon Egypt is utterly impossible at this time. In 700 BC, Greece was a semi-tribal society not yet emerged from the "Geometric" epoch. But if Shabaka actually reigned around 500 BC, and his Assyrian enemy Sargon II was the same person as Darius I of Persia, then the laurel-wreath crown makes perfect sense. By 500 BC, the Egyptians and Greeks were on the verge of establishing their long-standing anti-Persian alliance. We know from Herodotus that four years after Darius' defeat at Marathon, Egypt, clearly inspired by the Greek success, threw off the Persian yoke.[174]

Perhaps Darius' most important achievement was his defeat of the great Babylonian rebellion of Nebuchadrezzar III. We are told that the Babylonian insurrection began at the very outset of Darius' reign — an obvious reflection of the widespread refusal to accept his usurpation of the Great King's throne. It is known that this rebellion lasted a number of years, and that the neighboring Elamites aided and abetted the Babylonians.[175] Once again, the parallels with the life of Sargon II are striking. According to Sargon's annals, the Assyrians were forced to wage a long and bitter war in Babylonia against a Chaldean rebel named Marduk-apal-iddin (Merodach-Baladan), who led the insurrection against Assyria upon the accession of Sargon — again, an obvious reflection of the widespread refusal to accept Sargon's usurpation.[176] Just as the Elamites aided Nebuchadrezzar III against Darius, so they helped Merodach-Baladan against

---

173 J. Gardner Wilkinson, *A Popular Account of the Ancient Egyptians* (London, 1878) Vol. 2 p. 323.

174 However, it has to be admitted that even 500 BC seems a little too early for Shabaka to have adopted Hellenic insignia. It is unlikely that the Egyptians would have been formally allied to the Greeks until after the defeat of Xerxes' invasion in 480 BC. The answer may be simple. Evidence has recently emerged suggesting that Shabaka and Shabataka should swap places in the Nubian succession. Thus it could have been Shabataka who opposed Sargon II (Darius I) and Shabaka who waged war against Sennacherib (Xerxes). The laurel-wreathed Shabaka would therefore be dated some time after 480 BC.

175 Brian Dicks, The Ancient Persians: How they Lived and Worked (1979) p. 42.

176 C. H. W. Johns, *Ancient Babylonia* (1913) p. 117.

Sargon.[177] Both rebellions lasted quite a long time. We are told in the Neo-Assyrian annals that Sargon could not capture Babylon, and that he was compelled to leave Merodach-Baladan in control of the city for twelve years.[178] Similarly, Darius had great difficulty in capturing Babylon, and we are told that he almost despaired of ever taking the city.[179]

As was said earlier, the Merodach-Baladan who opposed Tiglath-Pileser III and Sargon must be identical to Merodach-Baladan I, last of the Kassites, who raised rebellion against Assyria after the death of Tukulti-Ninurta I. Now it is seen that both these men are also one and the same as Nebuchadrezzar III, last of the Chaldean, who raised rebellion against Persia after the death of Cambyses.

When Babylon finally did fall, Sargon's treatment of its citizens was relatively moderate. Some fortifications were destroyed, but there was also widespread restoration of temples and other public buildings. We are told that after his capture of the city, Uperi, the king of Dilmun (India) sent gifts to the Assyrian monarch.[180]

Darius' treatment of the conquered city was likewise moderate. Apart from the destruction of some fortifications, there was very little damage done, and the Persian Great King even brought women in from other regions to repopulate the metropolis.[181]

Finally, it should be noted that both Sargon and Darius died a soldier's death, campaigning on the northern frontier of the empire.

Xerxes and Sennacherib

When Darius the Great died he was succeeded by his son Xerxes, a man whose life and career we should expect to closely parallel that of Sargon's son and successor Sennacherib.

A random search of the internet produces the following for Xerxes and Sennacherib: "Like the Persian Xerxes, he [Sennacherib] was weak and vainglorious, cowardly under reverse, and cruel and boastful in success."[182] The writer of these words did not suspect any connection between the two kings, much less that they were the same person. Nevertheless, the similarities between them were so compelling that one apparently brought the other to mind.

---

177 Ibid.
178 Ibid.
179 Herodotus, iii, 151-60.
180 C. H. W. Johns, loc cit. The identification of Dilmun with India is controversial, but is proved really beyond question by Gunnar Heinsohn in his *Wer herrschte im Industal?* (Grafelfing, 1993).
181 Herodotus, iii, 160.
182 Cf. WebBible Encyclopedia at www. christiananswers. net/dictionary/sennacherib. html.

The writer's instincts did not betray him. The lives and careers of Xerxes and Sennacherib were so similar that were the thesis presented in these pages not proffered, scholars must wonder at the astounding parallels between the two.

One of Xerxes' first actions as king was an invasion of Egypt, which had thrown off the Persian yoke shortly after Darius' defeat at the hands of the Greeks.[183] This reconquest of Egypt was said to have taken place in Xerxes' second year. Similarly, one of the first actions of Sennacherib was a campaign against Egypt and her Palestinian and Syrian allies. This war against Egypt took place in Sennacherib's third year. The Assyrian inscriptions inform us how Hezekiah of Judah had rebelled and sought the assistance of

> the kings of Egypt (and) the bowmen, the chariot (-corps) and the cavalry of the king of Ethiopia (*Meluhha*), an army beyond counting — and they (actually) had come to their assistance. In the plain of Eltekeh (*Al-ta-qu-u*), their battle lines were drawn up against me and they sharpened their weapons.... I fought with them and inflicted a defeat upon them. In the melee of the battle, I personally captured alive the Egyptian charioteers with the(ir) princes and (also) the charioteers of the king of Ethiopia.[184]

Hezekiah was besieged, but not captured. Nevertheless, the outcome of this campaign was a complete victory for Sennacherib. Hezekiah sent tribute to the Great King:

> Hezekiah himself, whom the terror-inspiring glamour of my lordship had overwhelmed and whose irregular and elite troops which he had brought into Jerusalem, his royal residence, in order to strengthen (it), had deserted him, did send me, later, to Nineveh, my lordly city, together with 30 talents of gold, 800 talents of silver, precious stones, antimony, large cuts of red stone ... all kinds of valuable treasures, his (own) daughters, concubines, male and female musicians. In order to deliver the tribute and to do obeisance as a slave he sent his (personal) messenger.

Hezekiah would scarcely have sent this tribute to Sennacherib had his Egyptian allies not been totally defeated, a circumstance which has made many scholars suspect that he actually entered Egypt after his defeat of its army on the plain of Eltekeh.[185] This supposition is supported by the fact that Sennacherib described himself as "King of the Four Quarters," a term which, as stated above, traditionally implied authority over Magan and Meluhha (Egypt), regarded as the western-most "quarter" or edge of the world. It is also supported by both classical and Hebrew tradition. Thus Herodotus spoke of Sennacherib advancing against Egypt with a mighty army and camping at Pelusium, near the northeastern frontier (Herodotus, iii, 141), whilst Berossus, who wrote a history of

---

183 Herodotus, vii, 2-5.
184 J. Pritchard, *ANET* (Princeton, 1950) pp. 287-8.
185 The question is much debated. See e.g., A. T. Olmstead, *History of Assyria* (1923) pp. 308-9.

Chaldea, said that Sennacherib had conducted an expedition against "all Asia and Egypt."[186] Jewish tradition goes further and tells of the conquest of Egypt by the king and of his march towards Ethiopia. "Sennacherib was forced to stop his campaign against Hezekiah for a short time, as he had to move hurriedly against Ethiopia. Having conquered this 'pearl of all countries' he returned to Judea."[187] Talmudic sources also relate that after conquering Egypt, Sennacherib carried away from there the throne of Solomon.[188]

Sennacherib's second campaign against Egypt, not recorded in the Assyrian inscriptions, had, we have seen, a much less favorable outcome for the Great King.

The greatest event of Xerxes' reign was of course his momentous defeat in Greece. The story of his invasion is recorded in detail by the Greek authors, most particularly by Herodotus, and it is clear that Xerxes' failure to overcome the Hellenes represented the great watershed in Achaemenid history. From that point on the Persian Empire entered a period of prolonged decline.

Strange then that of all the wars waged by Sennacherib, the only opponents who are said to have come near to defeating him were the Ionian Greeks. In one well-known passage Berossus tells of a fierce battle between Sennacherib and the Ionians of Cilicia.[189] The Greeks, he says, were routed after a hard-fought hand-to-hand struggle.

The most important event of Xerxes' latter years was without doubt his defeat of yet another Babylonian rebellion. Although our sources are somewhat vague, it would appear that there were in fact two rebellions in Babylon during the time of Xerxes, the first of which occurred in his second year, and was led by Bel-shimanni, and the second some time later led by Shamash-eriba.

How peculiar then that Sennacherib too should face two major rebellions in Babylon, the first of which came within three years or so of his succession, and was led by Bel-ibni.[190] Rebellion number two came some years later and was led by Mushezib-Marduk. This second rebellion, one might guess, was one of the consequences of the Persian defeat in Greece, and there seems little doubt that Mushezib-Marduk of the Assyrian records and monuments is Shamash-eriba of the Persian.

---

186 Josephus, *Jewish Antiquities* X, i,4.
187 L. Ginzberg, *The Legends of the Jews* (Philadelphia, 1920) Vol. VI p. 365.
188 Ibid. Vol. IV p. 160.
189 H. R. Hall, The Ancient History of the Near East (London, 1913) p. 487.
190 C. H. W. Johns, *Ancient Babylonia* p. 120 It should be remarked here that Bel-shimanni and Bel-ibni, Babylonian rebel leaders during the times of Xerxes and Sennacherib, have virtually identical names. The elements "ibni" and "shimanni" are mere variants of the same word. Thus "shimanni" could also be written as "shibanni" or even "hibni".

Both Xerxes and Sennacherib were relatively mild in their treatment of the Babylonians after the first rebellion. However, after the second insurrection both kings subjected the city to massive destruction. But the parallels do not end there. Xerxes' terrible punishment of Babylon was partly in revenge for the Babylonians' murder of his satrap.[191] Similarly, Sennacherib's destruction of Babylon after the second insurrection was largely in vengeance for the Babylonians' kidnap and murder of his brother Ashur-nadin-shum, whom he had made viceroy of the city.[192] Xerxes tore down the walls of Babylon, massacred its citizens, destroyed its temples, and seized the sacred golden statue of Bel.[193] In the same way, Sennacherib razed the city walls and temples, massacred the people, and carried off the sacred statue of Marduk.[194] Bel and Marduk were one and the same; and the name was often written Bel-Marduk. In memory of the awful destruction wrought by Sennacherib, the Babylonian Chronicle and the Ptolemaic Canon define the eight years that followed as "kingless." The city, it is held, suffered no such catastrophe again until the time of Xerxes, supposedly two centuries later.

Xerxes' despoliation of Babylon is generally believed to have been accompanied by his suppression of the Babylonian gods, and it is assumed that his famous inscription recording the outlawing of the *daevas*, or foreign gods, in favor of Ahura Mazda, was part of the general response to the second Babylonian uprising:

> And among these countries (in rebellion) there was one where, previously, *daevas* had been worshipped. Afterward, through Ahura Mazda's favor, I destroyed this sanctuary of *daevas* and proclaimed. "Let *daevas* not be worshipped!" There, where *daevas* had been worshipped before, I worshipped Ahura Mazda.

How peculiar then that Sennacherib too should be accused of outlawing the Babylonian gods, especially Marduk, in favor of Ashur as part of his response to a second Babylonian rebellion? "A political-theological propaganda campaign was launched to explain to the people that what had taken place [the destruction of Babylon and despoliation of Bel-Marduk's shrine] was in accord with the wish of most of the gods. A story was written in which Marduk, because of a transgression, was captured and brought before a tribunal. Only a part of the commentary to this botched piece of literature is extant."[195] Nevertheless, it is clear that Sennacherib tried to "depose" or even "outlaw" Marduk. Thus we find that, "Even

---

191 Brian Dicks, The Ancient Persians: How they Lived and Worked (1979) p. 46
192 C. H. W. Johns, loc cit. pp. 121-2
193 Brian Dicks, loc. cit.
194 C. H. W. Johns, loc. cit. p. 122.
195 http://www. chn-net. com/timeline/assyria_study. html.

the great poem of the creation of the world, the Enuma elish, was altered: the god Marduk was replaced by the god Ashur."[196]

To summarize, then, consider the following:

Sennacherib	Xerxes
Made war on Egypt in his third year.	Made war on Egypt in his second year.
Fought a bitter war against the Greeks.	Fought a bitter war against the Greeks.
Suppressed two major Babylonian rebellions. First, in his second year, led by Bel-Shimanni. The second, years later, led by Shamash-eriba.	Suppressed two major Babylonian rebellions. First, in his third year, led by Bel-ibni. The second, years later, led by Mushezib-Marduk.
The Babylonians were well-treated after the first rebellion, but savagely repressed after the second, when they captured and murdered Sennacherib's viceroy, his own brother Ashur-nadin-shum.	The Babylonians were well-treated after the first rebellion, but savagely repressed after the second, when they captured and murdered Xerxes' satrap.
After the second rebellion, Sennacherib massacred the inhabitants, razed the city walls and temples, and carried off the golden statue of Marduk. Thereafter the Babylonian gods were suppressed in favor of Ashur, who was elevated almost to the position of supreme deity.	After the second rebellion, Xerxes massacred the inhabitants, razed the city walls and temples, and carried off the sacred golden statue of Bel-Marduk. Thereafter the Babylonian gods were suppressed in favor of Ahura-Mazda, who was made the supreme deity.

The parallels between Xerxes and Sennacherib are thus among the closest between an Achaemenid and a Neo-Assyrian. Added to the close parallels already observed between the Achaemenids and Neo-Assyrians that preceded these two, it becomes increasingly unlikely that we could be on the wrong track.

Yet even now we are not finished. There is yet one more striking comparison between the two monarchs, a comparison so compelling and so identical in the details that this one alone, even without the others, would be enough to demand an identification.

Assassination at the Palace

Xerxes died after a reign of 21 years (compare with Sennacherib's 22) in dramatic circumstances, murdered in a palace conspiracy apparently involving at least one of his sons. Popular tradition has it that the real murderer of Xerxes was Artabanus, the captain of his guard, and that this man then put the blame on

---

196 Ibid.

Darius, eldest son of the murdered king. Whatever the truth, it is clear that Artaxerxes, the crown prince, pointed the finger at Darius, who was immediately arrested and executed.[197] It is said that Artabanus then plotted to murder Artaxerxes, but that the conspiracy was uncovered by Megabyzus. No sooner had Artabanus been removed than Hystaspes, another elder brother of Artaxerxes, rose in rebellion. The young king then led his forces into Bactria and defeated the rebel in two battles.[198]

Of the above information, one feature is most unusual: the eldest son, Darius, who was *not* the crown prince, was accused of the murder by the crown prince Artaxerxes, who then had him hunted down and killed.

The death of Sennacherib compares very well with that of Xerxes. He too was murdered in a palace conspiracy involving some of his sons. But as with the death of Xerxes, there has always been much rumor and myth, though little solid fact, in evidence. The biblical Book of Kings names Adrammelech and Sharezer, two of Sennacherib's sons, as the killers (2 Kings 19:37). An inscription of Esarhaddon, the crown prince at the time, clearly puts the blame on his eldest brother, whom he hunted down and killed. Two other brothers are also named in complicity.[199]

In spite of Esarhaddon's clear statement, there has always been much confusion about the details — so much so that some have even implicated Esarhaddon himself in the deed. In view of such a level of confusion, the detailed discussion of the question by Professor Simo Parpola, in 1980, was sorely needed and long overdue. Employing commendable reasoning, Parpola demonstrated how a little-understood Babylonian text revealed the identity of the culprit, Arad-Ninlil.[200] A sentence of the document reads, "Thy son Arad-Ninlil is going to kill thee." The latter name should properly, according to Parpola, be read as Arda-Mulissi (identical to Adrammelech of 2 Kings). Motivation for the murder, said Parpola, was not difficult to find. After the capture and probable death at the hands of the Elamites of Sennacherib's eldest son and heir-designate, Ashur-nadin-sumi, the "second-eldest son, Arda-Mulissi, now has every reason to expect to be the next crown prince; however, he is outmaneuvered from this position in favor of Esarhaddon, another son of Sennacherib. This one is younger than Arda-Mulissi but becomes the favourite son of Sennacherib thanks to his mother Naqia ... Eventually, Esarhaddon is officially proclaimed crown prince."[201]

197 Percy Sykes, *A History of Ancient Persia* Vol. 1 (London, 1930) pp. 213-4.
198 Ibid. p. 214.
199 A. T. Olmstead, *A History of Assyria* (1923) p. 338.
200 R. Harper, *Assyrian and Babylonian Letters*, Vol. XI (Chicago, 1911) No. 1091.
201 Prof. Simo Parpola, "Death in Mesopotamia" *XXVIeme Rencontre Assyriologique International,e* ed. Prof. Bendt Alster, (Akademisk Forlag, 1980). Interestingly, Parpola explains how the

We need hardly go beyond that for a motive. It is not clear whether Arda-Mulissi personally delivered the death blow; it seems that one of his captains was responsible.

Of this death then we note the same unusual feature. The king was murdered by or on the orders of his eldest son, who was not however the crown prince. The eldest son was then pursued and executed by a younger son, who was the crown prince. The parallels with the death of Xerxes are precise. In both cases also a second brother is named in complicity, as well as various other conspirators. In both cases too the murder was not actually carried out by the prince but by a fellow conspirator; in the case of Xerxes by Artabanus, commander of the guard, and in the case of Sennacherib by a man named Ashur-aha-iddin — a namesake of Esarhaddon. And this calls attention to yet one more parallel. In both the murder of Xerxes and Sennacherib, the crown prince himself has repeatedly been named as a suspect. Thus the *Encyclopedia Britannica* has Artaxerxes I placed on the throne by Xerxes' murderer, Artabanus,[202] whilst Parpola refers to the common suspicion that Esarhaddon had a part in his father's death.[203]

Such striking similarities, when placed along with the multitude of other parallels between the two kings' lives, leave little doubt that we are on the right track.

Artaxerxes I and His Time

With Artaxerxes I (Artakhshathra) we come to one of the most remarkable men ever to sit on the Great King's throne. Although he began his reign as an avenger and executor of his father's murderers, it is for an opposite quality, that of mercy and humanitarianism, that he is best known. According to Plutarch, he was "among all the kings of Persia the most remarkable for a gentle and noble spirit."[204] The ancient authors "uniformly describe him as a brave and handsome man, a kindly and magnanimous ruler."[205]

For all that, the early part of his reign was marked by a series of rebellions in the satrapies, most particularly by a long drawn out and costly revolt in Egypt, which is said to have begun shortly after the new king's ascent of the throne in 465 BC, and lasted intermittently until 454 BC. The Egyptian leader was a man named Inaros, son of a prince Psamtek. With the help of Athenian troops the

god's name previously read as Ninlil, should in fact be rendered as Mulissi. This makes one wonder just how many other Akkadian and Babylonian names have been completely misinterpreted. The science of Assyriology is apparently still in its infancy.

202 *Encyclopaedia Britannica* Vol. 1 (15th ed.) p. 598.

203 Parpola, loc. cit.

204 Plutarch, "Artaxerxes" ch. i.

205 "Artaxerxes I" by Richard Gottheil www. jewishencyclopedia. com.

rebels enjoyed initial success and managed to liberate most of Lower Egypt. The Persian satrap Achaemenes, brother of the Great King, was killed. In 460 BC, however, a large Persian army under the leadership of Megabyzus, supported by three hundred Phoenician ships, succeeded in smashing the main body of the rebel army. The Greeks retreated to Prosopitis, where they withstood a siege of eighteen months. In order to bring the rebellion to a swift conclusion, Megabyzus negotiated the surrender of the Egyptians and their Hellenic allies, with the promise that there would be no reprisals. Accordingly, the Egyptian/Greek army laid down its arms, and Inaros was taken prisoner. After the capitulation of this force, some resistance to the Persians did continue in the Delta marshlands, where a leader named Amyrtaeus held out for over a decade.

It is remarkable that both in character and in terms of events surrounding his early reign, Esarhaddon offers a precise match with Artaxerxes I. Just as the Persian ruler, though famed for his humanitarianism, came to the throne after slaying his father's killers, so too did Esarhaddon. We are told that, "The verdict upon Esarhaddon has been as uniformly favorable as that upon his father has been condemnatory. He is characterised by 'a reasonable and conciliatory disposition,' a 'largeness of aim peculiarly his own'; he was 'a wise and strenuous king who left his vast domains with a fairer show of prosperity and safety than the Assyrian realm had ever presented at the demise of any of his predecessors.' He 'is the noblest and most sympathetic figure among the Assyrian kings.'"[206]

As with Artaxerxes I, the reign of Esarhaddon too is best known for the wars he waged against Egypt. In a series of well-documented campaigns he efficiently suppressed what he described as the "rebels" of Egypt. These campaigns we have already examined in some detail, and have identified Bey, the king-maker at the time of Tewosret and Seti II (whom we also place in the time of Sennacherib and Esarhaddon), with the satrap Achaemenes, earlier appointed by Xerxes, and slain by Inaros. Importantly, just as Esarhaddon faced initial failure in Egypt, so too did Artaxerxes I. The second, successful, campaign of Esarhaddon must be identical to the second and successful campaign of Artaxerxes I. We remember also that among the Egyptian rebels named by Esarhaddon (and his successor Ashurbanipal) were men with names like Nikuu (Necho), and Psamtek, names which occur again in the time of Artaxerxes I. We recall also the mention of Tirhaka in an inscription of Artaxerxes I's time, an occurrence that has caused considerable debate amongst scholars, who struggle to explain the apparently anachronistic reference to kings of supposedly the 7th century in a text of the 5th. Yet in our reconstruction the Necho of Esarhaddon's age, who allied himself

---

206 George Godspeed http://history-world. org/assyria_part_twelve. htm.

with Tirhaka, but was pardoned and restored to his kingdom by Ashurbanipal, is probably identical to Thannyras, son of Inaros, whom Herodotus informs us was restored to his father's kingdom by the Persians.[207] As we have seen, Inaros himself, who inflicted immense damage upon the Persians, was probably none other than Seti II.

Artaxerxes I was noted for the favor he showed to Babylon. He seems to have largely rebuilt the city after the destruction wrought by Xerxes. His successor, Darius II, was the illegitimate son of a Babylonian concubine.

How peculiar then that Esarhaddon too is noted as a great benefactor of Babylon. A text of his tells how the gods had decreed that the city should be a ruin for seventy years, but that they regretted their harshness, turned the tablet of destiny upside-down, and allowed the people to return after eleven years (in cuneiform, the numbers 70 and 11 relate to each other as our 6 and 9). Not only did Esarhaddon permit the inhabitants to return, he personally attended the ritual refounding of the city, along with his mother. In addition, we know that he married a Babylonian princess.[208]

Two Sons and two Mothers

The lives and careers of both Artaxerxes I and Esarhaddon were largely defined by the wars they waged in Egypt. Yet their lives had another very striking parallel. Both men were famously dominated by their mothers, and these women were among the most outstanding characters of their times.

Artaxerxes I was not the eldest son of Xerxes; yet he was the crown prince — and there can be no doubt whatsoever that he owed this advantage to his dominant and domineering mother, Amestris.

Amestris, whose name seems to connect her to the biblical Queen Vashti,[209] was the daughter of Otanes, one of the seven conspirators who killed the Median usurper Gaumata and placed Darius Hystaspes on the throne. For his support, Otanes was rewarded by marriage to Darius' own sister and Amestris was the fruit of this union. Upon reaching maturity, the young princess was married to the crown prince Xerxes, her first cousin, and when Darius died in 486 BC she became one of the most important women in the Empire. Herodotus describes her as a cruel despot:

---

207 Herodotus, iii, 15.

208 Donald A. MacKenzie, *Myths of Babylon and Assyria* (Kessinger Publishing, 2004) p. 471.

209 It is generally agreed that Vashti and Amestris are etymologically identical. Both names seem to derive from the Old Persian *vashishta* "beautiful," a word found in the *Avesta*. Whether the events related in the Book of Esther are historical or allegorical is a question much debated over the years. One thing is certain, if Esther is a factual account of events during the time of Xerxes, then the position of the apparently still exiled Hebrews was not nearly so favourable under the Persian kings as is generally imagined.

> I am informed that Amestris, the wife of Xerxes, when she had grown old, made return for her own life to the god who is said to be beneath the earth by burying twice seven children of Persians who were of renown.[210]

In short, to extend her own life, she sacrificed seven children of noble families. Evidently the woman had a fearsome reputation. Some hint of that cruelty is provided in the account given by Ctesias of Cnidus, who relates that Amestris was enraged by the actions of Megabyzus in Egypt who, after defeating Inaros' rebellion, had failed to punish those who had killed the satrap, her son Achaemenes. In order to shorten the war, Megabyzus had apparently negotiated the surrender of Inaros, promising to spare his life. We are informed that, intending to keep his word, Artaxerxes I permitted Inaros to live for five years, but that finally, capitulating to the incessant pressure of his mother, had the Egyptian leader, along with seven others, impaled.

We know slightly less of the details of Esarhaddon's mother Naqia, or Naqia-Zakutu, and yet of her life, "There are more sources ... than for all other Sargonid royal women combined."[211]

It was through the influence of Naqia that Esarhaddon, though not the eldest son of Sennacherib, became crown prince — a situation precisely paralleling that which led to Artaxerxes' succession.

Naqia Zakutu, just like Amestris, held powerful sway over both her husband and her son. Thus as well as being portrayed alongside Sennacherib, she is also — and unusually — portrayed alongside Esarhaddon, after he had become king. She is shown, for example, alongside her son attending the ritual refounding of Babylon. And when it came to Esarhaddon's appointment of his own successor, she was present again. Indeed, she was more than present; she played a key role. At the ritual marking the appointment, she "had thrown the weight of her influence into the balance and obtained from the Babylonians and their future viceroy [Shamash-shum-ukin] an oath of allegiance to the future ruler of Assyria."[212]

What manner of woman, one might ask, could exercise such a powerful influence upon husband, son and grandson? There is even evidence that she acted as regent — as ruling monarch in everything but name — whilst Esarhaddon campaigned in the west against Egypt and the states of Syria/Palestine.[213]

---

210 Herodotus, vii, 114.

211 www. helsinki. fi/science/saa/saas-09. html See Sarah C. Melville, "The Role of Naqia/Zakutu in Sargonid Royal Politics" *State Archives of Assyria Studies* Vol. IX (Helsinki, 1999).

212 G. Roux, *Ancient Iraq* (Penguin, 1980) pp. 303-4.

213 The Elamites, "ventured a raid into northern Babylonia (674 BC) while Esarhaddon was in the west, and his mother, Naqia, was acting as regent." George Godspeed, loc cit.

One final point. Historians are agreed that Naqia's name is not Assyrian, and it is widely accepted that she was a foreigner, probably a Babylonian or a Syrian. In this context, the second part of her name, Zakutu, is of particular interest. Zakutu represents the transcription into Latin letters of a cuneiform word composed of the consonants z (or s), k, and t; thus zkt. Vowels are conjectural. Since it is not always certain how a word should be reconstructed, it is possible that zkt or skt should actually be read as kst. Now the name Amestris is generally admitted to be a Greek rendering of the Persian Vashti, or more properly, Vashishti or Bashishti ("beautiful"). It is perhaps not impossible that the name Zakutu, or Kaztu/Kashtu is a Semitic version of this same word. Many languages mutate the "b" sound into a "k," and this may well be the case here.[214] Kaztu/Kashtu is thus perhaps the Babylonian version of Bashti/Bashishti, and Naqia Zakutu may therefore be identical to Amestris not only in terms of life and career, but also in terms of name.

Consider the following:

Esarhaddon	Artaxerxes I
Was not the eldest son of Sennacherib, but owed his position as crown prince to the influence of his powerful mother Naqia Zakutu (possibly Kashtu)	Was not the eldest son of Xerxes, but owed his position as crown prince to the influence of his powerful mother Amestris (Vashti/Vashishti)
His first action as ruler was the slaying of his father's murderers; yet he is regarded as the most humane of all Assyrian monarchs.	His first action as ruler was the slaying of his father's murderers; yet he is regarded as the most humane of all Persian monarchs.
Shortly after ascending the throne he fought a prolonged war against Egypt, where his enemies included men with names such as Tirhaka and Necho.	Shortly after ascending the throne he fought a prolonged war against Egypt, where his enemies included men with names such as Tirhaka and Necho.
Favored Babylon and began rebuilding the city after the devastation wrought by Sennacherib. Took at least one Babylonian wife.	Favored Babylon and began rebuilding the city after the devastation wrought by Xerxes. Took at least two Babylonian wives.
Esarhaddon's heir, the crown-prince Sin-iddin-apla, died near the end of his father's life, and the Great King was succeeded by Ashurbanipal, a man who may have had a Babylonian mother.	Artaxerxes I's heir, the crown prince Xerxes II, died shortly after his father, and the Great King was succeeded by Darius II, who had a Babylonian mother.

---

214 As for example the Q or K Celtic as opposed to the P or B Celtic dialects. Q Celtic Gaelic has the word "son" as *mac* (*macci*) whilst P Celtic Welsh has *mabi*.

The parallels between Esarhaddon and Artaxerxes I are thus specific and detailed, and they compare very well with those already identified between Sennacherib and Xerxes, as well as the other Neo-Assyrian and Persian monarchs who preceded them. There is however one major difference: reign lengths. We are told that Esarhaddon died in his twelfth year, on his way to Egypt. Artaxerxes I is reputed to have died in his fortieth or perhaps forty-first year. Notwithstanding all else we have said, if we cannot explain this remarkable dissonance, then the identification of the two men is brought into serious question.

We shall examine the reign-lengths of these kings in the final chapter. As we shall see, the answer is relatively simple. Artaxerxes I, we shall find, did not reign forty years, he merely lived forty years.

Darius II and Ashurbanipal

Chapter 2 showed that the lives of Darius II and Ashurbanipal displayed striking parallels in their respective relationships with Egypt. Thus Ashurbanipal appointed a character named Wenamon as governor of Natkhu, whilst a potentate named Wenamon controlled the shrine of Amon at Siwa during Darius II's time. In the same way, Ashurbanipal appointed Psamtek, son of Necho, as ruler of Athribis; whilst in Darius II's time a prince Psamtek, also apparently a son of a Necho, governed Egypt for many years in the name of the Great King.[215]

It was during the decadent reign of Darius II that the entire structure of the Achaemenid Empire weakened beyond repair. There were a whole series of revolts in the satrapies, and courtly intrigues caused further weakness and destabilization.[216] In the same way, the reign of Ashurbanipal was marked by a series of revolts in the provinces, culminating in the great rebellion coordinated by his brother Shamash-shum-ukin, an insurrection that involved virtually every vassal state of the empire.[217]

Just as Persia never quite recovered from the reign of Darius II, so Assyria never quite recovered from the reign of Ashurbanipal. He is held to have been the last Assyrian Great King, and after him the leadership of the Near East was taken

---

215 Psamtek and Necho were the "kings" of Egypt who left the famous Apis Bull burials at Sakkara. The Apis interments, which include one by Nekau Wehemibre, have often been seen as confirming the Manethoan system of dynasties (which placed Necho and Psamtek in the 7th century). Yet examination of the interments reveals those conducted under Necho (Nekau Wehemibre) and Psamtek to have been closely associated with, and in sequence with, those of the Persian kings. Thus burials by Cambyses and Darius, near the entrance, are followed by those of Necho and Psamtek, further in. In short, the Necho and Psamtek interments apparently came *after* those of Cambyses and Darius I.

216 Brian Dicks, The Ancient Persians: How they Lived and Worked (1979) p. 131.

217 C. H. W. Johns, *Ancient Babylonia* (1913) p. 124.

up by the Babylonians. In the same way, Darius II is held to have been the last true Achaemenid. After him the throne of Cyrus was occupied by men of largely Babylonian extraction, with the capital of the Empire actually being moved to Babylon.

It was perhaps in his dealings with Babylon that Ashurbanipal shows his most striking similarities with Darius II. Ashurbanipal in fact displayed, throughout his life, a pronounced pro-Babylonian bias. This phenomenon is observable right from the start of his reign, when one of his first actions was the restoration to Babylon of the great statue of Marduk, previously looted from the city by Sennacherib.[218] He showed great interest in rebuilding the city, and a stele, now in London, commemorates his restoration of Esagila.[219] But the king's pro-Babylonian leanings were most in evidence during and after the rebellion of his brother Shamash-shum-ukin. The latter, apparently an elder half brother of Ashurbanipal, had been appointed king of Babylon by their father Esarhaddon. In Ashurbanipal's seventeenth year, however, for reasons that are unclear, he rebelled. Indeed, if Ashurbanipal's records are anything to go by, he tried hard to organize a massive coalition against his brother. In spite of this, there is evidence that Ashurbanipal wished to avoid killing him or doing serious damage to Babylon. In the words of the *Encyclopedia Britannica*, "When Ashurbanipal discovered the plots he appealed directly to the Babylonians and perhaps tested their loyalty by imposing a special tax; only upon their refusal did he take military action. He seemed to move in ways that avoided direct danger to his brother, and worked more through siege warfare than through direct action."[220] When Babylon fell, the victor was not vindictive: "Ashurbanipal's own feelings toward the city are shown by his work of restoration and by his appointment of a Chaldean noble, Kandalanu, as his viceroy there."[221] Now Ashurbanipal was not well-known for his humanitarianism. His treatment of Thebes, which he plundered relentlessly and whose citizens he massacred, serves to illustrate what he was capable of. Yet he strove hard not to kill his brother and not to annihilate his city. What could have elicited such a favorable attitude?

As part of the same question we must also ask: Why would Ashurbanipal's and Shamash-shum-ukin's father Esarhaddon have given one son the kingship of Assyria and another and *elder* son the kingship of Babylon — placing the kingship of Babylon virtually above that of Assyria?

---

218 Wikipedia http://en. wikipedia. org/wiki/Shamash-shum-ukin.

219 Ibid. Another inscription records his restoration of the Nabu temple in Borsippa. Nabu was of course the chief god of Babylon.

220 *Encyclopaedia Britannica* Vol. I (15th ed) p. 629.

221 Ibid. There is good evidence to show that Kandalanu was none other than Ashurbanipal himself.

If what we have said in the present reconstruction is correct, then none of this presents a problem. Esarhaddon, as the alter-ego of Artaxerxes I, had a favorite concubine named Cosmartidene, a Babylonian woman who exerted great influence upon him.[222] Classical sources say that Cosmartidene was not the only Babylonian wife of Artaxerxes I. There existed another such woman, named Andia, whose daughter Parysatis was to become Darius II's chief wife. We are not told whether Andia also provided Artaxerxes I with a son, though it seems clear that, should any such offspring have existed, he would have been favored.

According to our reconstruction, there was such a son: the boy who would be named as his father as king of Babylon, Shamash-shum-ukin.

The Greek and Hellenistic authors assure us that Darius II too, half-Babylonian by blood, pursued a pro-Babylonian policy — taking as his chief wife his own half-sister Parysatis. Knowing of this we must now ask the question: Is there any evidence from the life of Ashurbanipal that he was illegitimate and that he himself married a Babylonian, or that his chief wife was of Babylonian extraction?

Such evidence exists.

Assyrian documents indicate that Ashurbanipal was not originally the crown prince. An elder brother, Sin-iddin-apla, had originally been groomed for kingship. When the latter died, apparently three years before their father, Ashurbanipal still had to contend with his elder brother Shamash-shum-ukin. Only the decisive action of Naqia, Esarhaddon's mother, secured the throne for Ashurbanipal, in face of opposition from court officials and parts of the priesthood.[223]

It would appear that Sin-iddin-apla was Xerxes II, only legitimate son of Artaxerxes I and Queen Damaspia. He is known to have served as Crown Prince, and according to Ctesias actually reigned as king for forty-five days, before being murdered by his half-brother Sogdianus, son of yet another Babylonian concubine, Alogyne. Nevertheless, it is questionable whether Xerxes II ever actually sat on the Great King's throne. No monuments or inscriptions of his survive, and even Ctesias admits he was only ever recognized in Persia.

Xerxes II's murderer Sogdianus was himself killed by Ochus/Darius II, who then became natural successor to Artaxerxes I. If Ashurbanipal was one and the same as Darius II, executor of the assassin Sogdianus, this would explain his rise to the kingship over and above the claims of his elder brother Shamash-shum-ukin.

---

222 As noted earlier, Esarhaddon did indeed have a Babylonian wife. Donald A MacKenzie, loc cit. p. 471.
223 Wikipedia http://en. wikipedia. org/wiki/Shamash-shum-ukin.

Ashurbanipal's wife was known as Ashur-sharrat, and a relief picturing her from Nineveh is the best-known representation remaining of an Assyrian woman. She was probably the same person as Parysatis.

Chapter 6. The Babylonian Achaeminids

The Influence of Babylon

If we are correct in identifying Darius II with Ashurbanipal, we are obliged to find where his successors fit into the picture. Three major Achaemenid kings — Artaxerxes II, Artaxerxes III, and Darius III — followed the second Darius, yet the Neo-Assyrian king-lists apparently end with Ashurbanipal. Only two or three ephemeral monarchs are named after the latter, and their combined reigns cannot have exceeded five or ten years, whereas the length of time between Artaxerxes II and Darius III was roughly seventy years.

According to the Neo-Assyrian lists, the next undisputed ruler of Mesopotamia after Ashurbanipal was named Nabopolasser, and this sequence is confirmed by the famous votive tablet of Adad-guppi, mother of king Nabonidus. The contents of the latter document, as well as others, make it seem likely that Nabopolasser was closely related to Ashurbanipal, quite probably a son. Because of scholarship's more or less unquestioning adherence to traditional biblical chronology, it has always been assumed that the Neo-Assyrians were one and the same as the Imperial Assyrians of the 8th century BC, whom the Greek historians report had been overcome by the Medes, in alliance with the Babylonians. Thus it was also assumed that the Babylonian king who allied himself with the Medes to overthrow Assyria was none other than Nabopolasser. The discovery of cuneiform documents of Nabopolasser in which he refers to his defeat of the Assyrians, who had long oppressed the nations "with their heavy yoke," seemed to confirm this identification. So it is not doubted that the cuneiform Nabopolasser was the Babylonian king who helped the Medes overcome the might of Assyria in the 7th century. Yet if everything we have discovered in the foregoing pages is not to be dismissed as complete fantasy, Nabopolasser must be identical to Darius II's successor Artaxerxes II. Furthermore, the next two important kings after Nabopolasser, Nebuchadrezzar and Nabonidus, must be the same as Artaxerxes III and Darius III.[224] The real founder of the Neo-Chaldean or Neo-Babylonian Empire was the "Kassite" king Burnaburiash, who, as I have demonstrated in another place, was identical to the Neo-Assyrian-age Nabu-apil-iddin.[225] The latter title would have been pronounced something like Nabopoladdan, or even Nabopolatsan, a name we might easily imagine later chroniclers such as Berossus confusing with Nabopolasser.

But if Nabopolasser, Nebuchadrezzar and Nabonidus were Persians, this can only mean that towards the end of the Persian epoch Babylon became more or less the center of the Empire, perhaps supplanting even Persepolis and Susa. Is there then any evidence to suggest that the influence of Babylon became paramount during the time of the last three or four of the Great Kings?

As seen in the final pages of the previous chapter, there is indeed very good evidence to that effect.

To recapitulate, Darius II was the son of Artaxerxes I by the Babylonian concubine Cosmartidene, in virtue of which he was popularly termed Nothus, "the Bastard." Darius II's wife, Parysatis, who was also his half-sister, was likewise the daughter of a Babylonian concubine. The accession of Darius II is thus normally held to mark the end of the pure Achaemenid line, and a period of increasing Babylonian influence is recognized in the years following.[226] Babylon was rebuilt and re-endowed after the massive destruction wrought by Xerxes, and in many ways the city was to supplant Persepolis as the true capital of the Empire.

Darius II died at Babylon (Xenophon, *Anabasis* i, 1, 2) and there is a strong suggestion that he lived most of his life there. His son and successor Artaxerxes II was perhaps even more closely associated with the city. Xenophon says that he was based at Babylon during the war against Cyrus the Younger, and from him as well as other Greek authors it seems fairly clear that he spent most of his life

---

224 In reality, the Babylonian, or Neo-Chaldaean (Neo-Sumerian) kings played no part in the destruction of the Akkadian/Assyrian Empire. In fact, southern Mesopotamia was devastated by the Gutians (ie. Scythians) for many decades before and after the fall of Nineveh, and a series of twenty-one Scythian kings reigned in Babylonia at this time. The Scythian dynasty was finally overcome by a Chaldaean/Sumerian king named Utu-khegal, who in turn was overthrown by the famous Ur-Nammu. It was this Ur-Nammu who founded the so-called Neo-Chaldaean Empire, an event which we cannot date earlier than 630 BC.

225 In my *Empire of Thebes* (New York, 2006). Nabu-apil-iddin was a contemporary of Shalmaneser III, normally placed in the 9th century BC, but really belonging to the late-7th and early-6th centuries.

226 See e.g., Brian Dicks, *The Ancient Persians: How they Lived and Worked* (1979) p. 131.

there. His son and successor Artaxerxes III was also heavily linked to the city, a fact confirmed both by the classical authors and by cuneiform texts which speak of prisoners captured in foreign wars being sent to the city.[227]

As was already argued in the previous chapter, it would appear that Ashur-banipal, in whom we see the alter-ego of Darius II, was the son of Artaxerxes' (Esarhaddon's) Babylonian concubine. That Esarhaddon favored Babylon is shown by the fact that he rebuilt the city after its destruction by Sennacherib, and gave the kingship to one of his favorite sons, Shamash-shum-ukin. The pro-Babylonian policy continued throughout the reign of Ashurbanipal, even after the defeat of Shamash-shum-ukin's conspiracy. Far from destroying the city, Ashurbanipal appears to have taken the hand of Bel, and ruled the metropolis under the name Kandalanu.[228]

After the death of Ashurbanipal the Neo-Assyrian kingdom was rent with civil discord. It was in the midst of this strife that Babylon was re-established as the true center of power in the Fertile Crescent. One son of the Great King, a man named Sin-shar-ishkun, inherited the throne of Assyria proper; but he was immediately opposed by Nabopolasser, the king of Babylon and apparently a relative of the former. A record of the great conflict which followed is preserved in a number of cuneiform documents, documents of course normally held to date from the latter 7th century. We hold however that these texts tell of the war of succession waged between Artaxerxes II and his brother Cyrus the Younger upon the death of Darius II.

Thus the accession of this king marks the almost complete Babylonization of the Achaemenid Empire. His reign was a time of disaster for the Persians, and, if what we have said is correct, even Egypt took part in the carve-up of the territories which formerly belonged to the Great King.

The next Achaemenid king, Artaxerxes III, did however display some of the qualities of the early rulers, and he reconquered many of the lost territories, including Egypt. He was also very much a Babylonian, naming himself Nebu-chadrezzar to emphasize the point — a fact which helps to explain the many (otherwise puzzling) traditions recalling a conquest of Egypt by a King Nebu-chadrezzar. This was the King Nebuchadrezzar who destroyed the tiny state of Judah, and who enslaved the last of the Twelve Tribes of Israel. His wars against Judah reflect the campaigns of Artaxerxes III against Egypt and her allies, and the pharaoh Necho whose assistance King Zedekiah vainly sought was actually Nectanebo II, the last native king of Egypt.

---

227 See e.g., S. Smith, *Babylonian Historical Texts* (1924) pp. 148 ff.
228 C. H. W. Johns, *Ancient Babylonia* (1913) p. 125.

Had he lived, Artaxerxes III could well have changed the course of history and reversed the Empire's decline. But it was not to be. In 338 BC, he was poisoned by his trusted eunuch Bagoas, who had grown fearful of his master's increasing violence. The crafty eunuch felt his position would be more secure with a weakling on the throne whom he could manipulate. The weakling in question was Arses III, whom Bagoas eliminated after a mere two years. Almost certainly Arses III is an alter-ego of the "Neo-Babylonian" Nergilasser, who reigned briefly after the death of Nebuchadrezzar.

The wily Bagoas now set about eliminating virtually all of the immediate royal family, being stopped only when a grandnephew of Artaxerxes III forced him to drink one of his own brews. This grandnephew was to go down in history as Darius III, last of the Achaemenids. He was also, in our reckoning, the King Nabonidus whose mother Adad-guppi left the famous votive tablet.

Thus the last of the Achaemenids named himself Nabonidus, and it must have been he who left the various chronological tablets counting many centuries between his time and that of early kings such as Naram Sin and Burnaburiash. According to the chronology proposed in the present volume, Naram Sin would have reigned in the 8th century and Burnaburiash, a contemporary of Akhnaton, would have flourished near the end of the 7th century, and thus would have been separated from the Nabonidus whom Cyrus is said to have conquered by no more than a few decades. However, this Nabonidus (Darius III) was indeed separated from Naram Sin and Burnaburiash by a number of centuries.

A more detailed look at the lives and careers of both Artaxerxes II and Artaxerxes III should serve to underline the clear parallels between them and the great 'Neo-Babylonian' kings Nabopolasser and Nebuchadrezzar.

Artaxerxes II

Artaxerxes II began life as Arsaces and is often referred to in Persian-Aramaic texts as Arshu. As crown prince, he grew up in Babylon, and his career was to be closely connected with that city. Not only was his mother Babylonian, but his father Darius II was himself half-Babylonian by blood. If we are to judge by lineage then the accession of Artaxerxes II marks the almost complete Babylonization of the Achaemenid dynasty.

Named Mnemon on account of his good memory, Artaxerxes II occupied the throne from 404 to 358 BC, a period of time marked by great events.

Very shortly after he mounted the throne the new monarch had to deal with one of the most serious rebellions ever faced by a Persian king. Although the new king was the first-born, his mother Parysatis favored his younger brother Cyrus, and made repeated attempts to have him proclaimed crown prince. This Cyrus, called the Younger, had earlier been made satrap of Asia Minor (including the Greek lands of Ionia and most of Anatolia), where he had become thoroughly acquainted with Hellenic culture and, importantly, Hellenic methods of warfare. No sooner had Artaxerxes II been declared king than Cyrus revolted and marched against him. An army of Greek mercenary soldiers, comprising over ten thousand men, joined him in this famous march. One of the leaders of the mercenaries, an Athenian named Xenophon, described the campaign into Babylonia, and the subsequent retreat from that region, in the *Anabasis* ("Going Up"). Cyrus, we are told, reached Babylon, only to be killed nearby in battle (401 BC).

During the next few years the Persian satrapies in Asia Minor were disturbed by repeated rebellions, and by the attempts of Sparta to liberate the Greeks of the Asian coast from Persian domination. Egypt was lost early in Mnemon's reign (401 BC), and the Egyptians were a continual source of trouble to the Great King throughout his life. The situation with regard to Egypt may be summarized thus:

> While Cyrus the Younger and Artaxerxes II were fighting over the Persian throne, Amyrtaios (404-399) organized a revolt in the marshes which spread to the whole delta. While they were fighting for their independence, Egyptian troops fought for Artaxerxes II at Cunaxa in Babylonia, where Cyrus the Younger fell. In 401 Amyrtaios' rule was recognized in Upper Egypt as well.
>
> Mention is also made of other contemporaneous kings, Amonher, Mutrud and Psammetic. The situation in Egypt remained unclear during much of the 4th century. The kings of Mendes formed the XXIX dynasty, Nepherites I ruling from 399 to 393, followed by Achoris (Hakor, 393-380), Psamouthes (380) and Nepherites II (379) ...
>
> Nepherites and Achoris resumed the traditional interventionist policies in Palestine. By erecting a fleet at great expense and diplomatic moves such as forming an alliance with the Spartans under Evagoras who had just conquered Cyprus, Rhodes and were holding Tyre at least for a few months, they hoped to extend their influence in the Middle East. Nepherites sent 500,000 measures of corn and the equipment for one hundred triremes to Evagoras to enable the Greeks to wrest control of the seas from the Persians. Achoris continued sending corn to his ally and fifty Egyptian triremes reinforced the Spartan fleet. After Artaxerxes, with a fleet of 300 ships, had reconquered Cyprus and Tyre, Evagoras took refuge in Egypt. When Achoris couldn't give him any further assistance he made his peace with the Persians.[229]

The above summarizes our general understanding of events early in Artaxerxes II's reign, and it is evident that historians see Egypt as a major player on the international scene at this time.

---

229 From Ancient Egypt WebRing "The last national dynasties: Dynasties XXVIII to XXX" at http://nefertiti. iwebland. com/reassertionofsovereignty. htm.

If Artaxerxes II/Mnemon is one and the same as Nabopolasser, then his great enemy Cyrus the Younger, whose power-base was to the north of Babylonia, must be identical to Nabopolasser's great enemy Sin-shar-ishkun, whose power-base was also to the north of Babylonia. Further, we should find that Egypt became a major opponent of Nabopolasser, and must have caused him much difficulty in the region of Syria/Palestine.

First, however, we note that the northern enemy of Artaxerxes II was his own brother. Can we say the same thing about Nabopolasser's enemy? It would appear that we can. In spite of attempts by historians to portray Nabopolasser as a patriotic hero liberating Babylon from the Assyrian yoke, several texts from Mesopotamia make it seem likely that he was a son of Ashurbanipal, and therefore a brother of his "Assyrian" enemy.[230] If this is correct, then he war between Nabopolasser and Sin-shar-ishkun was a dynastic war of succession, not a patriotic liberation struggle. True, Nabopolasser is said to have boasted of chasing from Akkad the Assyrians "who from days of old had ruled over all peoples and worn out the nations with their heavy yoke," a comment that we need to explain. Before attempting to do so, however, we should note that our knowledge of the war between Nabopolasser and Sin-shar-ishkun is patchy, to say the least. Most of what we know comes from the Babylonian Chronicle, combined with snippets of information from the Old Testament. Both sources certainly seem to portray the war as a conflict between Assyrians and Babylonians; yet there is much that we are ignorant of, even of the basics. For example, it is said that upon the death of Ashurbanipal, two brothers, Sin-shar-ishkun and Ashur-etil-ilani, battled over the throne. Some declare these two to have been twins, yet on the other hand, "The relationship between him [Ashur-etil-ilani] and his brother [Sin-shar-ishkun] is far from certain (it has even been hypothesized that he and Sin-shar-ishkun were in fact the same person)."[231]

In fact, we shall argue that Ashur-etil-ilani, to whom the Harran Inscription of Nabonidus ascribes a reign of three years, was indeed one and the same person as Sin-shar-ishkun.

The Babylonian Chronicle makes it certain that after only a short reign Sin-shar-ishkun was killed. How he died is not recorded, but it seems certain that he fell at the hands of Nabopolasser's troops. These events are said to have occurred in 623 BC, though, if we are correct, they are a Babylonian record of the defeat and death of Cyrus the Younger, in 401 BC.

---

230 The votive tablet of Adad-Guppi does not mention Nabopolasser's origins, but clearly states that Adad-Guppi, along with her son Nabonidus, was a descendant of Ashurbanipal. Furthermore, Nabonidus himself describes Esarhaddon and Ashurbanipal as his "royal forefathers".

231 Wikipedia, at http://en. wikipedia. org/wiki/Ashur-etil-ilani.

It is unfortunate that after the demise of Sin-shar-ishkun/Ashur-etil-ilani the Babylonian texts become less fragmentary. From these however we learn that after a short respite another enemy, Ashuruballit II, arose to challenge the Babylonian monarch. This second war appears to have dragged on for a number of years, for the cuneiform texts tell us of military action between the 10th and 17th years of Nabopolasser. The new enemy, Ashuruballit, has the support of the Egyptians, though Nabopolasser, here described as the "King of Akkad," obtains the assistance of a mysterious race of warriors called the "Umman-manda" or "Manda hordes." We are told that the:

> Ummanmanda, [who] had come [to hel]p the king of Akkad, put their armies together and marched to Harran [against Ashuruball]it who had ascended the throne in Assyria. Fear of the enemy overcame Ashuruballit (II) and the army of Eg[ypt *which*] had come [to help him] and they aban[doned] the city [...] they crossed. The king of Akkad reached Harran and he captured the city. He carried off the vast booty of the city and the temple.[232]

Believing this tract to refer to events near the end of the 7th century BC, historians normally assume that the Umman-manda are the Medes, or perhaps the Scythians. Yet nowhere else in ancient literature are the Medes or Scythians referred to by this name, and from this detail alone we might be justified in looking for another interpretation. It so happens that such an interpretation is readily available. The word *umman* is in fact very similar to *Jaman*, or *Iaman*, the normal Babylonian-cuneiform rendering of "Ionian." These Umman-manda were perhaps not Medes but Ionian Greeks. We may imagine that the lessons of his war against Cyrus would not have been lost upon Artaxerxes II/Nabopolasser, and he may have been quick thereafter to recruit Ionian hoplites in his own cause.

But if the Umman-Manda really were Medes or Scythians, this still does not present a problem. The Persian Empire long controlled the lands of the Medes and some of the Scythian races. Mede and Scythian detachments were employed by Persian kings throughout the whole of Achaemenid history.

The Babylonian Chronicle was written many years after the events it describes — from a pro-Babylonian perspective. Artaxerxes II was raised in Babylon and had a Babylonian mother. It is even possible that he viewed himself as a Babylonian, and certainly he would have endeavored to portray himself to the Babylonians, his own subjects, as the defender of their ancient rights. He certainly favored the city throughout his reign. Taking into account the fact that he also assumed a Babylonian throne-name, it is quite natural that the scribes who

---

232 Britsh Museum Text 21901.

compiled the Babylonian Chronicle would have seen in him one of their own, and have composed their history from this point of view.

But there is perhaps another, more personal reason for Nabopolasser's failure to describe himself as a son of Ashurbanipal. We know that Artaxerxes II only succeeded to the throne after repeated attempts by his own mother to have him disinherited in favor of his younger brother Cyrus. Artaxerxes II must have felt extremely bitter about this. His whole future, which he had perhaps earlier presumed to be secure, was thus made precarious by the weakness of his father. In such circumstances, we can well imagine him repudiating his paternal lineage. It may, against this, be argued that surely the young king would have reserved his ire for his mother. Yet sons are loathe to sever the bonds between themselves and their mothers — though notoriously all too willing to sever that with their fathers. It is even possible (though it must be admitted nowhere stated) that Cyrus and Artaxerxes II had two different mothers. This would certainly explain Parysatis' attempts to have Cyrus made heir to the throne.

The Babylonian Chronicle, although full of breaks, informs us that the Egyptians came to assist the king of Assyria, who is named Ashuruballit. Evidently the death of Cyrus did not put an end to Artaxerxes' dynastic problems, and it is quite probable that Ashuruballit was yet another rebellious brother. We know from other sources that the Egyptians did take part in the great battles of this period, including many engagements in Syria/Palestine. In these events Greek troops, both from Sparta and Athens, took part. Some fought for the Great King, others against.

From the Annals of Nabopolasser we are informed that for a period of seven years, between his 10th and 17th years (probably counted from his investiture as king of Babylon), the Babylonian ruler was in almost continual conflict with the Egyptians. By his twelfth year his Umman-manda allies had captured the city of Ashur. As late as Year 17, the Annals inform us, an Assyrian and Egyptian army crossed the Euphrates in an unsuccessful attempt to retake Harran.

Biblical sources would suggest that the "Babylonians" continued to be troubled by the Egyptians in northern Syria until the very end of Nabopolasser's reign. Yet there are serious discrepancies between the biblical and Babylonian chronologies, and it seems unlikely that the Egyptians gave much trouble after Nabopolasser's 17th year. It is apparent, however, that there was a protracted conflict in Syria between a rejuvenated Egypt and the great power of Mesopotamia, which at that time was centered in Babylon.

When Artaxerxes II died, in 359 BC, his son Ochus was proclaimed king under the name of Artaxerxes III. To ensure his succession against any attempted rebellion, he let all of his brothers and half-brothers, eighty in number, be killed.

The new Artaxerxes regarded the reconquest of Egypt as one of his chief tasks, a task which he did eventually accomplish, though not until the sixteenth year of his reign. We know that Nectanebo I died only a year before Artaxerxes II, and that he was replaced on the throne by a pharaoh known to the Greeks as Tachos. Well aware of the ruthless nature of the new occupant of the Great King's throne, Tachos made preparations to defend Egypt — part of which involved the recruitment of the legendary Spartan King Aegesilaus to his cause. Aegesilaus, by this time a very old man, was apparently delighted at the opportunity once again to do battle with the Persians. The Spartan veteran had been promised chief command by Tachos; but when he arrived in Egypt he found that the fleet had been placed in the hands of the Athenian general Chabrias, whilst Tachos himself retained overall supreme command. At this stage the pharaoh was in Syria, part of which had been occupied by him following the death of Artaxerxes II. In the meantime, a plot to place a nephew of his on the throne was being hatched. Aegesilaus threw his weight behind the conspirators, and effectively placed the nephew, known to history as Nectanebo II, on the throne.

When news of these developments reached Tachos in Palestine he fled northwards to the Persian king to ask forgiveness. Another two pretenders arose to challenge Nectanebo II, but these were quickly overcome with the assistance of Aegesilaus' hoplites.

Nine years later, which was also the ninth year of the reign of Artaxerxes III/ Ochus (350 BC), the Egyptians met the armies of the Great King on the borders of Egypt and threw them back towards Mesopotamia. The failure of this first expedition proved to be a major setback for Artaxerxes III, and his plan to reincorporate Egypt into the Empire had to wait another seven years (343 BC) for fruition. Thus Artaxerxes III's second, and successful expedition against Egypt occurred in his sixteenth year.

We are told that after this reconquest Ochus plundered the country mercilessly, repeating the depredations of Cambyses. There was a general massacre of the population and a violation of the temples and religious centers, even to the extent of slaying the sacred Apis bull and serving it at a feast. All of which is believable enough, considering what we know of his character from other sources. In the words of one commentator, the "chief characteristic" of Ochus was his

"savage cruelty."[233] How then does the life and military career of Nebuchadrezzar compare with that of Artaxerxes III?

Early in his reign, in his eighth or possibly ninth year, Nebuchadrezzar campaigned right to the borders of Egypt; it was then that he besieged Jerusalem,
removing its King Jehoiachin and replacing him with Zedekiah. It is known that
this campaign against Judah was actually but a small incident in a much greater
campaign against Egypt and its allies. But if such were the case, then the campaign was at best indecisive — no conquest of Egypt is recorded. Nevertheless, it
could not have been a complete disaster for the Babylonians, for Nebuchadrezzar
apparently retained control of Judah until Zedekiah's eighth year — at which
point the people of Judah once again threw off the Babylonian yoke.

Thus we see that Nebuchadrezzar, like Artaxerxes III, made a first and apparently largely unsuccessful attack on Egypt in his eighth, or possibly ninth,
year. But the parallels do not end there.

As we have noted, the Book of Chronicles records that in the eighth year of
Zedekiah, and therefore in the sixteenth year of Nebuchadrezzar, the Babylonian king again moved against Egypt and Judah. Once again, most, if not all, of
what we know of this campaign comes from the Jewish records, which were of
course concerned primarily with the devastation the war brought to their own
homeland. These sources report that on this occasion Nebuchadrezzar utterly
destroyed Jerusalem, pulling down the temple and deporting the entire population to Babylon.

This must have been part of the campaign against Egypt and its allies recorded in a much damaged tablet of Nebuchadrezzar. What is still legible has
been translated thus:

> The kings, the allies of his power and ... his general and his hired sol-
> diers ... he spoke unto. To his soldiers ... who were before ... at the way of ...
>   In the 37th year of Nebuchadnezzar, king of Babylon ... the king of
> Egypt came up to do battle [?] and ... es, the king of Egypt ... and ... of the
> city of Putu-Jaman ... far away regions which are in the sea ... numerous
> which were in Egypt ... arms and horses ... he called to ... he trusted ...[234]

The reference to the campaign against Egypt in Nebuchadrezzar's 37th year is
apparently puzzling, though it is possible, actually probable, that he was counting from his appointment as King of Babylon, a system he is known to have actually used. Whatever the case, it is certain that Nebuchadrezzar's second cam-

---

233 G. Rawlinson, *Ancient Monarchies* Vol. 3 (London, 1879) p. 510.
234 S. Langdon, Building Inscriptions of the Neo-Babylonian Empire (Paris, 1905) p. 182.

paign against Judah, and Egypt, occurred sometime between his sixteenth and seventeenth year.

Thus Nebuchadrezzar, like Artaxerxes III, made two assaults upon Egypt. The first, in the eighth or ninth year of both monarchs, was a failure; and the second, in the sixteenth or seventeenth year of both rulers, which was a success.

That Nebuchadrezzar actually conquered Egypt is suggested by a number of very powerful pieces of evidence. First of all, both Ezekiel and Jeremiah prophesied that he would do so; and since most of these "prophecies" were written in retrospect, or at least gained popular currency only after having been proved correct, we may be fairly certain that the prophesied invasion and defeat of Egypt actually took place. The conquest is predicted thus by Ezekiel (29:19-20):

> Therefore thus said the Lord God: Behold, I will set Nebuchadnezzar the king of Babylon in the land of Egypt: and he shall take her multitude, and take the booty thereof for a prey, and rifle the spoils thereof: and it shall be wages for his army. And for the service that he hath done me against it, I have given him the land of Egypt, because he hath labored for me, saith the Lord.

Secondly, the biblical sources say that Nebuchadrezzar was able to remove the Jewish refugees in Egypt to Babylon. He could not of course have done so unless he had entered and subjugated the country.

Thirdly, Josephus tells us that he conquered Egypt. We are informed that four years after the fall of Tyre, Nebuchadrezzar invaded the country and put its King Uaphris to death, installing a creature of his own upon the vacant throne.[235] Fourthly, and most importantly, artifacts of Nebuchadrezzar have actually been discovered in Egypt. These are "three cylinders of terra-cotta bearing an inscription of Nebuchadnezzar, an ordinary text referring to his constructions in Babylon ... These were said to come from the Isthmus of Suez, and they apparently belong to some place where Nebuchadrezzar had 'set up his throne' and 'spread his royal pavilion.' As he only passed along the Syrian road, and Daphnae would be the only stopping place on that road in the region of the isthmus, all the inferences point to these having come from Defenneh, and being the memorials of establishment there."[236]

In short, the prophecy of Jeremiah that the king of Babylon would spread his royal pavilion at the entrance of the pharaoh's house in Tahpanheth (Daphnae) was fulfilled. There can be little doubt; Nebuchadnezzar entered and conquered Egypt.

---

235 Josephus, *Jewish Antiquities* x,9,7.
236 F. Petrie, Tanis Pt II. Nebesheh and Defenneh p. 51.

It is of interest to note here that the cylinders were discovered at Daphnae, one of the Hellenic centers of the Delta, a garrison settlement of the pharaoh's Ionian bodyguard. This corresponds well enough with the contents of Nebucha-drezzar's tablet, which speaks of the city of Putu-Jaman. Jaman of course was the Babylonian for "Ionian."

Thus in a number of details the life and career of Nebuchadrezzar provides close parallels with that of Artaxerxes III:

- Both kings were rulers of Babylon, who clashed with Egypt.

- Artaxerxes III's first war against Egypt occurred in his eighth year, and ended in failure. Nebuchadrezzar's first war against Egypt took place in his eighth or ninth year and apparently ended in failure.

- The Egyptian enemy of Artaxerxes III was known as Nectanebo II. The Egyptian enemy of Nebuchadrezzar was known as Necho II.

- Artaxerxes III's second campaign against Egypt occurred in his sixteenth year and was successful. Nebuchadrezzar's second campaign against Egypt occurred in his sixteenth or seventeenth year and resulted in the conquest of the Nile Kingdom.

- Artaxerxes III's Egyptian enemy Nectanebo II used Greek mercenaries against the Great King. Nebuchadrezzar's Egyptian enemy Necho II used Greek mercenaries against him.

It is fairly evident then that here, once again, we find striking parallels in the lives and careers of two characters supposedly belonging to two different epochs separated by two centuries.

Before moving on, it should be noted that the Book of Judith, hitherto one of the most enigmatic of traditional Hebrew texts, takes on an altogether new sig-nificance in the light of the reconstruction proposed here. Judith is said to have lived during the time of a Nebuchadrezzar who is described as "King of Assyria." No king of Assyria of this name is said to be known. Yet this Mesopotamian monarch is involved in events strikingly similar to those of his namesake who deported the people of Judah. He is said to have summoned the peoples of the west, including the Egyptians, to assist him in a war against the Medes. When this summons is ignored, he sets out, in his eighteenth year, to punish the trai-tors, who include Egyptians and Jews (Judith 2). This march to the west recalls the action taken by the other Nebuchadrezzar in the same region in his sixteenth year. Could it be that the Book of Judith provides an account of an otherwise ob-scure episode of the war against Nebuchadrezzar in the time of King Hezekiah — the war which we have identified as Artaxerxes III's second campaign against

Egypt? One striking detail in the Book of Judith seems to confirm this. We are told that Nebuchadrezzar's general Holofernes, whom Judith assassinates, had a eunuch named Bagoas (Judith 12:11). Yet Bagoas was the name of the trusted eunuch who assassinated Artaxerxes III. Even more to the point, Artaxerxes III also had a general named Holofernes. According to Diodorus, this Holofernes was a Cappadocian who accompanied Artaxerxes III in his campaign against the Egyptians.[237]

Strange then that the Book of Judith would name as servants of Nebuchadrezzar two characters with names identical to two servants of Artaxerxes III!

End of the Empire

The Neo-Babylonian Empire did not long survive the death of Nebuchadrezzar. Indeed little more than six years or so are accorded to the series of kings who briefly occupied the throne in the bloody events which followed his demise. But the fate of the Achaemenid Empire offers a precise parallel with that of the Neo-Babylonian.

Within a year of his Egyptian victory, Nebuchadrezzar II died and was succeeded by his son Amel-Marduk (Evil-Merodach), a man who reigned barely two years and of whom very little is known. We do know however that he did not die a natural death. A conspiracy was hatched against him by a brother-in-law named Nergilissar, who rose in rebellion and placed himself on the throne. Nergilissar, we are told, reigned just three years himself, and was succeeded by his son Labash-Marduk, who occupied the throne no more than a few months. He was beaten to death in the palace, and one Nabu-na-id (Nabonidus) was placed on the throne in his stead.

This Nabonidus is generally believed to have been the last king of an independent Babylon, and it is universally assumed that he was the king overthrown by Cyrus the Great. Yet according to the reconstruction of history proposed here, he was not a contemporary of the first Persian Great King, but was himself the last of the Persian Emperors — Darius III.

The final years of the Achaemenid state, like those of the Neo-Babylonian, involved assassination and courtly intrigue. However, as with the Neo-Babylonian history, sources are meager and we must rely solely on a passage from Diodorus (xvii, 5) for our knowledge. We are told that Bagoas, who had been an invaluable help to Ochus in his reconquest of Egypt, began to fear that he would be the next victim of his master's paranoid violence. Acting pre-emptively, he offered the king a poisoned brew, which left the throne vacant and the empire shaken to its foundations. Intent on survival, the courtier now eliminated all the king's elder

---

237 Diodorus Siculus, xviii, 6, 1.

sons and set a younger brother, Arses (known as Artaxerxes IV), on the throne. Yet after only three years the crafty eunuch felt he detected too independent a spirit in his youthful protégé and eliminated him, too. Bagoas now set about ridding himself of virtually the entire immediate royal family, before finally Codomannus, a prince of a minor branch of the royal line, turned the tables and forced the eunuch to drink his own brew. Codomannus now ascended the throne as Darius III. His reign was to be as short as it was momentous. Within a couple of years, the armies of Alexander were crossing the Hellespont.

How does this history correlate with the "Neo-Babylonian"?

In this reconstruction, Nergilissar, who reigned for three years, is probably identical to Arses, who sat on the Achaemenid throne for the same period. Who then, it might be asked, was Amel Marduk, who occupied the Babylonian throne for just under two years? The Diodorus account does not mention anyone who could be identified with him and it covers this entire period in just a few lines; but archaeology has supplied the want. According to the King List of Uruk (*ANET* 3, 566), a prince named Nidin-Bel seized the throne of Babylon immediately after the death of Artaxerxes III. Aside from this man's name, we know virtually nothing about him, though he was probably a son of Artaxerxes III by a Babylonian woman and he almost certainly reigned only a short time. In our reconstruction, he is probably to be identified as Amel Marduk (Bel and Marduk were regarded as identical gods), who reigned less than two years before being slain by Nergilissar.

Knowledge of events surrounding the assassination of Arses/Artaxerxes IV and the rise of Darius III/Codomannus is again confined to a line or two in Diodorus. We are informed that Bagoas killed all of Arses' sons before himself being slain by Codomannus. However, it does not make sense that Bagoas would kill all of Arses' progeny. He must, logically, have preserved at least one to serve as a puppet. In any event, translated into "Neo-Babylonian" history this one surviving royal prince would have been Labash-Marduk, who was in turn murdered after only a few months. In both Neo-Babylonian and Persian histories the next ruler, the last of both empires, i.e., Nabonidus (Nabu-na-id) and Darius III, was not closely related to the main branch of the royal family.

A final point. A detail of an inscription of Nabonidus' mother strongly suggests that both he and the entire Neo-Babylonian royal family was of Persian origin. In this document Adad-Guppi offers a prayer to the Babylonian god Sin:

> May your return to your town [Babylon] take place so that (its)
> black-headed inhabitants can worship for all days to come your great
> godhead.[238]

But the term "black-headed" was one used by the light-skinned and often
fair-haired Indo-Aryan Medes and Persians to describe the dark-haired inhabitants of Mesopotamia. Thus we find an inscription of Cyrus stating that he "did
always endeavour to treat according to justice the black-headed whom he (Marduk) had made him conquer."[239] Is it likely then that a native king of Babylonia,
prior to the advent of the Persians, would have used a term for his own subjects
later used by the conquering Indo-Europeans, for whom black hair was quite
unfamiliar?

Extent of the Neo-Babylonian Empire

According to the classical authors, the Babylonian Empire which arose after
the fall of Imperial Assyria in the 7th century BC was confined to central and
southern Mesopotamia. The Greek writers for example made it very clear that
it was the Medes, and not the Babylonians, who were chiefly responsible for
Assyria's demise, and they devoted considerable space towards outlining the
power of this people, whom they described as the "Mighty Medes." These authors further affirm that Babylon did not even survive as an independent power
after the fall of Assyria. On the contrary, the whole of Lower Mesopotamia was
dominated for a period of eighty years by the Scythians, a barbarian race which
had initially allied themselves with the Assyrians, but which had stayed in the
region to plunder and to conquer. From the classical writers we learn that whilst
the Scythians took southern Mesopotamia, the Medes occupied the whole of
northern Mesopotamia as well as large parts of Anatolia. These regions became
an integral part of the Mede Imperium, and so remained for a number of generations. From Herodotus we find the Medes involved in a prolonged conflict with
the other great power of the time — Lydia. According to the Father of History,
the border between the Mede and Lydian kingdoms lay at the Halys River, right
in the middle of Anatolia.

The Old Testament however, which recounted the deeds of apparently "Neo-
Babylonian" monarchs such as Nebuchadrezzar, seemed to describe a very different history. From the pages of the Old Testament we learn of a "Neo-Babylonian"
empire whose power encompassed the whole of the Fertile Crescent, right to

---

238 Pritchard, *ANET* p. 311.
239 Ibid. p. 315.

the borders of Egypt. Indeed, the Bible even seems to claim a Neo-Babylonian conquest of that country.

With the advent of modern archaeology, in the 19ᵗʰ century, discoveries in Mesopotamia and elsewhere seemed to provide stunning confirmation of the biblical version of history and refutation of the classical. It was found, for example, that post-Neo-Assyrian northern Mesopotamia was not controlled by the Medes at all, but by the Neo-Babylonians. Throughout the region archaeologists found ample evidence, in the form of monuments, inscriptions and cuneiform documents, of Neo-Babylonian rule.[240] In addition, the translation of texts such as the Nabopolasser Chronicle appeared to question the importance of the Medes and to refute the idea of a "Scythian epoch" in the south. The Nabopolasser Chronicle and other documents in fact entirely rewrote history, appearing to show, as they did, that it was the Neo-Babylonians themselves who had conquered Assyria. From the time of Nabopolasser, whose armies crushed the last Assyrian power, Babylon was the dominant force throughout Mesopotamia and beyond. This was confirmed both by textual and archaeological evidence.

Of the Medes, whom the early explorers had expected to find, archaeologists uncovered not a trace.

The apparent disappearance of the Mede Empire from the archaeological record is now held to be one of the greatest of all historical mysteries.

But the extent of "Neo-Babylonian" power, it seemed, was even under-estimated in the pages of the Old Testament. This conclusion was reached upon the discovery of a business archive in Cappadocia — well into Anatolia — which named Nebuchadrezzar II as the ruling monarch.[241]

Thus archaeology and the Old Testament combined to refute the classical and Hellenistic authors. The Medes, it seemed, may have destroyed the cities of Assyria; but they did not build on the ruins they left. They must then have been transitory semi-nomads. Their power, furthermore, did not extend into the regions claimed by the Greek authors. It was the Babylonians, and not the Medes, who controlled northern Mesopotamia, the whole Fertile Crescent, and a large part of Anatolia. It was the Babylonians who were rivals of the Lydians, not the Medes.

Yet such drastic rewriting of history is unnecessary. The "Neo-Babylonian" kings, after all, were not Neo-Chaldeans of the 7ᵗʰ and 6ᵗʰ centuries, but Persians of the 4ᵗʰ century. Nabopolasser, Nebuchadrezzar II and Nabonidus could leave monuments all through the Fertile Crescent and Anatolia because they were Per-

---

240 See e.g., *Proceedings of The Assyrian National Convention in Los Angeles*, (September 4, 1999), Journal of Assyrian Academic Studies, Vol. XIII, No. 2, 1999.
241 See e.g., C. H. W. Johns, *Ancient Babylonia* (1913).

sian Great Kings who really ruled in those regions. In the same way, Nebucha-drezzar II could conquer Egypt because he was none other than Artaxerxes III, who really did conquer Egypt in 340 BC.

The true Neo-Babylonians, or more properly, Neo-Chaldean, the rulers of an independent Babylon which arose in the 7ᵗʰ century upon the ruins of the Assyr-ian (i.e., Akkadian or "Old Assyrian") Imperium, were great enough kings in their own right; but their authority did not extend beyond Lower Mesopotamia. These men were contemporaries and opponents of the (supposedly) 9ᵗʰ and early 8ᵗʰ century "Neo-Assyrian" kings (who were in fact Medes). Thus the well-known Shalmaneser III, believed to have reigned in the second half of the 9ᵗʰ century BC, was actually the Mede Emperor Cyaxares (the second of that name).[242] His Babylonian contemporary and opponent, Nabu-apil-iddin (or Nabopoladdan) was the man who re-established Babylonian independence, around 630 BC, after many years of Scythian (i.e., "Gutian") rule. Nabu-apil-iddin also had a "Kassite" name; and it was under this title, Burnaburiash, that he appears in the most fa-mous correspondences of the period, the Amarna Letters.

One of Nabu-apil-iddin's successors, Kurigalzu, was also known as Nebu-kudur-utsur (Nebuchadrezzar). He was the first Babylonian monarch of the name, and he reigned roughly between 600 and 570 BC.

The last of these true Neo-Chaldean kings, the man conquered by Cyrus the Great, was named Nabu-nutsur (Nabonasser), a title sadly confused with Na-bonidus (Darius III).

Nabonasser and Nabonidus

From what has been said in the present work, it is clear that we view virtually all of the historical material pertaining to Egypt and Assyria, which is presently dated to the 8ᵗʰ and 7ᵗʰ centuries BC, as belonging in the Persian epoch, from the mid-6ᵗʰ to the 4ᵗʰ century BC. But how could such a monumental misplacement have occurred? The Hebrews, we recall, apparently placed Tiglath-Pileser in the 8ᵗʰ century, and his successors Sennacherib and Esarhaddon at the start of the 7th. Even Herodotus placed a king named Sennacherib early in the 7ᵗʰ century, and it was he who bequeathed to us the 7ᵗʰ century chronology of Egyptian kings from Necho I through to Psammetichus and Necho II. By contrast, the system presented in the foregoing pages would suggest that no king named Psammeti-

---

242 As I have explained in some detail in *Empire of Thebes: Ages in Chaos Revisited* (New York, 2006). The Akkadian or Old Assyrian Empire actually fell before the Mitanni (Medes) between 720 and 690 BC. Southern Mesopotamia, including Babylon, was then controlled by the Guti, or Gasa (Sa. Gaz, Saka), the Scythians, until around 630 BC, when the region was liberated by Nabu-apil-iddin, also called Burnaburiash and Ur-Nammu.

chus ever lived in the 7th century, and that the Psammetichus of Herodotus was Psamtek of Sais, who lived during the time of Darius II.

How is it then that the Persian epoch came to be relocated two centuries in the past, and Persian monarchs took on the *personae* of Assyrian kings?

As well as answering this question, we must also address the series of documents/inscriptions dating from the final years of the Neo-Babylonian Empire, which appear to put the accepted chronology on an unassailable basis. These documents, it is said, show that the last Neo-Babylonian king, Nabonidus, was in direct line of succession from the Neo-Assyrian kings (i.e., Sennacherib, Ashurbanipal, etc.) and that he himself was overthrown by Cyrus of Persia.

Let us deal first with the latter point.

On the face of it there can be no denying that the "Neo-Babylonian" documents do seem to provide a formidable defense of accepted chronology, and the present writer was compelled to dig deep into the fundamentals of Neo-Babylonian and Persian historiography in order to unravel the truth.

Five or six major historical inscriptions of this period are known, all of which are presented in Pritchard's *Ancient Near Eastern Texts*. One document, from the time of Nabopolasser, describes the fall of Assyria and the rise of the Neo-Babylonians under the latter ruler. Another, written as a eulogy for Adad-Guppi, mother of Nabonidus, describes this woman's life and touches also on the circumstances surrounding the rise of her son to the kingship. Two inscriptions, and two only, describe the fall of Nabonidus and the conquest of Cyrus. These are the so-called Nabonidus Chronicle and the famous Prism of Cyrus. The Nabonidus Chronicle, the lengthier of the two, describes how Cyrus of Anshan became master of the Mede Empire after his defeat of Astyages (Ishtumegu), and chronicles his victory over Lydia, as well as his conquest of Babylon.

To all intents and purposes, the above documents do appear to put conventional chronology beyond question. Nevertheless, two points need to be considered:

(a) None of these inscriptions, with the possible exceptions of the Cyrus Prism and the Stela of Adad-Guppi, were actually written contemporary with the events they describe. This is important, for reasons that will become apparent as we proceed.

(b) Neither of the inscriptions dealing with the conquest of Babylon by Cyrus — the Nabonidus Chronicle and the Cyrus Prism — refer to any Neo-Babylonian or Neo-Assyrian king other than Nabonidus. This is important because, as we shall see, these documents do not belong with the others loosely grouped together as "Neo-Babylonian." In fact, there were two "Babylonian" kings named Nabonidus. The first of these, the man defeated by Cyrus, lived two centuries before another Nabonidus, the latter being the same man as Darius III. The earlier Nabonidus is usually known as Nabonasser, the contemporary and adversary of Tiglath-Pileser III of Assyria, whom the present writer regards as an alter-ego of Cyrus.

The names "Nabonasser" and "Nabonidus" look very different, written this way. However, the Babylonian versions, Nabu-nasir (or Nabu-n-atsir) and Nabu-na-id, tell a different tale. The titles mean, respectively, "Nebo protects" and "Nebo protecting," and are rendered more fully into English by the translators as "Nebo protects (me)" and "Nebo (is) protecting (me)"[243] Bearing this in mind it becomes readily understandable that these two monarchs could be confused.

For the reign of the earlier of these two, commonly called Nabonasser, there is hardly a brick or inscription, though he was an important king whose lifetime was viewed as marking the start of a new epoch. The Ptolemaic Canon begins with his reign.

Given Nabonasser's importance, and the apparent non-appearance of documents relating to him, I will argue that much of the "Nabonidus" material actually belongs to Nabonasser, and that cuneiform translators have simply interpreted the same name according to their preconceived notions of chronology. Thus when a document of King Nabu-nat-sir/Nabu-na-id also mentions Cyrus of Anshan, the name is simply transliterated as Nabonidus. Such inscriptions (as the Nabonidus Chronicle) are then grouped in modern publications — such as Pritchard's *Ancient Near Eastern Texts* — alongside others which tell of the second Nabonidus, and the impression is given of a smoothly-running, seamless sequence from Neo-Assyrians to Neo-Babylonians to Persians.

But it has to be admitted that it is not only modern scholars who have had difficulty in differentiating these two men. The ancients themselves, faced with two kings who not only shared almost the same name but in many ways the same fate (both were the last kings of their dynasty and both were overthrown by a mighty conqueror), had problems in deciding which was which. Both Babylonian and Jewish chroniclers of a later date confused not only the two Naboniduses, but also their conquerors.

This confusion, we have seen, is extensively reflected in the Jewish literature. We recall how the prophet Daniel, although believed to have flourished in the time of Darius I, also mentions the Macedonians and the Romans, and is therefore almost certainly a contemporary of Darius III, not Darius I. We saw too

---

243 G. Rawlinson, *Ancient Monarchies* Vol. 3 (London, 1879) p. 82. I have recently been informed however by Lisa Liel of Israel that Nabu-na'id should really be read as "Nabu praised" or "Nabu is praised." Not being an authority on ancient Akkadian I can only give the two translations I have heard from those who are.

how, at the other end of the timescale, the prophet Isaiah mentions both Tiglath Pileser III and Cyrus the Great, two characters supposedly separated from each other by 200 years. All this duplicating stems from the initial error of equating Nabonidus I (or Nabonasser), who was overthrown by Cyrus/Tiglath-Pileser III, with Nabonidus II/Darius III, who was overthrown by Alexander the Great.

The confusion of Nabonidus I and II has in fact bedeviled Near Eastern historiography for over two thousand years. Thus whilst we claim that it was Alexander (the conqueror of Nabonidus II), who unleashed the Jews from their Babylonian captivity, Jewish tradition insists that it was Cyrus. But the identities of Cyrus and Alexander have been confounded in much of Near Eastern tradition. Even Islamic scholarship is affected. To this day, Iranian scholars and clerics hold the name of Cyrus in contempt, though they honour Zoroaster and the monotheistic religion of Achaemenid times. But Cyrus is not identified with this noble faith; he is rather identified with the Macedonian destroyers of Iran and her culture — with Alexander, no less. One of Islam's holy books specifically links Alexander with Cyrus. We are told: "Alexander had a hairstyle curved like two horns, as did Cyrus. In Daniel 8:6 [we read]: 'and he came to the ram with two horns'. The last word in Hebrew is 'Karanaim': *krnym*. In Arabic it is *Zialgharein* or *Zelgarne* or *Zelranain* ... Many Arab and Persian scholars have referred to Zelranain as Alexander who destroyed Persian and Indian culture."[244]

A Chronology in Chaos

It is evident then that the confusion over the two Naboniduses must take a large part of the blame for the chaotic chronology we now possess. Yet other factors played their part. To begin with, there was the Achaemenid habit of aping the great empires of the past — particularly the Assyrians and Babylonians. In many ways the Persians regarded themselves as the inheritors of Assyria's mantle. Thus when Darius I seized the Persian throne he adopted the name Sargon "Legitimate King," apparently in direct imitation of the Akkadian/Old Assyrian Sargon I, who was also a usurper. The later kings of Persia also adopted Assyrian-style names, and, as we have seen, maintained Assyria as one of the main administrative regions of the Empire. The Hebrews, who compiled their sacred scriptures primarily during the Hellenistic and Roman epochs, eventually got the real Assyrians of the 8th and 7th centuries hopelessly confused with the later "Neo-Assyrian" Persians, whom they projected back into the Assyrian epoch. Similarly, the Egyptian enemies of the Neo-Assyrians (Tirhaka, Necho, and Psammetichos), were also relocated back to the 8th/7th centuries. Error was

---

244 David Roth, quoting Ali Rezah Saheb, from a talk given at the SIS Ancient History Study Group. Published in *SIS Chronology and Catastrophism Workshop* (1995) No. 1 p. 4 .

eventually compounded on error when the last of the Achaemenid monarchs, from Darius II onwards, began to use Babylonian rather than Assyrian names. Things were made even worse by the fact that the Babylonian names they chose — Nabopolasser, Nebuchadrezzar, and Nabonidus, were strongly reminiscent of the titles of the Neo-Chaldean Babylonian kings who had earlier reigned in the 6th and 7th centuries. At this time there actually did reign a series of kings who named themselves Nabu-apil-iddin (Nabopoladan), Nebuchadrezzar (I) and Nabu-natsir (Nabonasser).

We need also to consider the fact that after the initial conquest of Palestine by Tiglath-Pileser/Cyrus, numbers of Hebrews were continually being transported to Mesopotamia and the Median territories. With the fall of the northern kingdom of Israel during the time of Shalmaneser V/Cambyses and Sargon II/Darius I, huge numbers of Hebrews were transported eastwards. These persons did not, as many suppose, immediately lose their identity. On the contrary, as the Scriptures themselves make perfectly clear, they continued as a distinct culture and people for many years — surviving indeed until the arrival in exile of their Judaic cousins over a century later. During these years, the exiled Ten Tribes interacted with their Persian conquerors, and some of the books of the Old Testament deal with the fortunes of these exiles under the various Persian Great Kings. However, even as the captive Israelites recorded their fortunes as exiles in Persia and Mesopotamia, the still free people of Judah also continued to keep records — records which told of their struggle for survival against the great power to the east which had already enslaved their Israelite cousins. The chroniclers of Judaic history however called this power and its kings by their Semitic names, whereas the chroniclers of the history of the exiled Israelites, living as they did in the Persian homeland, probably used the Persian names. Thus two parallel histories, one compiled by the free Jews, the other by the exiled Israelites, seem to have developed. When the Scriptures were being written in their final form, during the first century BC, the two distinct traditions were available. Clearly the use of totally different names for the same kings must have caused profound confusion, and eventually the parallel traditions were put in sequence rather than kept as they should have been, contemporary.

The misplacement of Persian history also therefore had the effect of throwing Hebrew history into chaos. It is a fact noted frequently by commentators that the Jews, most assiduous of record-keepers, left not a single document or even note from the time of Ezra (supposedly fifth century BC) until the time of the Maccabees, in the mid-second century BC. Thus, in a period where we should have expected a rich tradition to have survived, there are 250 years of Hebrew history totally unaccounted for. The only Jewish writer to cover the third and fourth centuries is Josephus, but his sources are entirely Hellenistic; and he tells us virtually nothing about the Jews themselves in this epoch. (He does however mention that Alexander came to Jerusalem and honored the Jewish God — rather in the way Cyrus honored the same God).[245] Even worse, Rabbinical Jewish tradition, just like Matthew's genealogy of Jesus, places the Babylonian Exile and the rebuilding of the Temple in the fourth century (around 350 BC) rather than the sixth. This is a perplexing problem which generations of academics have failed to solve.

In fact, there is absolutely no material in the Old Testament to cover the period from the reign of Artaxerxes I (c.450 BC) and the Seleucid Antiochus Epiphanus (175 BC). Two books, Ezra and Nehemiah, are said to document the period between Cyrus the Great and Artaxerxes I, but there is nothing afterwards until the First Book of Maccabees, which begins around 175 BC. Thus in the Old Testament we have the following:

550 BC	Cyrus	Covered in Books of Ezra
500 BC	Darius I	and Nehemiah and (partly)
450 BC	Artaxerxes I	In Haggai and Zechariah.
		NOT CHRONICLED IN HEBREW LITERATURE
200 BC		Covered in Books of
150 BC	Antiochus IV (Epiphanus)	Maccabees 1 and 2
100 BC		

It will be immediately obvious that this constitutes a "hiatus" or even a "dark age" comparable to the hiatus observed in Mesopotamian archaeology, where the entire Persian period is missing. This is a dark age in the true sense of the term in that no events, characters or genealogies exist to fill the gap. But this dark age is observed also in the archaeology. Thus a recent conference laments the non-appearance of Persian material in the region: "The topic of our symposium, 'Judah and the Judeans in the Persian Period,' leads us into the realm of mystery. The word mystery evokes a twofold feeling of sadness and of hope: Sadness, because we know so little and would like to know so much more; hope, because there is still much work to be done in this area.... The Hebrew Bible contains very

---

245 There is in fact one striking parallel between the "Cyrus" of the Bible and Alexander as described by Josephus. Just as Cyrus, at the start of the Book of Ezra, links his mastery of the whole world to his honouring of the Jewish God, so Alexander honours the holy name of Yahweh and explains to his followers how the Jewish High Priest had appeared to him in a dream promising him the conquest of the entire Persian Empire (*Jewish Antiquities*, Bk. XI, viii, 4-5).

few passages that address Achaemenid rule over Judah and the Judeans (539-332 BCE). Very few events are illuminated or given any kind of value judgement.... The existing extrabiblical sources contain little or no reference to the Judeans or Judah. There are only a few archaeological and epigraphic finds. Thus, Herbert Donner justifiably refers to the Persian era as the 'dark ages.'"[246] But Rabbinical Jewish tradition recognizes no such gap, and, placing the return from Babylonian Exile in the latter 4th/early 3rd century, makes Ezra and Nehemiah, who organized the rebuilding of the Temple and the city of Jerusalem, immediately precede the Maccabees.

This of course is the correct chronology. The Books of Ezra and Nehemiah, though containing some material actually written by Ezra and Nehemiah themselves, were almost certainly completed after the Maccabean Wars; and it should be noted in this context that a priestly character named Ezra occurs in the Second Book of Maccabees.[247] It is highly likely that this Maccabean age Ezra was the author of the book which bears the same name. The Maccabean Ezra is said to have read from the "holy book," by way of a blessing to the Jewish soldiers. In the same way, the Ezra of the Book of Ezra reads at length to the people from the sacred scriptures.[248] We hold therefore that these texts do not cover the first century of the Persian Empire, but the otherwise totally unattested first two centuries of the Seleucid Empire. Both books report that the money contributed towards the Temple's rebuilding was in gold drachmas (Ezra 2:69 and Nehemiah 7:69-71). This of course is a Greek unit of currency. That the kings mentioned in Ezra and Nehemiah, who give their blessing to the Temple-building project, have Persian-sounding names, should come as no surprise. As rulers and inheritors of the Persian homeland the Seleucids adopted Persian dress, styles, religion, and to some extent even language. The exiled Jews in Babylon would have known these rulers by their oriental names. Probably only after their return to the west did they begin to use the Seleucid monarchs' Greek names.

By placing Ezra and Nehemiah in the third and second centuries BC, we make them contemporaries of the Septuagint authors, whose task it was to translate the Jewish Books of the Law (the Torah) into Greek. In later years, other Jewish scriptures were added to the latter, to form what we now call the Old Testament. But this did not occur before the first century BC (or even later), by which time the true heroes and villains of the Babylonian Exile had become obscure. During the period of the Maccabees, the Jews came into violent conflict with Seleu-

---

246 Oded Lipschits and Manfred Oeming (eds.) "Judah and the Judeans in the Persian Period" Conference Winona Lake, Indiana: (Eisenbrauns, 2006) No. XXI p. ix.
247 2 Maccabees 8:23.
248 2 Ezra 8:1-12.

cid kings, descendants of the men who freed their own ancestors from Babylon. Under such circumstances, we may well understand how the post-Maccabean chroniclers would have been reluctant to recognize their debt to earlier Seleucids. In time it was entirely forgotten. The Persian kings, the real villains of the piece, were gradually transformed into Assyrians — whilst the Macedonians, whose liberalism eventually freed the Jews, were cast forever in the role of villains and tyrants.

There remains, finally, the problem of explaining how Herodotus, just like the Hebrew chroniclers, managed to misplace the Assyrian alter-egos of the Persians in the 8th and 7th centuries. He too, we recall, placed Sennacherib 150 years before Cyrus; and he made Psamtek and the other "Saite" kings, who were contemporaries of Artaxerxes I and Darius II, live 200 years earlier than we say they did. Herodotus, we know, traveled to Egypt in the final decades of the 5th century. The great events associated with Xerxes/Sennacherib and Psamtek would have been fresh in people's minds at the time. How then could the Father of History have made such a monumental mistake?

We need to remember here that the entire sequence of Herodotus' Egyptian history is thoroughly confused. Famously, he made the pyramid-builders Cheops, Chephren and Mycerinus, come just two reigns prior to Shabaka of the Twenty-Fifth Dynasty. Much debate has centered round this problem, but it seems evident that when dealing with foreign rulers, Herodotus' Egyptian informants were themselves confused. In another place I have explained how this probably happened.[249] Briefly, the Fifth Dynasty, which supplanted Cheops' line, was of Elephantine (i.e., Nubian) extraction, and the later kings of the Twenty-Fifth Dynasty copied Fifth Dynasty art, architecture and royal titles assiduously. The Fifth Dynasty was then supplanted by the Sixth (Pepi I and II), whom I have identified as the Great Hyksos (Apepi I and II), as well as the Empire Assyrians of the 8th century BC. So, Herodotus' Egyptian sources knew that a Nubian dynasty came immediately after the Fourth, and also that this Nubian dynasty was conquered by the Assyrians. By Herodotus' time Egypt had again been conquered by another mighty empire from the east. These kings bore Persian names, but also occasionally employed Assyrian titles. Different temples and scribal colleges had their own records. Some of these called the Persian kings by their Persian names; some probably used the Assyrian titles. The earlier Assyrian kings became confused, in some quarters, with these latter-day Neo-Assyrians.

---

249 In my *Pyramid Age* (2nd ed. New York, 2007).

Remember also that Herodotus' informants were native Egyptians who may not necessarily have spoken perfect Greek. Misunderstandings are all too easy when communicating in a second language.

With regard to the "Saite" kings, the Nechos and the Psamteks, whom we now know lived in the Persian period, it would appear that Herodotus' Egyptian sources were telling him of recent history, which he somehow misunderstood as being older history. We should consider also at this point the influence of unfamiliar pronunciations. As Velikovsky said, the titles of certain Nineteenth Dynasty pharaohs, as for example, Seti-Ptah-Maat, could easily have been heard by a Greek as something like Psammetich.

All in all, the wonder is not that Herodotus or his priestly informants got confused at times, but that they actually succeeded in passing on so much accurate information.

In this way, then, it would appear that Herodotus, through no fault of his own, bequeathed to us his somewhat chaotic, though intriguing, history of the Nile Kingdom. Yet it seems evident that Herodotus' mistake was also instrumental in formulating the erroneous biblical chronology that we now possess. For the Jewish scribes who came after the original Septuagint authors, working in Hellenistic Alexandria, were almost certainly influenced by what appeared to be the unassailable authority of Herodotus in placing Sennacherib (whom they knew about from their own traditions) precisely where Herodotus placed him, a century and a half before Cyrus.

Chapter 7. Questions and Answers

A fundamental principle of the present work is that the Medes and Persians do not appear in the archaeological record in Mesopotamia. It is true, of course, that the Persians have left plentiful evidence of their existence in Persia itself. The great cities of Persepolis, Susa and Ecbatana are replete with evidence of the Achaemenid Empire. Yet outside the Persian heartland, the evidence of the Achaemenids is patchy to say the least. Indeed it is almost non-existent. Archaeology cannot point to a single notable monument of Achaemenid date outside the Iranian plateau.

In the case of the Medes, the situation is even worse. Not only are the Medes an unknown quantity in the lands they conquered, namely Assyria and parts of Anatolia, but they left virtually no trace of their existence even in their own heartland, in the Iranian highlands. So complete is this Median disappearing act that some scholars have come to doubt the very existence of any such entity as a Mede Empire. A conference in Padua in 2001, called to discuss the subject of Mede archaeology, came to the conclusion that the Mede Imperium was virtually non-existent archaeologically, at least in the Late Iron Age strata in which it was sought. Papers included M. Roaf, "The Median Dark Age"; R. Schmitt, "Die Sprache der Meder — eine grosse Unbekannte"; and John Curtis, "The Assyrian heartland in the period 612-539 BC." All the scholars contributing expressed exasperation at the difficulties in trying to "pin down" the historical Medes. Roaf, for example, stated: "This survey of the evidence, both textual and archaeological for the Medes between 612 and 550 BC, has revealed almost nothing. Media in the first half of the sixth century is a dark age."[250] In a similar vein John Curtis laments that, "It has to be admitted at the outset that there is not the slightest archaeological indication of a Median presence in Assyria after 612 BC."[251]

Now the non-existence of a recognizably Mede stratum in Assyria is normally explained by the proposition that Assyria was a wasteland during the Mede epoch — that the Mede conquerors had not only burned the cities of Assyria, but massacred and denuded the population of the entire country. This is a claim which, though universally held to be true, is flatly contradicted by the evidence, some of which shall be examined presently.

But it is not only the Medes who make no appearance in Assyria. The Persians do likewise. There is not a single major structure in the whole of Assyria that can unequivocally be identified as Persian; and indeed even small artifacts, such as cuneiform tablets and cylinder seals, are extremely uncommon, if not non-existent. "Unfortunately there are no cuneiform tablets from the Assyrian heartland that are securely dated to the Achaemenid period.... We are not confident in our ability to identify Achaemenid pottery.... At the same time, there is no evidence for major urban centers, with the possible exception of Erbil, and it is doubtful whether they existed."[252]

Yet this presents scholars with a major problem. The Greek writer Herodotus described Assyria as among the wealthiest regions of the Persian Empire, and claimed that the people of Assyria contributed an enormous proportion of the tribute received annually by the Great King. "In power the land of Assyria counts as one third of all Asia. Rule over this country — which rule is called by the Persians a satrapy — is of all the satrapies by far the greatest."[253] Not bad for an uninhabited wasteland! As an explanation, scholars generally hold that by "Assyria" Herodotus meant the whole of Mesopotamia, and indeed there is evidence to suggest that he did mean the whole land of the Two Rivers. Nevertheless, as we shall see, Herodotus did regard northern Mesopotamia, i.e., the historic land of Assyria, as an important and wealthy part of the Achaemenid state.

Admitting for one minute however that by "Assyria" Herodotus was really referring to Babylonia, this does not solve the problem for conventional scholars. For Babylonia too is virtually devoid of Persian archaeology. Thus in *The Cam-*

250 "Continuity in Empire (?) Assyria, Media, Persia: Proceedings of the International Meeting in Padua," (26th — 28th April, 2001) *History of the Ancient Near East. Monographs* V. Padova. S. a. r. g. o. n. , (2003) Giovanni Lanfranchi, Michael Roaf, Robert Rollinger (eds) R. Roaf, "The Median Dark Age" p. 12.

251 Ibid. John Curtis, "The Assyrian heartland in the period 612-539 BC" p. 165.

252 John Curtis, "The Achaemenid Period in Northern Iraq," (November, 2003) www. aina. org/ articles/curtis. pdf.

253 Herodotus, i, 192.

bridge Ancient History, A Kuhrt, one of the most experienced archaeologists in the field, remarks that, "Archaeological material from Babylonia for the [Persian] period as a whole and for its earlier phase in particular is unfortunately not extensive," whilst "the material culture of the Babylonians under the Achaemenids is a difficult and unrewarding subject."[254] Yet the Persian disappearing act in Babylonia is a complete conundrum, for there is no justification whatsoever in seeing it as a wasteland during the age in question. On the contrary, the ancient writers insisted, at great length and on numerous occasions, that Babylon was a major center, perhaps the major center, of the Achaemenid monarchy, during the entire period of the Empire. Thus in the words of A.T. Olmstead, "For contemporary Greeks, the three residences of the Achaemenid monarch were Babylon, Ecbatana, and Susa.... For the Jews, likewise, the Persian capitals were Babylon, Ecbatana the fortress, and Shushan the palace."[255]

We shall return to this question at a later stage. Not only was Mesopotamia and Babylon a major economic and administrative region of the Persians, there is evidence to show that it became, in a very real sense, the true capital of the empire, replacing and supplanting Pasargadae and Ecbatana. Yet the Achaemenids left, apparently, no recognizable trace of their stay in the region!

Before looking at this evidence however we need to say something more about the land of Assyria.

Was Assyria a Wasteland after the Mede Conquest?

The complete absence of Mede and Persian remains in Assyria is normally explained by the hypothesis that the destruction wrought by the Medes was so complete that in the aftermath the entire region became a virtual wasteland. Yet there is much evidence to show that this is quite untrue, and that the region continued to be a vastly productive and wealthy territory.

Much of the relevant material was presented at The Assyrian National Convention in Los Angeles, September 4, 1999, and published in the *Journal of Assyrian Academic Studies,* Vol. XIII, No.2, 1999. The question is put thus:

> What happened to the Assyrians after the fall of Assyria? This is a question that is not easy to answer for two reasons. Firstly, the issue has hardly been touched by Assyriologists. Most of them seem to tacitly agree with the idea of a more or less total wipe-out, as suggested by Sidney Smith in 1925: "The disappearance of the Assyrian people will always remain a unique and striking phenomenon in ancient history. Other, similar kingdoms and empires have indeed passed away but the people have lived on... No other land seems to have been sacked and pillaged so completely as was Assyria."

254 A. Kuhrt, "The Persian Empire: Babylonia from Cyrus to Xerxes" in *CAH* Vol. 4 (2nd ed.) p. 119.
255 A. T. Olmstead, *History of the Persian Empire* (Chicago, 1948) p. 162.

Yet the idea of a genocide or vast depopulation is firmly rejected. On the contrary, there is much evidence that no such thing happened, and that there was both economic and cultural continuity that lasted into the hellenistic period. I will quote the published text here at length, for it is of much interest:

> Yet it is clear that no such thing as a wholesale massacre of all Assyrians ever happened.... Assyria was a vast and densely populated country, and outside the few destroyed urban centers life went on as usual. This is proved by a recently discovered post-imperial archive from the Assyrian provincial capital Dur-Katlimmu, on the Chabur river, which contains business documents drawn up in Assyrian cuneiform more than a decade after the fall of Nineveh. Apart from the fact that these documents are dated by the regal years of a Babylonian king, Nebuchadnezzar II, nothing in their formulation or external appearance would suggest that they were not written under the Assyrian Empire. Another small archive discovered in Assur, written in a previously unknown, presumably Mannean variety of cuneiform, proves that Assyrian goldsmiths still worked in the city in post-empire times, though now under Median command.
>
> Moreover, over a hundred Assyrians with distinctively Assyrian names have recently been identified in economic documents from many Babylonian sites dated between 625 and 404 BC, and many more Assyrians undoubtedly remain to be identified in such documents. We do not know whether these people were deportees or immigrants from Assyria; their families may have settled in Babylonia already under the Assyrian rule. In any case, they unequivocally prove the survival of many Assyrians after the empire and the continuity of Assyrian identity, religion and culture in post-empire times. Many of these names contain the divine name Ashur, and some of the individuals concerned occupied quite high positions: one Pan-Ashur-lumur was the secretary of the crown prince Cambyses under Cyrus II in 530 BC.
>
> Distinctively Assyrian names are also found in later Aramaic and Greek texts from Assur, Hatra, Dura-Europus and Palmyra, and continue to be attested until the beginning of the Sasanian period. These names are recognizable from the Assyrian divine names invoked in them; but whereas earlier the other name elements were predominantly Akkadian, they now are exclusively Aramaic. This coupled with the Aramaic script and language of the texts shows that the Assyrians of these later times no longer spoke Akkadian as their mother tongue. In all other respects, however, they continued the traditions of the imperial period. The gods Ashur, Sherua, Istar, Nanaya, Bel, Nabu and Nergal continued to be worshiped in Assur at least until the early third century AD; the local cultic calendar was that of the imperial period; the temple of Ashur was restored in the second century AD; and the stelae of the local rulers resemble those of Assyrian kings in the imperial period. It is also worth pointing out that many of the Aramaic names occurring in the post-empire inscriptions and graffiti from Assur are already attested in imperial texts from the same site that are 800 years older.
>
> Assur was by no means the only city where Assyrian religion and cults survived the fall of the empire. The temple of Sin, the great moon god of Harran, was restored by the Babylonian King Nabonidus in the mid-sixth century BC, and the Persian King Cyrus claims to have returned Ishtar of

Nineveh to her temple in Nineveh. Classical sources attest to the continuity of Assyrian cults in other Syrian cities until late antiquity; in Harran, the cults of Sin, Nikkal, Bel, Nabu, Tammuz and other Assyrian gods persisted until the 10th century AD and are still referred to in Islamic sources. Typically Assyrian priests with their distinctive long conical hats and tunics are depicted on several Graeco-Roman monuments from Northern Syria and East Anatolia.

Little is known of the political status of Assyria in the decades following its fall, but it seems that the western part of the Empire as far as the Tigris fell into the hands of the Babylonians, while the eastern Transtigridian areas, including the Assyrian heartland north of Assur, came under Median rule. Under the Achaemenid Empire, the western areas annexed to Babylonia formed a satrapy called Athura (a loanword from Imperial Aramaic Athur, "Assyria"), while the Assyrian heartland remained incorporated in the satrapy of Mada (Old Persian for "Media"). Both satrapies paid yearly tribute and contributed men for the military campaigns and building projects of the Persian kings. Assyrian soldiers participated in the expedition of Xerxes against Greece (480 BC) according to Herodotus, and Assyrians from both Athura and Mada participated in the construction of the palace of Darius at Susa (500-490 BC).

Interestingly, it was the "Median" Assyrians who executed the gold works and glazing of this palace, whereas the Assyrians from the satrapy of Athura provided the timber for the palace from Mt. Lebanon. In the Babylonian version of the Persian inscription, the name Athura is at this point rendered Eber nari, "land beyond the river (Euphrates)." This shows that the Western, originally Aramean, half of the Assyrian Empire was already at this time firmly identified with Assyria proper, an important issue to which we shall return later on.

We thus see that by Achaemenid times, Assyria, though split in two, had re-emerged as a political entity of considerable military and economic strength. In 520 BC, both Athura and Mada joined the revolt against Darius, trying to regain their independence. This revolt was a failure, but in a sense the Assyrian Empire had already been re-established long ago. Actually, in the final analysis, it had never been destroyed at all but had just changed ownership — first to Babylonian and Median dynasties, and then to a Persian one.

Echoing very closely the position argued in the present work, namely that the Mede and later Persian conquerors of the Assyrian Empire actually posed as Assyrian kings and tool upon themselves the titles and privileges of Assyrian monarchs, the authors of the report note:

> Contemporaries and later Greek historians did not make a big distinction between the Assyrian Empire and its successors: in their eyes, the "monarchy" or "universal hegemony" first held by the Assyrians had simply passed to or been usurped by other nations. For example, Ctesias of Cnidus writes: "It was under [Sardanapallos] that the empire (*hegemonia*) of the Assyrians fell to the Medes, after it had lasted more than thirteen hundred years."
>
> The Babylonian King Nabonidus, who reigned sixty years after the fall of Nineveh and actually originated from an Assyrian city, Harran, refers to Ashurbanipal and Esarhaddon as his "royal forefathers." His predecessor Nebuchadnezzar and the Persian kings Cyrus and Artaxerxes are corre-

spondingly referred to as "Kings of Assyria" in Greek historical tradition and in the Bible. Strabo, writing at the time of the birth of Christ, tells us that "the customs of the Persians are like those of the Assyrians," and calls Babylon a "metropolis of Assyria" (which it, of course, in fact was too, having been completely destroyed and rebuilt by the Assyrians in the early seventh century BC).

The Babylonian, Median and Persian empires should thus be seen (as they were seen in antiquity) as successive versions of the same multinational power structure, each resulting from an internal power struggle within this structure. In other words, the Empire was each time reborn under a new leadership, with political power shifting from one nation to another.

Of course, the Empire changed with each change of leadership. On the whole, however, the changes were relatively slight, one could almost say cosmetic only. The language of the ruling elite changed, of course, first from Assyrian to Babylonian, Median, and Persian, and finally to Greek. In its dress the elite likewise followed its national customs, and it naturally venerated its own gods, from whom its power derived. Thus Ashur was replaced as imperial god first by the Babylonian Marduk, and then by the Iranian Ahura Mazda, Greek Zeus, etc.

Assyrian culture and religion was retained and copied by the Medes and Persians — and strikingly, Ashur was completely identified with Ahura Mazda.

On the whole, however, the old structures of the Empire prevailed or in the long run gained the upper hand. Cuneiform writing (now in its Babylonian, Elamite and Old Persian forms) continued to be used for monumental inscriptions. Aramaic retained the status of imperial *lingua franca* which it had attained under the Assyrian Empire. The gods of the new elites gradually became assimilated to Assyrian gods. The supreme god of the Persians, Ahura Mazda, was now represented by the winged disk of Ashur; the Iranian goddess Anahita acquired features of the goddess Ishtar and finally became to all practical purposes fully assimilated to her. The same happened to the god Mithra, who was transformed into the Iranian equivalent of the Assyrian savior gods Nabu and Ninurta.

The list could be made much longer. The Assyrian calendar and month names remained in use in the whole Near East, as they still do today. So did other imperial standards and measures, the taxation and conscription system, royal ideology in general, the symbolism of imperial art, organization of the court, court ceremony, diplomatic practices, and so on. The continuity of Assyrian imperial culture was certainly aided by the fact that the Babylonians and Medes had for centuries been vassals of Assyria, while the Persians, as former vassals of the Elamites and the Medes, had long been subjected to Assyrian cultural influence. Both conquerors of Nineveh, the Babylonian Nabopolassar and Median Kyaxares, had previously served as Assyrian governors in their respective countries.

Thus, the Assyrian Empire continued to live on despite the fact that the Assyrians themselves were no longer in control of it. However, they still contributed to its government and expansion. An analysis of the inscriptions of Nabonidus shows that this Babylonian king employed scribes who had been trained in Assyria and were familiar with its literary traditions; later on, the same scribes served the Persian king, Cyrus. The role of Assyrian artists in the construction of Susa and Persepolis has already been referred to. The governorship of the Persian satrapy Athura seems to have been often in the hands of Assyrians. The Book of Ezra (c. 450 BC) refers to a governor with the name Sanballat (Assyrian Sin-ballit), and the Greek historian Xenophon writing in 400 BC mentions a governor with the Aramaic name Abracomas.

Even the Assyrian language, it seems, was used by the Persians in normal diplomatic correspondence.

The Greek historian Thucydides reports that during the Peloponnesian wars (c. 410 BC), the Athenians intercepted a Persian named Artaphernes, who was carrying a message from the Great King to Sparta. The man was taken prisoner, brought to Athens, and the letters he was carrying were translated "from the Assyrian language. " The language in question of course was Aramaic, which, as already noted, continued as the lingua franca in the Achaemenid Empire, as it had done in Assyria.

So deeply-ingrained was Assyrian culture that it survived well beyond the Persian period, into the time of the Seleucids and beyond. By this time, however, the country and its culture came to be known as Syrian, a word which, nevertheless, as the authors of the report emphasise, is identical to Assyrian.

We thus see that two hundred years after its fall, the Empire created by the Assyrians and its language were still prominently associated with Assyria, and this with a markedly Aramaic tint. This state of affairs continued under the Macedonian rulers of the Seleucid Empire. The area of the Seleucid kingdom initially largely covered that of the Assyrian Empire, and its capital soon moved from Babylonia to Syria/Assyria. Despite the heavily Greek orientation of the ruling elite and the imposition of Greek as the official language, the Seleucid kings were commonly referred to in Greek sources as "kings of Syria," a designation that still retained a strong association with Assyria.

The Greek word Syria and the adjectives Syrios and Syros derived from it are originally simple phonetic variants of Assyria and Assyrios, with aphaeresis of the unstressed first syllable. The dropping of the first syllable is already attested in Imperial Aramaic spellings of Ashur, and the variation in Greek is thus likely to derive from corresponding variation in Aramaic. In Greek texts, both variants are usually freely interchangeable and can refer to both the Persian province Athura and the Assyrian Empire. For example, Strabo writes that "the city of Ninus was wiped out immediately after the overthrow of the Syrians," while his older contemporary Diodorus, quoting Herodotus, writes that "after the Assyrians had ruled Asia for five hundred years they were conquered by the Medes." Only in Roman times, do the two forms start to acquire the distinct meanings that Assyria and Syria have today.

Syria and Assyria are still interchangeable and refer to the Assyrian Empire in the Geography of Strabo, who however makes a distinction between Assyrians at large and the Assyrian homeland on the Tigris, to which he refers to as Aturia/Assyria:

The country of the Assyrians borders on Persis and Susiana. This name is given to Babylonia and to much of the country all around, which latter, in part, is also called Aturia, in which are Ninus [...], Nisibis, as far as the Zeugma of the Euphrates, as also much of the country on the far side of the Euphrates ... and those people who in a special sense of the term are called by the men of today Syrians, who extend as far as the Cilicians and the

Phoenicians and the sea that is opposite the Aegyptian Sea and the Gulf of Issus. It seems that the name of the Syrians extended not only from Babylonia to the gulf of Issus, but also in ancient times from this gulf to the Euxine.... When those who have written histories of the Syrian empire say that the Medes were overthrown by the Persians and the Syrians by the Medes, they mean by the Syrians no other people than those who built the royal palaces in Babylon and Ninus; and, of these Syrians, Ninus was the man who founded Ninus in Aturia, and his wife, Semiramis, was the woman who succeeded her husband and founded Babylon. These two gained the mastery of Asia... But later the empire passed over to the Medes.

Two generations later, Pliny the Elder (c. AD 70), while utilizing the work of Strabo, already prefers the name Assyria for the Empire. His contemporary Flavius Josephus likewise consistently refers to the Empire as Assyria, and uses Syria in referring to the Seleucid Empire and the Roman province of Syria. This terminology anticipates the situation after the reign of Trajan, who after his campaign against the Parthians (AD 116) created a province called Assyria in the east, probably annexing the semi-independent state of Adiabene which the Assyrians had succeeded in establishing in their ancient homeland.

The new distinction made between Syria (in the west) and Assyria (in the east) recalls the split of the Assyrian Empire into the Achaemenid satrapies Athura and Mada and can be explained as follows.

In the Strabo passage just cited, the adjective Syros is used both in a historical sense referring to inhabitants of the Assyrian Empire and as an ethno-linguistic designation referring to speakers of Aramaic who identified themselves as Assyrians. The area called "Syro-Media" was the Assyrianized part of Media where Aramaic was commonly spoken instead of Iranian languages. This entire Aramaic-speaking area, that is Assyria/Syria, had long been controlled by the Seleucid Empire. At the time when the Seleucid state was annexed to the Roman Empire, 64 BC, its area had however shrunken to encompass only the Transeuphratian part of Assyria/Syria, which now became the Roman province of Syria. As the remnant of the Seleucid Empire, this area still was strongly identified with Assyria; there was no need to distinguish it from ancient Assyria. Only later, when the Roman Empire expanded further eastward, there arose a need for further distinctions. The name Syria now became established for the Roman province, while Assyria was reserved for the Transtigridian Aturia/Adiabene and by and by for ancient Assyria as well. It is likely that this distinction reflects linguistic realities, the Aramaic words for Assyria having lost the initial syllable in the west but retained it in the eastern dialects.

To sum up the long discussion, whatever their later meanings, in Greek and Latin usage, Syria and Assyria originally both referred to the Assyrian Empire, while speakers of Aramaic were identified as Assyrians and the script they used as Assyrian script. How, when and why did this intrinsic association of Assyria and Assyrians with Arameans and Aramaic come about?

The Empire extended beyond the Euphrates already in the 12th century BC and from that point on Arameans constituted the majority of its population. In the 9th century BC, Assyrian kings initiated an active policy of assimilation and integration, the goal of which was to put a definite end to the endless revolts that had vexed the Empire in the past. The results of this new policy were soon to be seen. Rebel countries were now annexed to the Empire as new provinces, whereby hundreds of thousands of people were deported to other parts of the Empire and the annexed country was totally reorganized in Assyrian fashion. This involved imposition of a uniform taxation and conscription system, uniform standards, weights and measures, the conversion of the local royal city into an Assyrian administrative center, and, above all, the imposition of a single universal language and script, Aramaic.

By the end of the 8th century the provincial system covered the entire Levant from Palestine to central Iran, and it was further expanded in the seventh century. At this time Aramaic was already spoken all over the Empire, and Assyrian imperial culture had been dominant everywhere for centuries.

All these features survived the fall of the Assyrian Empire and helped give its successors their specifically Assyrian stamp, despite the alien customs and cultural elements introduced by the new overlords. It can even be surmised that the foreign habits of the new rulers may rather have strengthened the Assyrian identity of the masses. This will have been the case especially in the areas longest attached to Assyria, that is, the later Achaemenid/Roman province of Athura/Syria and, of course, the Assyrian heartland itself.

Several writers and philosophers of late antiquity born in Roman Syria identify themselves as Assyrians in their writings, for example the second-century bellestrist Lucian of Samosata, who introduces himself as "an Assyrian ... still barbarous in speech and almost wearing a jacket in the Assyrian style." Another second-century writer, a certain Iamblichus who wrote a novel set in Babylonia, "was a Syrian by race on both his father's and mother's side, a Syrian not in the sense of the Greeks who have settled in Syria, but of the native ones, familiar with the Syrian language and living by their customs." The famous namesake of this writer, the Neoplatonian philosopher Iamblichus, also originated from Syria. The name Iamblichus is a Greek version of the Aramaic name Ia-milik, which is already attested in Assyrian imperial sources.

All these self-professed Assyrians were well-versed in Greek culture but at the same time perfectly aware of the greater antiquity and value of their own cultural heritage. The second-century Church Father Tatian, in his Oratio adversus Graecos, describes himself as "he who philosophizes in the manner of barbarians, born in the land of the Assyrioi, first educated on your principles, secondly in what I now profess," and then goes on to reject Greek culture as not worth having.

Since Late Antiquity, Christianity in its Syriac elaboration has constituted an essential part of Assyrian identity. As I have tried to show elsewhere, conversion to Christianity was easy for the Assyrians, for many of the teachings of the early Church were consonant with the tenets of Assyrian imperial religion. In fact, it can be argued that many features and dogmas of early Christianity were based on practices and ideas already central to Assyrian imperial ideology and religion. Such features include the central role of asceticism in Syriac Christianity, the cult of the Mother of the god, the Holy Virgin, and belief in God the Father, his Son and the Holy Spirit, formalized in the doctrine of the Trinity of God.

Was Babylonia a Wasteland after the Persian Conquest?

Just as Assyria revealed no recognizable trace of its Mede conquerors, so Babylonia, it seems, has left precious little trace of its Persian conquerors. Now the absence of the Medes in Assyria, we have seen, is explained by the belief that the conquerors had reduced the territory to a wasteland. But the same could certainly not be said of Babylonia after the rise of the Persians; for it was here, as we have seen, the ancient authors placed the very epicenter of Persian economic and administrative power.

During the course of a debate that was to draw out over a period of three years I put this point to Professor Trevor Palmer of Stoke University in England. Initially, he agreed that Babylonia had been a major center during the Achaemenid period, but challenged my (and Gunnar Heinsohn's) assertion that the region was almost devoid of Persian archaeology. On the contrary, he said, Persian material was "abundant" in Babylonia.[256] One source provided for this assertion was Robert Koldewey's *Excavations at Babylon*, a record of the archaeological work carried out at the site in the early years of the 20th century. Yet nowhere in the text does Koldewey describe the Persian remains as "abundant," or anything remotely approximating to it. On the contrary, all the great archaeologist could find was the remains of a small aristocratic Persian house, which he described as a "kiosk," along with a typically Persian *apadana* (pillared hall), plus a couple of seals and some inscribed tablets — this in a city which for over two centuries was right at the center of the Persian Empire. We recall that Herodo-

---

256 Trevor Palmer, "A Test of Beards," *Society for Iinterdisciplinary Studies Review and Workshop Combined* No. 1 (2004).

tus described Assyria (i.e., Mesopotamia) as "by far the richest of all the Persian provinces" with its tribute alone counting for a third of everything received from the Great King's Asiatic satrapies. The whole region should be overflowing with monumental Persian architecture. Yet all that can be found in the region's capital is a small house!

Repeating a claim made first by Lester Mitchum of New Zealand in 1987 that Koldewey had discovered a clearly-defined Persian stratum above that of the Neo-Babylonians, Palmer held that this provided a definitive rebuttal of my entire thesis.

What Koldewey had actually found is related by him on pages 239 and 240 of *Excavations*, where he discusses the stratigraphy of the Merkes area of the city, the best-defined archaeological stratification at the site. Here the ancient remains rose 10 meters above the level of the surrounding landscape (level 0). The top two to three meters contained the "scanty ruins of the Parthian period."[257] Immediately below this, at seven meters above zero (and three below the surface) Koldewey found "Greek sherds and tablets with dates of the Persian period...."[258] This then is the "Persian" stratum referred to by Mitchum and Palmer. Immediately beneath this, at five-and-a-half meters above zero, lay Neo-Babylonian bricks with the stamps of Nabonidus and Nebuchadrezzar.[259]

The actual strata appeared thus:

Meters above zero	Cultural Strata
10	Parthians
7	"Persians" — but exclusively Greek pottery and writings
5.5	Neo-Babylonians
2.5	Kassites
-1	Old Babylonians

Before saying anything else, we should first of all note that the so-called Persian stratum seemed to produce only Greek pottery and tablets. If it were a Persian stratum, why no Persian pottery or inscriptions? Secondly, it is notable that this "Persian" layer, with its Greek material, lies immediately beneath the Parthian layer. This means that, should we regard the stratum as Persian, then the entire Greek or Hellenistic stratum, lasting two centuries (from 331 to 139 BC) is missing.

---

257 R. Koldewey, *The Excavations at Babylon* (London, 1914) p. 239.
258 Ibid. p. 240.
259 Ibid.

From all this, it is clear that the stratum immediately following the Neo-Babylonian one, at five-and-a-half to seven meters above zero, the stratum which could produce only Greek pottery and inscriptions, was the otherwise missing Hellenistic layer. Thus Babylon, like the rest of Mesopotamia, is completely devoid of a recognizably Persian stratum. Koldewey evidently decided that the post Neo-Babylonian layer must, in spite of its Greek pottery and inscriptions, be Persian, for the simple reason that that is what conventional historical wisdom demanded. If this layer were not Persian, then no Persian layer existed at the city — in complete defiance of the ancient historians who insisted that Babylon was an important center at the time. Thus Koldewey was willing to ignore what he actually found — Greek material — in order to make his discoveries agree with a preconceived chronology.

Another reference provided by Palmer was G. Roux's *Ancient Iraq* (Penguin, 3rd ed., 1992). In order to be absolutely fair I got hold of this book and looked up the pages cited. Once again, however, the relevant text made no mention of the word "abundant," and once again the source says exactly the opposite of what Palmer claimed. Thus on pages 409-410 Roux mentions an "arsenal" as well as the small house (described as a "palace" by Roux) and the *apadana* referred to by Koldewey, all of which he assigns to Darius I. He makes no mention of any other Persian remains in the city. On the contrary, he tells us that "The entire period between the accession of Xerxes (485 BC) and the conquest of Alexander (331 BC) *is exceedingly poor in architectural remains and building inscriptions*" (my italics). He continues, "In southern Iraq business documents found *in situ* prove that Babylon, Barsippa, Kish, Nippur, Uruk and Ur ... were alive, some of them even fairly prosperous, *but none of their monuments appears to have been rebuilt or repaired* [in the Persian period]" (p. 410) (my italics).

Having demonstrated beyond reasonable doubt that the Persian material in Babylonia was as scarce as I had claimed, Professor Palmer now changed tack completely, and in a subsequent article argued that we should not, after all, expect to find much of the Persians in Babylonia, because it too, just like Assyria, was an exploited wasteland during the Achaemenid period.[260]

Before going on, it will be obvious to the reader that such a remarkable *volte face* is the infallible sign of a faltering argument.

But how important was Babylon during the Persian period? We have seen that Herodotus makes it the very center of Achaemenid power. Other ancient writers tell a similar story, and, as we saw earlier, there is good evidence to sug-

---

260 Trevor Palmer, *Chronology and Catastrophism Workshop*, 2005 No. 1 *SIS* (February, 2005) Letter, "With Reference to Trevor Palmer's 'Test of Beards' and Clark Whelton's Response."

gest that towards the second half of the Achaemenid period the empire actually became Babylonian, even in blood. This is indeed asserted very explicitly in all of the literature, and before the age of archaeology, it was assumed that the Persian kings, from the time of Darius II onwards, had more or less moved the capital to Babylon. We have already seen how this latter king was the son of Artaxerxes I by the Babylonian concubine Cosmartidene, in virtue of which he was popularly named Nothus, "the Bastard." We have noted too that Darius II's wife, Parysatis, who was also his half-sister, was likewise the daughter of a Babylonian concubine. This and other factors have prompted historians to view the accession of Darius II as marking the end of the pure Achaemenid line, with a veritable "Babylonian Period" following. (See e.g. Brian Dicks, *The Ancient Persians: How they Lived and Worked* (1979) p. 131).

Darius II died at Babylon (Xenophon, *Anabasis* i, 1, 2) and there is a strong suggestion that he lived most of his life there. His son and successor Artaxerxes II was perhaps even more closely associated with the city. From Xenophon we know that he was based at Babylon during the war against Cyrus the Younger, and from him as well as other Greek authors is seems fairly clear that he spent most of his life there. His son and successor Artaxerxes III was also heavily linked to the city, a fact confirmed both by the classical authors and by cuneiform texts which speak of prisoners captured in foreign wars being sent to the city. (See e.g. S. Smith, *Babylonian Historical Texts* (1924) pp.148 ff.).

Thus the historical evidence would lead us to expect a rich Persian stratum in Babylonia and throughout Mesopotamia. Instead, we have virtually nothing. No recognizable Persian stratum at all, anywhere in the region. Thus the logic of the archaeology, as it is commonly interpreted, would have us believe that the land of the Two Rivers was heavily populated during the Neo-Assyrian and Neo-Babylonian periods, but completely abandoned during the Persian Period, only to be again heavily peopled (in exactly the same settlements) during the Hellenistic period. Worse still, the folk who re-peopled Mesopotamia during the Hellenistic period, after two centuries of abandonment, used exactly the same material culture as the inhabitants who had earlier occupied the land during the Neo-Assyrian and Neo-Babylonian period. This goes for both Assyria and Babylonia.[261]

The improbability, not to say utter absurdity, of such a scenario, hardly needs to be stressed. Yet this is just the view that that orthodox interpretation of existing strata demands.

---

261 For the continuity of material culture in Assyria from Neo-Assyrian times through to the Seleucid epoch see as above The Assyrian National Convention in Los Angeles, (September 4, 1999) *Journal of Assyrian Academic Studies*, Vol. XIII, No. 2, 1999.

The Judgment of Archaeologists

What do the professional archaeologists make of this remarkable Persian disappearing act? Professor Gunnar Heinsohn and I have made three basic assertions about the Achaemenid Empire. These are:

- There is very little archaeological evidence for the Empire (outside Persia proper).

- The history of the Empire is derived almost entirely from ancient literary sources: archaeology has added little or nothing to the picture, and the two sources — literary and archaeological — are in basic disagreement.

- We must seek the elusive Persians in the satrapies under the guise of local rulers and potentates, using the art, culture and iconography of those regions.

Here's what Heleen Sancisi-Weerdenburg, one of the most senior Iranologists of our times, has to say on these issues:

> When one decides to look from the bottom [i.e., from an archaeological perspective] it is often hard to see the empire. In other words, it is very difficult to perceive the impact, let alone the administrative structure of, the Achaemenid empire....
>
> This situation [i.e., that there was a monolithic empire as revealed by literature but an amalgam of culturally distinct and politically semi-independent areas as revealed by archaeology] is clearly unsatisfactory. Unless we are prepared to settle for two divergent views of the empire, an "archaeological" one and a "historical" one, an attempt must be made to integrate the divergent evidence into a synthesis....
>
> In looking for traces of the Persian empire, the search has so far been mostly confined to phenomena that betray an Iranian influence.... Frankly the results of such a search have been disappointing.
>
> [Nevertheless,] Iranian "traces" are ... not the only kind of evidence which can lead us to detect the impact of the Persian empire. [We must search for] elements from the various venerable traditions that preceded the rise of Persia.

She specifically mentioned the artistic and religious iconography of Mesopotamia as being employed by the Persians.

> "Cyrus chose elements from the pictographic repertoire of the Mesopotamian tradition and used both the languages and the cultural codes of the preceding tradition in quite a direct way.... Most attempts at tracing the existence of such a structure [i.e., Achaemenid Empire] archaeologically have failed since what has usually been looked for were phenomena which could be identified as either Persian or Achaemenid or even Iranian. Since, however, much of the effective means of control must have passed

through native individuals and offices, we should clearly be looking for something else. [262]

Sancisi-Weerdenburg is saying almost exactly word for word what Professor Heinsohn and I have been saying for years. In short, the absence of recognizably Persian material in Mesopotamia can only be explained by the proposition that the Persians do appear, but under the guise of local Mesopotamian princes and potentates — in short, under the guise of Neo-Assyrian and Neo-Babylonian monarchs.

Alter-egos and Reign-lengths

A basic thesis of the present work is that the Mede and Persian emperors appear, in Mesopotamia, as Mesopotamian kings, complete with Mesopotamian names. They are even portrayed in Mesopotamian dress and worshipping Mesopotamian deities. In recent years there has been much criticism over the idea that ancient monarchs could have had alter-egos at all. Much of this criticism, I feel, stemmed originally from the disillusionment of the British "Velikovskians" when they discovered that (as they saw it) the great man's chronology — as outlined in the *Ages in Chaos* series — was untenable. In the present work and elsewhere I have argued that the jettisoning of the whole of *Ages in Chaos* was a grievous mistake, a mistake which has hitherto blocked the possibility of completing the revision of ancient history in a satisfactory way. Ancient kings *were* known by more than one name, and this is a phenomenon accepted even by orthodoxy. It would, for example, be a brave Egyptologist who would contend that Nimmuria and Naphuria of the Amarna Letters were not identical to Amenhotep III and Akhnaton (which incidentally gives the latter three well-used names, for he was originally known as Amenhotep [IV]). Similarly, biblical scholars have no problem at all in seeing Uzziah of Judah as an alter-ego of Azariah, whilst the king now universally known as Solomon was only accorded that title after his death. Again, Tiglath-Pileser III is widely believed to be identical to Pul, ruler of Babylon, whilst Ashurbanipal is generally believed to have taken on the name Kandalanu as ruler of the same city.

But even as rulers of Assyria itself, the Neo-Assyrians had more than one title. Thus Esarhaddon (Ashur-ahhe-iddin) appears also to have borne the name Ashur-etil-ilani-mukin-apil.

Conventional history also knows the Persian kings themselves by multiple titles. These, in some cases, were mere nicknames, such as for example Artaxerx-

---

262 All quotes from Dr Heleen Sancisi-Weerdenburg and H. Kuhrt (eds.) "The quest for an elusive empire" *Achaemenid History IV: Centre and Periphery* (Leiden, 1990).

es I "Longimanus" (or "Macrocheir" to the Greeks), or Artaxerxes II "Mnemon." Some, however, were not nicknames; thus Darius I is and was commonly referred to as Hystaspes, his original title. And virtually all of the Persian kings changed their names, or adopted a new name, upon ascending the throne. Yet they continued, at times, to also employ their old titles.

It would seem from this, then, that the only people who deny the use of royal alter-egos are revisionist historians who want to decry the chronologies of other revisionist historians.

Let me repeat also a point I made previously on more than one occasion. Ancient kings bore names which reflected their exalted status as temporal representatives of the gods. In a multi-ethnic polity such as the Persian it is unlikely that the Great Kings would have been known by their Iranian names in the non-Persian regions. These names, as for example Xerxes (Khshayarsha), were religiously meaningless and quite possibly unpronounceable to the intensely religious inhabitants of Mesopotamia. In such circumstances, it is entirely to be expected that the Semitic-speakers of Mesopotamia would have had their own religiously significant name for this ruler.

Another question raised by the reconstruction proposed in the present pages is that of reign-lengths. There is no question, as Palmer and others have said, that the reign-lengths of the Achaemenids as we have them differ greatly — as a general rule — from those of the Neo-Assyrians and Neo-Babylonians. However, as I emphasized repeatedly, reign-lengths are a veritable minefield when it comes to reconstructing ancient history. The kings of antiquity used a whole variety of methods of calculating their years on the throne, i.e., beginning at the start or end or half-way through a co-regency, beginning at their appointment as kings or satraps of an individual city or province, beginning at birth, or beginning at the beginning of the reign of the previous monarch (if he were deemed illegitimate). Such being the case, the evidence of reign-lengths should not be regarded as carrying great weight (in spite of the opinion of my critics). Carl Olof Jonsson, who has made an intensive study of the chronology of the biblical kings, has admitted that it is impossible to make the reigns of the kings of Judah and Israel agree with each other, and that co-regencies etc — not mentioned in the biblical texts — must be postulated.

It should not be forgotten also that our knowledge of some of these kings is minimal. Very often for the Achaemenid period a line or two in Diodorus is our sole complement of information. Similarly, knowledge of Neo-Assyrian and Neo-Babylonian rulers may at times comprise little more than a line or two of cuneiform or a paragraph in the Old Testament. Such, for example, is the case with Shalmaneser V, in whom we see an alter-ego of Cambyses. Frequently the reign-lengths of these rulers is nowhere stated, and is only arrived at by modern scholars through various efforts of extrapolation or calculated guesswork.

Two deviations from the given reign-lengths of Achaemenid rulers (on the one hand) and Neo-Assyrian and Neo-Babylonian rulers (on the other) are outstanding. They are the sequence Artaxerxes I (40 years) followed by Darius II (18 years) — which contrasts greatly with their proposed Neo-Assyrian equivalents Esarhaddon (12 years) and Ashurnasirpal (40 or 41 years); and Artaxerxes II (46 years) followed by Artaxerxes III (21 years), which contrasts sharply with the proposed Neo-Babylonian equivalents, Nabopolasser (21 years) and Nebuchadrezzar II (43 or more likely 46 years).

It is true, of course, that the 40 years attributed to Artaxerxes I and the 18 years attributed to Darius II look very different from the reign-lengths of their Neo-Assyrian alter-egos. In this case, the Neo-Assyrian dates seem fairly well established by virtue of the numerous inscriptions attributed to these kings. There is some evidence, admittedly circumstantial, for believing that Esarhaddon may have reigned a little longer than 12 years;[263] yet even if this were to be true, it hardly solves the problem. There is still a great difference between a reign of perhaps 16 or 17 years and one of 40.

Note that the reign-length of Artaxerxes I seems fairly well established. The discovery of a cuneiform archive belonging to the Murashu firm of Nippur provided a great number of dated tablets from the end of Artaxerxes I's time. This collection is described as "the largest available documentary source for Achaemenid Babylonia in the years between Xerxes and Alexander."[264] Almost all the tablets are dated to the reigns of Artaxerxes I and his successor Darius II, and the greatest number by far belong to the last two years of Artaxerxes I and the first seven of Darius II.

A number of other such tablets exist, all from southern Mesopotamia, referring to the 40th or 41st year of Artaxerxes I. How then is this to be equated with the 12 or so years attributable to Esarhaddon?

---

263 The Esarhaddon Chronicle mentions how in the king's second year, "the army of Assyria went to Egypt. It fled before a storm." In view of the highly unusual nature of this entry — armies do normally flee before storms — it has often been supposed that this is a reference to the events of Sennacherib's second and unsuccessful expedition to Egypt, where his soldiers too were defeated by some natural event. Since Sennacherib's records do not mention the disaster, it is difficult to ascertain exactly when it occurred. Nevertheless, the silence of Assyrian records for the final nine or ten years of Sennacherib's reign suggest that it probably took place then. Now, if the entry in the Esarhaddon Chronicle really does refer to the disaster of Sennacherib's reign, this implies a profound confusion on the part of the chroiclers. However, an even more probable explanation is that the writers of the document (working it should be said, long after Esarhaddon's death) themselves believed it to refer to Sennacherib's defeat, and so lopped off several years from Esarhaddon's reign to make it "right".

264 V. Donbaz and M. W. Stolper, *Istanbul Murashu Texts* (Istanbul, 1997) p. 4.

Before taking another step, we should note a remarkable fact. Although Artaxerxes I is regarded as the second-longest reigning monarch of the Persian epoch, he has left us, in material terms, almost nothing: "there are no archaeological remains of the reign of Artaxerxes I with the exception of a single inscription on a building in Susa and an alabaster vase in Paris which bears his name.... All information concerning him is derived from the accounts of the Greeks writers."[265] Strange indeed that a king said to have reigned forty years has left so little.

All of the texts attributing a 40-year reign to Artaxerxes I come from Babylonia; the great majority, in fact, from Nippur. As Great King Artaxerxes I favored Babylon, and he possessed several highly honored Babylonian concubines. Bearing this in mind, I initially considered the possibility that Artaxerxes I had been appointed satrap of Babylon 28 or so years prior to ascending the Great King's throne. This system of regnal calculation was in fact, as we shall see, employed by Artaxerxes III. Yet I soon discounted this in the case of Artaxerxes I. If Esarhaddon and Artaxerxes I were the same person, then he cannot have been much more than 50 or so upon his death — for he was in the act of marching with his army against Egypt when he died. Thus he would need to have been little more than a child upon ascending the Babylonian throne, if he had reigned 40 years in the city. Besides, we know who the rulers of Babylon were during Sennacherib's time, and Esarhaddon's name does not appear among them.

It is here, however, that the real meaning of the 40-year reign emerges. Esarhaddon/Artaxerxes I was a great friend of Babylon. He it was who re-peopled the city and began its reconstruction after the devastation wrought by Sennacherib.

We should not underestimate the symbolic significance either of Babylon's destruction under Sennacherib or its restoration under Esarhaddon. Ancient texts describe the horror felt by the inhabitants of Mesopotamia upon Sennacherib's action. In destroying the city — he claims to have razed it to the ground and left it looking like a meadow — he had "broken the axis between heaven and earth" (symbolized by the Esagila Temple). Such sacrilege had a profound impact, and there can be little doubt that Esarhaddon's restoration of Esagila had an equal import. A king responsible for such a reverential act would have been honored in a special way. Marduk himself acted through such a man.

Thus it would appear that the inhabitants of Babylonia began to honor Esarhaddon/Artaxerxes I as a virtual incarnation of Marduk. Like any god, his reign began not with his coronation, but with his birth.

---

265 Richard Gottheil, "Artaxerxes I" www. jewishencyclopedia. com We also note however a tomb at Naksh-i Rustam said to belong to Artaxerxes I, though his name does not appear on it.

Here then is the explanation for the scarcity of material remains from the time of Artaxerxes I. The Great King did not reign 40 years; he merely lived 40 years.

As for Darius II, his reign of (perhaps) 18 years is calculated primarily by allowing for a 40-year span for his predecessor. Nowhere in ancient literature is there any definite information as to how long Darius II sat on the throne. If, however, he is identical to Ashurbanipal, then he was Great King for a total of 40 years; and this four decades "fills in" much of the time that needs to be allotted to the Persian Kings in order to make their chronology agree with that of the Greek world.[266]

Of the second set of alter-egos, namely Artaxerxes II and Artaxerxes III versus Nabopolasser and Nebuchadrezzar II, this concept of reign-lengths dated according to local reckoning is very definitely a factor we need to consider.

The Nebuchadrezzar who is said by Ptolemy to have reigned 43 years (or 46/7 years according to the Sippar tablets), may appear very different from his proposed alter-ego Artaxerxes III, who is said to have reigned 21 years. But the difference is not as great as it seems. As I mentioned in an article published in 2003 there is a good deal of evidence to indicate that Artaxerxes III shared a long co-regency with his father Artaxerxes II and that he dated his reign from his appointment as satrap of Babylon, an event which occurred long before his father's death.

The dates normally given for these kings are as follows:

Artaxerxes II	46 years
Artaxerxes III	21 years

This contrasts with the canonical dates for their prospective alter-egos, which are as follows:

Nabopolasser	21 years
Nebuchadrezzar	43 years (but 46/7 years according to the Sippar Tablets)

The reader will note the strange correspondences in the above reign-lengths. The two sets of kings look like virtual mirror-images of each other, with father-son roles reversed. This is not coincidental. I would suggest that in his 21st year Artaxerxes II appointed his son, the future Artaxerxes III, as satrap of Babylon

---

266 Nevertheless, even reducing Artaxerxes' reign to 12 years does not bring complete agreement between the Persian and Neo-Assyrian/Neo-Babylonian chronologies; and there is some evidence to suggest that the Persian epoch may need to be shortened by as much as a decade or even two. Incidentally, it is quite probable that the Hellenistic epoch is also too long — perhaps by as much as two or three decades.

— a position the latter occupied for the remaining 25 years of his father's life. Thus when Artaxerxes II died, Artaxerxes III was already in his 26th year as king of Babylon, and his accession to the Great King's throne did not change the dating system among his Babylonian subjects. In this way, when Artaxerxes III died, 21 years later, he was actually in his 47th year as king of Babylon (though of course only in his 21st year as Persian Great King). The true situation then, as I see it, is as follows:

Artaxerxes II/Nabopolasser:	46 years (but only 21 as king of Babylon)
Artaxerxes III/Nebuchadrezzar:	21 years (but 46/7 years if period as king of Babylon is counted)

My examination of the reign-lengths of the Achaemenid and Neo-Assyrian/ Neo-Babylonian kings has in fact proved consistent with a pattern I have found in all other areas. The differences and contradictions, which to begin with appeared great or even insurmountable, tended to evaporate upon closer examination. Indeed, close investigation invariably revealed startling new correspondences that I had previously never even suspected.

Who Were the Old Babylonians?

My study of the history and archaeology of Mesopotamia would not be complete without some mention of the Old Babylonians. According to conventional ideas, this people were the first to establish Babylon as the pre-eminent city of Mesopotamia. Their greatest king was known as Hammurabi, a man generally dated to early in the second millennium BC.

I would scarcely consider it important to mention the Old Babylonians here, since they belong to an age earlier than that examined in the present volume, were it not for the fact that my colleague Gunnar Heinsohn has repeatedly identified them as alter-egos of the Persians. Thus for example he sees Hammurabi, who promulgated a famous table of laws, as an alter-ego of Darius the Great, who was reputedly the first king to produce a written legal code.

Whilst over the years I have generally been in agreement with Heinsohn, on this crucial identification I part company with him.

The true historical position of the Old Babylonians is revealed in the stratigraphy of Babylon. Here, as seen earlier in the present chapter, Robert Koldewey discovered evidence of these kings at the very bottom-most layer of the city, occurring at one meter below zero and immediately underneath the earliest of the Kassites. The Kassites were contemporaries of the Egyptian Eighteenth and Nineteenth Dynasties, a fact confirmed in innumerable ways and doubted by no one. It was a well-known Kassite king, Burnaburiash, who sent a series of petulant missives to Amenhotep III and Akhnaton.

Before taking another step, we should note here that were we to equate the Old Babylonians (coming before the Kassites), with the Persians, then we must as a consequence place the Kassites, as well as the Egyptian Eighteenth and Nineteenth Dynasties, *after* the Persians. This alone, in and of itself, completely refutes the equation of Old Babylonians and Persians. But if they were not Persians, who were they?

In order to answer that question, we need to examine the broader sweep of Mesopotamian history and archaeology in the light of our new chronology.

Like the Kassites in southern Mesopotamia, the Mitanni in northern Mesopotamia were also contemporaries of the Eighteenth Dynasty. I am in agreement with Heinsohn in seeing the Mitanni as the Mede conquerors of the Old Assyrian (Akkadian) Empire, an event that must have occurred around 700 BC. Now, whilst the Mitanni immediately replaced the Akkadians in northern Mesopotamia, in southern Mesopotamia their place was eventually taken (in some areas at least) by the so-called "Neo-Sumerian" Third Dynasty of Ur. These kings, with names like Ur-Nammu, Shulgi, and Ibbi-Sin, are rightly identified by Heinsohn with the Neo-Chaldeans (as distinct from Neo-Babylonian) kings who controlled Babylonia during the time of the Medes. Thus the last of these men, Ibbi-Sin, who was carried in bonds to Anshan, was identical to the Nabonidus of the Cyrus Prism, who was also carried off in bonds to Anshan.

For me, therefore, and for Heinsohn, the Third Dynasty of Ur was contemporary, in part at least, with the Egyptian Eighteenth and Nineteenth Dynasties. Yet we have already seen that the Kassites, who occur at many sites in southern Mesopotamia, were also contemporary with the Egyptian Eighteenth and Nineteenth Dynasties. Hence it is hardly open to question that the Kassites and Ur Dynasty 3 kings were one and the same Neo-Chaldeans Dynasty.

Yet here there arises a difficulty. If the Kassites and Ur Dynasty 3 rulers were alter-egos of each other, this means that the latter kings, just like the Kassites, have to come after Hammurabi's Old Babylonians. Again, we must ask: Who, then, were they?

Classical sources record that after the fall of Assyria the Medes took northern Mesopotamia, but Babylon was ruled for a period of about eighty years by a dynasty of Scythian kings. Only after this time, which by our reckoning must have been around 620 BC, did the Neo-Chaldean take control of the region. These Neo-Chaldean, or Kassites, or Neo-Sumerians, were led to power by the great leader Nabu-apil-iddin (Nabopoladdan), also known (in his Chaldean guise) as Ur-Nammu and (in his Kassite guise) as Burnaburiash. It was this mighty Babylonian king who corresponded with Akhnaton, probably around 620 BC.

The Old Babylonian dynasty, the line of kings which directly preceded that of Nabopoladdan/Ur-Nammu/Burnaburiash, was that of the Scythians (or Gutians), the former nomads who seized Lower Mesopotamia, and held it for 80 years.

Hammurabi was no Persian — he was a Scythian.

Before finishing, I wish to state that Heinsohn is not to be blamed for the confusion that surrounds the Old Babylonian question. The term has been applied far too loosely to kings and dynasties that were actually centuries apart. Thus Heinsohn is right in seeing Ibbi-Sin, threatened by the Martu, as the Neo-Chaldean Nabonidus (Nabu-natsir) threatened by the Persian Mardians. But the Martu were not the Old Babylonians, as Heinsohn has stated. Their kings, apparently, had names reminiscent of some borne by the Old Babylonians, and this may go some way to explain the confusion. Yet the Old Babylonians did not follow the Third Dynasty of Ur, they actually preceded them, though in the "Sumerian" cities over which the Third Dynasty ruled, they were called Gutians. Only in the Kassite (Semitic-speaking) regions were they known as Old Babylonians.

Epilogue

We have completed, in the foregoing pages, an enterprise that commenced in 1952 when Velikovsky's first volume of *Ages in Chaos* appeared in the bookshops. It is now perfectly clear why Velikovsky could not close the circle and complete his reconstruction. Always he came up against the apparently immutable measuring-rod of biblical chronology. No one at the time, least of all Velikovsky, imagined there would ever be a need to mount a challenge to that chronology. Yet the present volume shows that the unquestioning acceptance of biblical timescales was probably, more than any other single factor, responsible for the gross distortion of ancient history that we now find in the textbooks.

With the advantage of hindsight it is now seen that the need to challenge biblical dates should have been glaringly obvious from the beginning. Jewish genealogies, as for example that of Jesus in Matthew's Gospel, show the Babylonian Exile to be an event occurring in the mid-4th century, not the early 6th century, as "traditional" chronology insists. The same genealogy would place Abraham around 1050 BC, in contrast to the traditional date of circa 2000 BC.

In my *Genesis of Israel and Egypt* (1997), which may be regarded as the first volume of my own, smaller, "Ages in Chaos" series, I demonstrated in some detail how the Abraham legend referred to a migration from Mesopotamia to Egypt at the very dawn of civilization, and that "Abraham" is a contemporary of Menes, the first pharaoh. Yet the birth of high civilization did not occur around 3000 BC, as the textbooks would suggest, but, just as the Hebrew genealogies state, as the beginning of the first millennium BC.

The second volume of my reconstruction, entitled *The Pyramid Age* (2007), dealt with events chronologically subsequent to those in *The Genesis of Israel and Egypt*. Here the reader saw that Egypt's Pyramid Age occurred after the catastrophic disturbances which marked the Israelite Exodus — an event which brought to an end the Early Dynastic epoch.

In *The Pyramid Age* too we found that the Assyrian conquest of Egypt, which the Egyptians recalled as the invasion of the Hyksos, occurred early in the 8th century BC, and was accomplished by a king known to history as Sargon I, founder of the Akkadian (or Old Assyrian) Empire. Sargon (or Sharek, as the Egyptians remembered him) easily overthrew the Egyptian army because he employed weaponry far in advance of anything possessed by the Egyptians. The most notable of the new weapons was the two-wheeled, horse-drawn chariot — a device well-known to have been introduced by the Hyksos.

The Hyksos/Assyrians were expelled from Egypt around 720 BC, when the Medes (or Mitanni) overwhelmed their northern Mesopotamian heartland. It was then that the great imperial dynasty of Egypt, the Eighteenth, was established. It was then too that the mighty United Kingdom of the Israelites rose to power under its first kings Saul and David.

This period of Egypt's history, which was the subject of Velikovsky's *Ages in Chaos* Vol. 1, was covered by the present author in his *Empire of Thebes* (2006). There it was shown that, apart from the absolute dates, which were two centuries too early, Velikovsky was generally right about the details. In one important area, however, he was indeed mistaken — that of the Amarna Letters. The latter documents, from the time of Amenhotep III and Akhnaton, were believed by Velikovsky to have been written during the reigns of the Hebrew kings Ahab and Jehoshaphat. Here he was nearly right, but not quite. In fact, the Amarna Letters were written a generation before this period, in the time of Baasha (and Omri) of Israel and Asa of Judah. Apart from that, *Ages in Chaos* Vol. 1 was a veritable masterpiece, a masterpiece that was however rejected by the scholarly world. Yet, to paraphrase one well-known biblical prophet, this building-block that was rejected has become the veritable cornerstone of ancient history.

Indeed, now that the reconstruction of Near Eastern history has been completed, we can only look in wonder and admiration at Velikovsky's achievement. Not one of his published volumes is wrong completely; and one at least, *Peoples of the Sea*, is completely right — both with regard to dates and character identifications. *Ages in Chaos* Vol. 1 is also largely right in terms of character identifications and synchronisms — only the overall timescale, as we have said, is at fault. Even the most "wrong" of his historical books, *Ramses II and his Time*, is actually spot on with regard to dates, for Ramses II really did reign in the first half of the 6th century — only the attempted synchronizations with the Jewish and Babylonian histories were mistaken.

Thus for a pioneering effort Velikovsky's historical work was astonishingly accurate, and all of us, who over the years have enjoyed countless pleasant hours poring over and discussing his ideas, owe him an immense debt of gratitude. We can only hope that the wider academic world will eventually also come to realize this.

Neo-Assyrian and Achaemenid Parallels

TIGLATH-PILESER III
Was the founder of a new dynasty and not the son of the previous king of Assyria. During his time Assyrian power reached the borders of Egypt. Ruled Babylon and "took the hand of Bel."

CYRUS
Was the founder of a new dynasty and not the son of the previous king of Persia. During his time Persian power reached the borders of Egypt. Conquered Babylon and "took the hand of Bel."

SHALMANESER V
Reigned only six years. Campaigned in the direction of Egypt.

CAMBYSES
Reigned seven and a half years. Conquered Egypt.

SARGON II
Was a usurper and not the son of the preceding king. Described himself as King of the Four Quarters, implying rule from Magan (Egypt) to Dilmun (India). Defeated a major insurrection in Babylon led by Merodach-Baladan (III). Boasted of expelling the Ionians (Jaman) from their island homes.

DARIUS I
Was a usurper and not the son of the preceding king. Described himself as King of the Four Quarters, ruling from Egypt to India. Defeated a major insurrection in Babylon led by Nebuchadrezzar (III). Cleared the Ionian islands of their inhabitants.

SENNACHERIB
Reigned 22 years. Defeated two major insurrections in Babylon and destroyed the city after the second. Thereafter suppressed the Babylonian deities in favor of Ashur, who was elevated to the position of supreme god. Was murdered in a palace conspiracy involving at least one of his sons.

XERXES
Reigned 21 years. Defeated two major insurrections in Babylon and destroyed the city after the second. Thereafter suppressed the Babylonian deities in favor of Ahura Mazda, who was elevated to the position of supreme god. Was murdered in a palace conspiracy involving at least one of his sons.

ESARHADDON
Was not the eldest son of Sennacherib, but was appointed crown-prince through the influence of his powerful mother Naqia, who dominated her son. Had to suppress a series of rebellions in Egypt and appointed Egyptian potentates with names like Necho and Psamtek. Began rebuilding Babylon.

ARTAXERXES I
Was not the eldest son of Xerxes, but was appointed crown-prince through the influence of his powerful mother Amestris, who dominated her son. Had to suppress a series of rebellion in Egypt and appointed Egyptian potentates with names like Necho and Psamtek. Began rebuilding Babylon.

ASHURBANIPAL
Was not the original crown-prince, but was appointed to rule after the death of his brother Sin-iddin-apla. Faced rebellions in Egypt, where he honored a prince named Wenamon. During his time Assyrian control of Egypt began to weaken.

DARIUS II
Was not the original crown-prince, but was appointed to rule after the death of his brother Xerxes II. Faced rebellions in Egypt, where he honored a prince named Wenamon. During his time Persian control of Egypt began to weaken.

NABOPOLASSER

Was based in Babylon and associated with that city. Appears to have been a son of Ashurbanipal, but had to fight for control of the Assyrian Empire against another son named Sin-shar-ishkun

NABUCHADREZZAR

Appears to have conquered Egypt, after a second attempt, where he brought to an end the reign of Necho II. Destroyed Egypt's ally Judah. According to the Book of Judith had a servant named Bagoas and a general named Holofernes. Was known for his savage cruelty.

NABONIDUS

Was not the son of Nebuchadrezzar, but from a minor branch of the royal family. Last native Babylonian king.

ARTAXERXES II

Was based in Babylon and associated with that city. Son of a Babylonian mother and a half-Babylonian father. Upon his accession had to battle for control of the Persian Empire against a younger brother named Cyrus.

ARTAXERXES III

Conquered Egypt after a second attempt, where he brought to an end the reign of Nectanebo II. Brought all the nations of Syria/Palestine under his control. According to Diodorus Siculus had a servant named Bagoas and a general named Holofernes. Was known for his savage cruelty.

DARIUS III

Was not the son of Artaxerxes III, but from a minor branch of the royal family. Last native Persian king.

CHRONOLOGY OF MAJOR EVENTS FROM THE FINAL YEARS OF THE 19ᵀᴴ DYNASTY TO THE END OF THE PERSIAN EPOCH

BC	EGYPT	ISRAEL	MESOPOTAMIA	GREECE
550	Ramses II	Uzziah of Judah	Tiglath-Pileser III (Cyrus) conquers the Medes and annexes Babylon	Solon visits Egypt
	Merneptah	Prophet Isaiah active		
525	Amenmesse (Amasis) dies		Shalmaneser V (Cambyses) conquers Egypt	
520	Shabataka (Sabako) invades Egypt		Sargon II (Darius I) seizes the throne	
490				Persians defeated at Marathon
480	Rebellion of Seti II (Sethos or Inaros))			Persians defeated in Greece
475	Seti II (Inaros) allied with Tirhaka, defeats Persians	Hezekiah of Judah	Army of Sennacherib (Xerxes) destroyed on Egyptian border	
465	Seti II (Inaros) captured and deported to Assyria.		Esarhaddon (Artaxerxes I) reconquers Egypt	
440	Necho I appointed		Ashurbanipal (Darius II) defeats Egyptians	
	Psamtek and Wenamon		Satrap Arsames resident in Babylon	
430	Ramses XI and Psamtek			Beginning of Peloponnesian War
420	Nekht-hor-heb Herihor			First phase of Peloponnesian War ends.
405	Amyrtaeus II rebels against the Persians		Nabopolasser (Artaxerxes II) fights for the throne	Xenophon with the Ten Thousand marches on Babylon
	Egypt proclaims independence			
395			Battle of Carchemish	

380	Ramses III (Nectanebo I) ascends the throne	
370		Pharnabazus de- feated in Egypt
340	Ramses IV (Tachos)	Egypt Reconquered by Nebuchadrezzar (Artaxerxes III)
335	Alexander en- ters Egypt	Conquest of Persia by Alexander

BIBLIOGRAPHY

Books

Akurgal, E. *The Birth of Greek Art* (Methuen, 1968)

Breasted, J. H. *A History of Egypt* (1951)

Campbell-Thompson, R. *The Prisms of Esarhaddon and Ashurbanipal* (London, British Museum, 1931)

Delaporte, L. *Malatya* (Paris, 1940)

Dicks, B. *The Ancient Persians: How they Lived and Worked* (1979)

Donbaz, V. and M.W. Stolper, *Istanbul Murashu Texts* (Istanbul, 1997)

Fakhri, A. *Siwa Oasis* (1940)

Fossing, P. *Glass Vessels before Glass Blowing* (Copenhagen, 1940)

Frankfort, H. *The Art and Architecture of the Ancient Orient* (Penguin, New York, 1988)

Galling, K. (ed.) *Biblisches Reallexikon* (Tübingen, 1977)

Gardiner, A. H. *Egypt of the Pharaohs* (Oxford, 1966)

Garland, H. and C. Bannister, *Ancient Egyptian Metallurgy* (London, 1927)

Ginzberg, L. *The Legends of the Jews* 7 Vols. (Philadelphia, 1920)

Gjerstad, E. et al. *The Swedish Cyprus Expedition, 1927-1931* 4 Vols. (Stockholm, 1934-37)

Glueck, N. *The Other Side of the Jordan* (1970)

Hall, H. R. *The Ancient History of the Near East* (London, 1913)

Harper, R. *Assyrian and Babylonian Letters*, 13 Vols. (Chicago, 1911)

Heinsohn, G. *Assyrerkönige gleich Perserherrscher!* (Gräfelfing, 1996)

Heinsohn, G. *Die Sumerer gab es nicht* (Frankfurt, 1988)

Heinsohn, G. *Wann lebten die Pharaonen?* (Frankfurt, 1990)

Hyatt, J. P. (ed.), *The Bible in Modern Scholarship* (1965)

Johns, C. H. W., *Ancient Babylonia* (London, 1913)

Junker, H. and L. Delaporte, *Die Völker des antiken Orients* (Freiburg, 1933)

Koldewey, R., *The Excavations at Babylon* (London, 1914)

Kramer, S. N., *The Sumerians* (Chicago, 1963)

Langdon, S., *Building Inscriptions of the Neo-Babylonian Empire* (Paris, 1905)

Layard, A. H., *Discoveries in the Ruins of Nineveh and Babylon* (London, 1853)

Lepsius, C. R., *Denkmäler aus Aegypten und Aethiopien* 2 Vols. (1897-1904)

Luckenbill, D. D., *Ancient Records of Assyria and Babylonia* 2 Vols. (Chicago, 1926-7)

MacKenzie, D. A., *Myths of Babylon and Assyria* (Kessinger Publishing, 2004)

MacQueen, J. G., *The Hittites* (London, 1975)

Maspero, G., *History of Egypt* 13 Vols. (London, 1906)

Montet, P., *Psousennes* (Paris, 1951)

Moscati, S. et al, *The Phoenicians* (New York, 1999)

Murray, A. S., A.H. Smith, and H.B. Walters, *Excavations in Cyprus* (London, British Museum, 1900)

Naville, E., *The Mound of the Jew* (London, 1894)

Nolte, B., *Die Glasgefässe im alten Aegypten* (Berlin, 1968)

Olmstead, A. T., *History of Assyria* (Chicago, 1923)

Olmstead, A. T., *History of the Persian Empire* (Chicago, 1948)

Petrie, F., *A History of Egypt* 3 Vols. (1905)

Petrie, F., *Egyptian Architecture* (London, 1938)

Petrie, F., *Tanis* Pt II

Piepkorn, A. C., Historical Prism Inscriptions of Assurbanipal (Chicago, 1933)

Pritchard, J. B. (ed.), *Ancient Near Eastern Texts* (Princeton, 1950)

Rawlinson, G., *Ancient Monarchies* 3 Vols. (London, 1879)

Rohl, D., *A Test of Time* (London, 1995)

Roux, G., *Ancient Iraq* (Penguin, 1980)

Sancisi-Weerdenburg, H. and H. Kuhrt (eds.), *Achaemenid History IV: Center and Periphery* (Leiden, 1990)

Smith, S., Babylonian Historical Texts Relating to the Capture and Downfall of Babylon (London, 1924)

Sweeney, E., *Empire of Thebes* (New York, 2006)

Sweeney, E., *Genesis of Israel and Egypt* (London, 1997)

Sweeney, E., *The Pyramid Age* (2nd ed. New York, 2007)

Sykes, P., *A History of Ancient Persia* 2 Vols. (London, 1930)

Velikovsky, I., *Ages in Chaos* (London and New York, 1952)

Velikovsky, I., *Peoples of the Sea* (London and New York, 1977)

Velikovsky, I., *Ramses II and his Time* (London and New York, 1978)

Wilkinson, J. G., A Popular Account of the Ancient Egyptians 2 Vols. (London, 1878)

Woldering, I., *Egypt: The Art of the Pharaohs* (Baden-Baden, 1963)

Woolley, L., *Carchemish III* (1952)

Articles

Albright, W. F., "Syria, the Philistines, and Phoenicia" in The Cambridge Ancient History Vol.2 part 2 (3rd ed.)

Badawi, A., «Das Grab des Krönenprinzen Scheschonk, Sohnes Osorkon's II, und Hohenpriesters von Memphis»; Annales du Service des Antiquites, Vol. 54 (1956)

Bennett, R. D., "Phoenician-Punic Art" in Encyclopedia of World Art, XI (New York, 1966)

Bimson, J., "An Eighth-Century Date for Merneptah," Society for Interdisciplinary Studies Review Vol.III No.2 (1978)

Bimson, J., "Can There be a Revised Chronology Without a Revised Stratigraphy?," Society for Interdisciplinary Studies: Proceedings, Glasgow Conference (April, 1978)

Bimson, J., "Finding the Limits of Chronological Revision," Proceedings of Society for Interdisciplinary Studies, Conference: Ages Still in Chaos? (London, September, 2002)

Chassinat, E. "Le Mot seten 'Roi', Revue de l'Egypte Ancienne II (Paris, 1929)

Cooney, J. D. "Three Early Saite Tomb Reliefs," Journal of Near Eastern Studies 9 (1950)

De Rouge, M. «Étude sur quelques monuments du règne de Taharka,» Mélanges d'Archéologie Vol.1 (1873)

Dhorme, H. «Premiere traduction des textes phèniciens de Ras Shamra,» Revue biblique Vol.XL (1931)

Drower, M. S. "Syria Before 2200 BC." in The Cambridge Ancient History Vol.1 part 2 (3rd ed.)

Faulkner, R. O. "Egypt: From the Inception of the Nineteenth Dynasty to the Death of Ramesses III" in The Cambridge Ancient History Vol.2, part 2 (3rd ed.)

Fecht, G. "Der Moskauer 'literarische Brief' als historisches Dokument," Zeitschrift für Aegyptische Sprache 87 (1962)

Grayson, A. K. "Assyria: Tiglath-Pileser III to Sargon II (744-705 BC)" in The Cambridge Ancient History Vol.3 part 2 (3rd ed.)

Greenberg, L. "The Lion Gate at Mycenae Revisited," Society for Interdisciplinary Studies: Proceedings of Conference 'Ages Still in Chaos' (14th-15th Sept 2002)

Güterbock, H. G. Journal of Near Eastern Studies (1945)

Hall, H. R. "The Ethiopians and Assyrians in Egypt" in The Cambridge Ancient History Vol.3 (1st ed. 1929)

Hawkins, J. D. "The Neo-Hittite States in Syria and Anatolia" in The Cambridge Ancient History Vol.3 part 1(3rd ed.)

Hrozny, B. «Les Ioniens à Ras-Sharma,» Archiv Orientální Vol.IV (1932)

Jones, M. "Some Detailed Evidence from Egypt against Velikovsky's Revised Chronology," Society for Interdisciplinary Studies Review Vol.VI

Kuhrt, A. "The Persian Empire: Babylonia from Cyrus to Xerxes" in The Cambridge Ancient History Vol.4 (2nd ed.)

Melville, S. C. "The Role of Naqia/Zakutu in Sargonid Royal Politics," State Archives of Assyria Studies Vol.IX (Helsinki, 1999)

Munn-Rankin, J. M., "Assyrian Military Power 1300-1200 BC." in The Cambridge Ancient History Vol.2 part 2 (3rd ed.)

Oppenheim, A. L., "The Babylonian Evidence of the Achaemenian Rule in Mesopotamia" in The Cambridge History of Iran Vol.1 (Cambridge, 1985)

Palmer, T., "A Test of Beards," Society for Interdisciplinary Studies Review and Workshop Combined No.1 (2004)

Parpola, S., "Death in Mesopotamia," XXVIeme Rencontre Assyriologique Internationale ed. Prof. Bendt Alster, (Akademisk Forlag, 1980)

Ray, J. D., "Egypt 525-404 BC" in The Cambridge Ancient History Vol.4 (2nd ed, 1988)

Schuler, F., "Ancient Glassmaking Techniques. The Egyptian Core Vessel Process," Archaeology Vol.15 (1962)

INDEX

A

Achaemenes, 34, 37, 134, 136
Achaemenid, 17, 24, 31, 45, 47, 49, 52, 66-67, 101-104, 108, 123, 129, 131, 138-139, 143-146, 149, 155-156, 162, 165, 169-171, 173, 175, 177-179, 181-183, 185-186, 189, 195, 201
Adad-guppi, 143, 146, 156, 160
Adad-Nirari, 5, 15-16, 78, 90
Adad-Nirari III, 5, 15-16, 90
Adrammelech, 132
Aegesilaus, 151
Aegeus, 47
Aeolia, 12
Agog, 77
Ahab, 13-14, 194
Ahasuerus, 106
Ahaz, 119
Ahiram, 92-93
Ahmose, 19-20, 77, 98
Ahura Mazda, ii, 104-106, 116, 130, 174, 195
Akhnaton, 10, 13, 29-30, 77, 96-97, 146, 184, 189-190, 194
Akkad, 119, 125, 148-149
Akkadian, 10-11, 25, 80, 158, 162, 172, 190, 194
Akurgal, Ekrem, 87
Albright, William F., 83
Allumari, 120
Alogyne, 140

Amarna Letters, 10, 78, 159, 184, 194
Amasis, 16, 19-21, 24, 45, 56, 98, 196
Amathus, 93
Amenhotep, 65-66, 73, 77, 79, 93, 184, 189, 194
Amenhotep III, 73, 77, 79, 93, 184, 189, 194
Amenmeses, i, 19-22, 24, 26-28, 98
Amenmesses, 16, 61
Amennakht, 63
Amenophis, 33-34
Amestris, 135-137, 195
Amon, 25, 28-30, 33, 42, 56-57, 65, 77, 138
Amon-Ra, 23, 28
Amyrtaeus, 43, 48, 134, 197
Anatolia, 9-10, 84-85, 87, 89, 104, 147, 157-158, 169, 173, 202
Andia, 140
Anshan, 122, 160-161, 190
Antiochus, 164
Anysis, 70
Apis, 26, 55-56, 151
Apopi, 77
Apries, 17, 19-20
Aramaic, 26, 46, 172-178
Arbaces, 16-17
Arsa, 23-24, 49, 54, 60, 66
Arsaces, 146
Arsames, 24, 46, 49-50
Arses, 146, 155-156
Arshu, 146
Artabanus, 131-133